Narratives in Conflict

American Society of Missiology Monograph Series

The ASM Monograph Series provides a forum for publishing quality dissertations and studies in the field of missiology. Collaborating with Pickwick Publications—a division of Wipf and Stock Publishers of Eugene, Oregon—the American Society of Missiology selects high quality dissertations and other monographic studies that offer research materials in mission studies for scholars, mission and church leaders, and the academic community at large. The ASM seeks scholarly work for publication in the Series that throws light on issues confronting Christian world mission in its cultural, social, historical, biblical, and theological dimensions.

Missiology is an academic field that brings together scholars whose professional training ranges from doctoral-level preparation in areas such as scripture, history and sociology of religions, anthropology, theology, international relations, interreligious interchange, mission history, inculturation, and church law. The American Society of Missiology, which sponsors this series, is an ecumenical body drawing members from Independent and Ecumenical Protestant, Catholic, Orthodox, and other traditions. Members of the ASM are united by their commitment to reflect on and do scholarly work relating to both mission history and the present-day mission of the church. The ASM Monograph Series aims to publish works of exceptional merit on specialized topics, with particular attention given to work by younger scholars, the dissemination and publication of which is difficult under the economic pressures of standard publishing models.

Persons seeking information about the ASM or the guidelines for having their dissertations considered for publication in the ASM Monograph Series should consult the Society's website—www.asmweb.org.

Members of the ASM Monograph Committee who approved this book are:
    James R. Krabill, Mennonite Mission
    Judith Lingenfelter, retired from Biola University
    Roger Schroeder, SVD, Catholic Theological Union

Previously Published in the ASM Monograph Series

Randall G. Prior, *Contextualizing Theology in the South Pacific: The Shape of Theology in Oral Cultures*

P. V. Joseph, *An Indian Trinitarian Theology of Missio Dei: Insights from St. Augustine and Brahmabandhab Upadhyay*

Kevin George Hovey, *Guiding Light: Contributions of Alan R. Tippett Toward the Development and Dissemination of Twentieth-Century Missiology*

Narratives in Conflict

Atonement in Hebrews and the Qur'an

MATTHEW AARON BENNETT

☙PICKWICK *Publications* • Eugene, Oregon

NARRATIVES IN CONFLICT
Atonement in Hebrews and the Qur'an

American Society of Missiology Monograph Series 42

Copyright © 2019 Matthew Aaron Bennett. All rights reserved. Except for brief quotations in critical publications or reviews, no part of this book may be reproduced in any manner without prior written permission from the publisher. Write: Permissions, Wipf and Stock Publishers, 199 W. 8th Ave., Suite 3, Eugene, OR 97401.

Pickwick Publications
An Imprint of Wipf and Stock Publishers
199 W. 8th Ave., Suite 3
Eugene, OR 97401

www.wipfandstock.com

PAPERBACK ISBN: 978-1-5326-7766-3
HARDCOVER ISBN: 978-1-5326-7767-0
EBOOK ISBN: 978-1-5326-7768-7

Cataloguing-in-Publication data:

Names: Bennett, Matthew Aaron, author.
Title: Narratives in conflict : atonement in Hebrews and the Qur'an / by Matthew Aaron Bennett.
Description: Eugene, OR: Pickwick, 2019 | Series: American Society of Missiology Monograph Series 42 | Includes bibliographical references and index.
Identifiers: ISBN 978-1-5326-7766-3 (paperback) | ISBN 978-1-5326-7767-0 (hardcover) | ISBN 978-1-5326-7768-7 (ebook)
Subjects: LCSH: Bible. Hebrews—Criticism, interpretation, etc. | Atonement—Biblical teaching. | Christianity and other religions—Islam—Biblical teaching. | Qur'an—Relation to the Bible.
Classification: BS2775.6.A8 B46 2019 (print) | BS2775.6.A8 (ebook)

Manufactured in the U.S.A.   NOVEMBER 8, 2019

Biblical quotations, unless otherwise noted, are from The Holy Bible, English Standard Version, copyright © 2001 by Crossway Bibles, a publishing ministry of Good News Publishing. Used by permission. All rights reserved.

Qur'anic quotations, unless otherwise noted, are from *The Qur'an: Text, Translation, and Commentary,* copyright © 2005 by Abdullah Yusuf Ali, Elmhurst, NY: Tahrike Tarsile, Qur'an.

To my wife, Emily, whose efforts in the process of seeing this project completed far exceed my own:
Thank you and I love you.

To my Egyptian brothers and sisters, whose love of the gospel and hope for its transformative power in their communities is fuel for my own passion:
الف شكر يا كنيسة مصرية

And to Dr. Bruce Riley Ashford and Dr. Heath Aaron Thomas who have labored long with me in the process of seeing this project through. Your character and integrity in academics and the Christian life have left an impression on me that goes far beyond this dissertation. Thank you.

Contents

Preface ix
Tables xi
Abbreviations xii

1. Introduction: Atonement in Hebrews and the Qur'an 1
2. Blood, Story, and Worldview: The Day of Atonement in Leviticus 43
3. Hebrews and Atonement: A Re-Envisioning of Israel's Narrative in the Light of Christ 77
4. The Qur'an and Atonement: A Conspicuous Absence 113
5. Hebrews and the Qur'an: Conflicting Worldviews and the Narratives That Form Them 149
6. Hebrews and Contextual Communication: The Cross-Cultural Communicative Power of the OBN 185

Bibliography 213
Appendix A: Kaffāra (Noun – Atonement) in the Qur'an 225
Appendix B: Kaffara (Verb – To Atone) in the Qur'an 227
Appendix C: Sacrificial Vocabulary in the Qur'an 230
Appendix D: Ransom Vocabulary in the Qur'an 237

Preface

As the last 1,400 years of Christian-Muslim dialogue have demonstrated, there are several areas of Islamic theology and Qur'anic claims that conflict with the message of the Bible. One such conflict arises when considering an area of vital concern to the Bible: the concept of atonement. In the Hebrew Bible atonement is a logically unified concept whereby God grants his people means of achieving forgiveness and purification by accepting the blood of a sacrificial animal as a ransom-purgation. The book of Hebrews highlights the way the Christ event accomplishes atonement by connecting Jesus' death, resurrection, and ascension with the ritual actions of the high priest on the Day of Atonement.

The Qur'an, however, despite both claiming to continue and complete prior revelation and while including similar language often understood to mean atonement, teaches a very different doctrine of forgiveness. Despite the presence of the component parts of biblical atonement—sacrifice, forgiveness, purification, ransom, blood—the Qur'an keeps each aspect conceptually separate from the others. Such separation is most clearly seen in the Qur'an's refusal to acknowledge blood's role in achieving forgiveness or purification. Thus, while atonement language and the concepts of forgiveness and purification are present in both texts, there is an underlying disunity in the biblical and qur'anic ideas of atonement (conveyed through the Arabic word, *kaffāra*).

Where many scholars accuse the Qur'an of being blatantly mistaken or ill-informed in its retelling of quasi-biblical narratives, this dissertation will show that a generous reading of the Qur'an reveals a potentially nuanced intertextuality resulting in a different understanding of continuation. Exegesis of *Sura* 5 demonstrates that the Qur'an sees sacrifice as a demarcation given to mark off new dispensations of revelation. This understanding of the purpose of sacrifice gives the Qur'an the ability to claim to stand in the stead of Judaism and Christianity without having to account for some of the details of underlying meaning and overt ritual. Thus, rather than assuming the Qur'an to be negligent in its treatment of Jewish and Christian atonement, the Qur'an simply makes a different claim to continuation than the book of Hebrews makes.

Ultimately, Hebrews offers a narrative-driven answer to the question, "Why did the Christ event occur as the Bible indicates?" In so doing, it challenges the qur'anic claims to continuation of prior revelation more forcefully than does the mere factual question, "Did the Christ event occur as the Bible indicates?" The affirmative answer given to the latter question gains impact through understanding the whole biblical narrative that the Christ event brings to a climax. The book of Hebrews demonstrates the climactic nature of the Christ event, and thus its portrayal of Christian atonement coheres more seamlessly with biblical ritual, metanarrative, and worldview than does the disjunctive metanarrative suggested by the Qur'an. Ultimately, the argument of this dissertation is that Christ's fulfillment of the Day of Atonement, as presented in the book of Hebrews, exposes distinct worldviews between the Qur'an and Bible, and can be used to challenge qur'anic claims to completing prior revelation.

Tables

1.1 Bevans' Six Models of Contextual Theology | 10

1.2 Schlorff's Seven Models of Ministry to Muslims | 13

1.3 Fusion of Bevans and Schlorff | 17

1.4 Assessment and Proponents of Contemporary Offerings | 33

2.1 The Day of Atonement In Leviticus 16–17 | 65

2.2 Worldview Questions and Answers from Leviticus 16–17 | 76

3.1 The Day of Atonement Comparison: Leviticus 16–17 and Hebrews | 95

3.2 Worldview Questions and Answers Comparison: Leviticus 16–17 and Hebrews | 107

5.1 Worldview Questions and Answers Comparison: Hebrews and the Qur'an | 166

5.2 Communication Barriers and OBN Resolution | 181

6.1 Trialogical Critical Contextualization Model | 197

Abbreviations

ACCOS – Ancient Christian Commentary on Scripture

CMB – Christian from a Muslim Background

CPM – Church Planting Movement

EI – Encyclopedia of Islam

EMQ – *Evangelical Missions Quarterly*

IJFM – *International Journal of Frontier Missions*

MIR – *Missiology: An International Review*

NICNT – New International Commentary on the New Testament

NICOT – New International Commentary on the Old Testament

SFM – *St. Francis Magazine*

WBC – Word Biblical Commentary

ABC – Anchor Bible Commentary

1

Introduction
Atonement in Hebrews and the Qur'an

THE QUESTIONS THAT DRIVE this project began to take shape in my mind on August 15th, 2013 at six in the morning, as I stood on the bloody streets of Alexandria, Egypt. It was Islam's annual Feast of the Sacrifice (*'id al Aḍha*), and the makeshift butchers that had been set up throughout the city's neighborhoods were already surrounded by the carcasses of sacrificial animals. Trickling out from under piles of these carcasses, the puddles of blood already filling the streets were not unexpected. The bustling city of five million people requires butchers to start early to accommodate all of the worshippers celebrating the feast.

What was curious, however, was the Egyptian tradition of using the blood of the sacrifices to adorn the walls and doorways of storefronts and apartment buildings. Dipping their hands in the blood, residents and owners of such buildings made bloody handprints around their dwellings as an element of their ritual. Most attributed the habit to superstition, but the echoes of Passover blood applied to doorposts mixed with the celebration of the feast commemorating Abraham's near sacrifice of his son evoked multiple questions: What is the role of blood in Islam? How does Islam see itself relating to previous religious cultus? What is the relationship between sacrifice, blood, and atonement in the Qur'an? With so much commonality and shared history, why does it prove so difficult to explain Christian atonement to Muslims? Are there places in the Bible that might be used to effectively explain Christian views of atonement?

This last question in particular has served to lay the foundational inquiry for this particular monograph.

Initial investigation of these questions, however, uncovered the fact that this project will not be the first to ask what parts of Scripture are most helpful for sharing the Christian message with Muslims. Though much contemporary missiological scholarship concerns itself with how far one might go in accommodating cultural and religious forms before falling into syncretism, a few scholars have argued that one must consider issues such as the selection of Scripture prior to advocating for a contextual expression of faith.[1]

For example, some apologists argue for engaging Islam in a point-by-point, propositional manner, using biblical proof texts to establish the Christian position on a given doctrine.[2] Other missiologists have identified a particular book of the Bible, suggesting that the selected book serves as an especially appropriate text for reaching Muslim people. Colin Chapman's selection of the book of Luke stands as an especially well-known example of this approach.[3] Yet others have proposed selecting portions of Scripture from the Old and New Testaments in order to provide an overview of redemption history while accommodating various worldview distinctives.[4]

While this book both recognizes the importance of the concerns and affirms the relative merits of each approach given above, the focused purpose will be to ask, "What section of Scripture might be helpful in explaining the difference between biblical and qur'anic understandings of the atonement, while also providing a challenge to the qur'anic

---

1. Douglas, "Ongoing Strategy Debate," 70, writes, "Conversations regarding contextualization center on questions of 'how much' to contextualize and where to draw the line."

2. See Geisler and Saleeb, *Answering Islam*, whose work will appear below under the methodological approach referred to as "combative."

3. See Chapman, *Cross and Crescent*, 322–23, who argues for using Luke due to Luke's use of the parable of the prodigal son (Luke 15:11–32), its christology, and the manner in which it connects to the book of Acts. Chapman's work will appear below under the methodological approach referred to as "conversational."

4. See Brown, "Selecting and Using," 10–25. Others have followed Brown's recommendation, creating story sets of their own. See Smith and Kai, *T4T*, whose C2C suggestion can be told in a single telling, or broken into multiple lessons. Also, see McIllwain, *Building on Firm Foundations*, whose curriculum comes in a five-volume set, the first story-set for evangelism being seventy lessons long. Brown, Smith, and McIllwain appear below under the methodological approach referred to as "overarching biblical narrative" (OBN).

perspective?" This question ultimately led to the research contained herein. While the inquiry began as a personal curiosity following the *'id al Adha* observations mentioned above, the question generated answers that are instructive for Christians attempting to contextually explain the Christian faith to their Muslim friends.

Simply stated, then, the purpose of this project is to argue for a biblical starting point for explaining a biblical view of atonement to those operating out of a qur'anic worldview. However, as missiologist and anthropologist Paul Hiebert indicates, potential problems abound when employing the word worldview due to the various ways that philosophers, anthropologists, sociologists, and missiologists have used it.[5] Since worldview will provide a key aspect of this book's content, it is important to first pause to define what worldview means within this project from the outset.

Reinforcing Hiebert's claim regarding the wide-ranging ways that worldview is discussed in the academy, David Naugle has dedicated an entire monograph to conducting a historical analysis of the different approaches to—and even rejections of—worldview.[6] Therein, Naugle finds that for philosophers following Immanuel Kant, the word worldview refers to "an intellectual conception of the universe from the perspective of a human knower."[7] Thus, worldview is the product of one's intellectual examination of the world.

Taken in a different direction, however, Naugle highlights Wilhelm Dilthey as an influential philosopher who uses the word worldview to describe an inherent, intuitive response to the world that is not intellectually constructed, but which exists in the social and historical environment into which one is born and which is further formed as one lives in a particular environment.[8] Further distilling Dilthey's perspective, authors Craig Bartholomew and Michael Goheen summarize Dilthy's understanding of worldview by stating that reason cannot simply produce a

---

5. See Hiebert, *Transforming Worldviews*, 13–30, whose first chapter provides a historical overview of the varied uses of worldview within a variety of disciplines.

6. Naugle, *Worldview*. While some criticize and reject the worldview discussion for being so broad as to dissolve into meaninglessness (See the discussion and rebuttal to such dismissal offered by Sire, *Naming the Elephant*, 112–15), the definition proffered herein will provide sufficiently limited parameters to allow the concept to serve as a helpful heuristic device for the comparative religious work undertaken herein.

7. Naugle, *Worldview*, 59.

8. Naugle, *Worldview*, 86–87.

worldview because worldview is the foundation for both science and philosophy.[9]

While multiple other uses of worldview exist, these two examples suffice to determine the importance of positioning one's use of the word on the spectrum of its intended meaning. This project will use the word worldview, then, following Dilthey through the work of Bartholomew and Goheen and intending to communicate a subconscious, foundational way of seeing the world. Worldview, in other words, will mean what N. T. Wright describes as the "presuppositional, pre-cognitive stage of a culture or society."[10] Such an approach understands worldview as the latent framework underlying a person's and a society's understanding of the world that is yet accessible through intentional investigation. Worldview is the subconscious substructure formed by a culture or society's stories that provides answers to basic questions regarding reality, provides the symbols and rituals that tell, rehearse, and reinforce their stories, and which govern the subsequent manner of living in the world.[11]

Therefore, the following chapters attend to the stories told by the Bible and the Qur'an at the point of each text's discussion of atonement. To do so, chapters 2 and 3 will investigate the biblical concept of atonement through the lens of both the Hebrew Bible and the book of Hebrews, then chapter 4 will turn to the Qur'an in order to understand how parallel component parts (sacrifice, blood, forgiveness, cleansing, and atonement) serve divergent purposes, driven by alternative stories and undergirded by different worldviews.

Beyond highlighting the incompatibility of the worldview of Hebrews and the worldview of the Qur'an at the point of each tradition's teaching on atonement, the following chapters will investigate how the book of Hebrews might be used to explain a Christian understanding of atonement to those whose worldview draws on the Qur'an's influence. In the process of this investigation, the current project will capitalize on the narrative-driven explanation of atonement found in Hebrews in order to provide a challenge to the Qur'an's teaching on the same topic while also providing a means to communicate a biblical worldview in which atonement fits in continuity with the teaching throughout the Hebrew Bible.

---

9. Bartholomew and Goheen, *Christian Philosophy*, 19.
10. Wright, *People of God*, 122–24.
11. Wright, *People of God*, 123–24.

Ultimately, this monograph argues that Christ's fulfillment of the Day of Atonement, as presented in the book of Hebrews, exposes distinct worldviews between the Qur'an and Bible, and can be used to challenge qur'anic claims to completing prior revelation.

Communication: Words, Stories, and Worldviews

Basic cross-cultural communication can be an arduous task when the message is simple. The further attempt to explain complex concepts such as atonement across linguistic, geographic, and religious barriers is additionally problematic when the receptor culture or religious tradition uses similar vocabulary loaded with alternative meaning.[12] Missiologist Jackson Wu provides an example of this in his book, *One Gospel for All Nations*, showing that, translated into Chinese and viewed through Chinese culture, the words "law" and "guilt" communicate very different things to an Asian audience than what a Westerner intends when sharing the widely used "Four Spiritual Laws" tract.[13]

Setting the stage for such potential miscommunication between Christians and Muslims, Sidney Griffith, a renowned scholar of Middle Eastern culture and faiths, notes that when Christians began to write theology in Arabic, it was often done in response to Islamic polemic against Christianity and thus shaped by Islamic concerns.[14] Likewise, the Qur'an,

---

12. Reed, *Preparing Missionaries*, 134.

13. Wu, *One Gospel*, 11, gives the example of the use of common Western evangelistic tools in the broader world, writing, "A missionary from America might uncritically translate a presentation like 'the Four Spiritual Laws' or the 'Romans Road' without consideration as to whether categories like 'law' and 'guilt' convey the same thing in a place like East Asia as they do in the American 'Bible Belt.'"

14. Griffith, *Church in Shadow*, 75, notes that Christians writing in Arabic adopted the vocabulary and idiom of Islam, allowing Islamic contention against Christianity to shape subsequent discussions. He writes, "Christians sought to defend the reasonableness of their distinctive doctrines in terms of the same religious idiom as that employed by their Muslim interlocutors and counterparts, who, in accord with the teachings of the Qur'an, often rejected the central Christian doctrines. In contrast with the previously standard modes of Christian discourse in Greek or Syriac, for example, the Arabic-speaking Christian writers often built their arguments on ways of thinking that the Muslims had initially elaborated in view of commending their own faith in the Qur'an and the traditions of the prophet Muhammad." Furthermore, and also citing Griffith's work, see Bridger, "Christian Exegesis of the Qur'an," 25, who summarizes Griffith's findings, saying, "Griffith demonstrates that Christian adoption of Arabic as a theological language resulted in a degree of Islamicization in the diction

along with its underlying theology, has served to shape the Arabic language itself, even when employed by Christian writers and translators of Scripture.[15] Therefore, the vocabulary Christians use in Arabic can prove a barrier to communication with Muslims who use the same words with different meaning and for different purposes.

As the following chapters demonstrate, the Christian concept of making atonement, carried in Arabic by the word *kaffara* (كَفَّر), is prone to such misunderstanding when used in discussion with a Muslim audience.[16] Because the Qur'an and Islamic theology have exerted so much influence on the language of Arabic, then, Christian use of the term must be distinguished by its use in biblical context rather than understood to mean independently as a mere shared lexeme.[17] The biblical narrative provides both the context for the meaning of atonement and the formative basis for a biblical worldview.

In recent decades several notable biblical scholars have made such a point about the relationship between biblical narrative and worldview. Authors such as Kevin Vanhoozer, Craig Bartholomew, Michael Goheen, Michael Williams, and N. T. Wright have all convincingly argued that one of the effects of the biblical story is the shaping of the worldview of its audience.[18] Building on such scholarship, then, this project recognizes

---

and phraseology of early Arabic Christian theology."

15. Griffith, *Bible in Arabic*, 209–10.

16. The verbal root *kaffara* (كَفَّر) and its derivative forms, which are used in the Arabic translation of the OT (e.g., Lev 16) and the NT (e.g., Heb 2:18), and which are found in the Qur'an (e.g., Qur'an 2:271), are translated by derivations of the verb "atone" in English.

17. Griffith, *Bible in Arabic*, 209, explains the earliest emergence of Christian theology and biblical translation in Arabic, saying, "Arguably, it was due in no small part to the religious provocation of Islamic scripture and its influence on the linguistic development of Arabic that Arabic emerged as the *lingua franca* of the newly emerging Islamic polity, becoming the public language even of the newly subject Jewish and Christian communities. It followed as a natural development that the Arabic Qur'an became a stimulus for the first written translations of the Bible into Arabic. . . . It was under the shadow of the Qur'an and a developing Islamic religious discourse that the language of the early translations of the Bible into Arabic took on the Muslim cast that was, as we have seen, a discernable feature in their diction, especially among the Christians."

18. As will be considered in chapter 6, the biblical story provides a context and a plotline that serves to form a biblical worldview within which the Christian life might appropriately situate itself throughout the ages and across cultures. This point has been extensively and convincingly argued by Vanhoozer, *Drama of Doctrine*. See also Bartholomew and Goheen, *Drama of Scripture*; and Williams, "Systematic Theology."

that merely attempting to define atonement lexically will prove unhelpful without giving attention to its function within the larger narrative in which it is situated and the subsequent impact upon the biblical worldview.

Concurring with Wright and Vanhoozer from an anthropological and missiological perspective, Paul Hiebert claims, "To understand Scripture, we must seek to understand the worldview themes that underlie the whole. The unity of Scripture lies first in its insistence that all the biblical events are part of one great story—in other words, a central diachronic worldview theme."[19] Therefore the overarching biblical narrative context in which Christian perceptions of atonement are located carries a great deal of explanatory weight, giving meaning to the words and shaping the concepts employed within Scripture. Simply stated, the story itself is a key to understanding the individual concepts located within its narrative.

Hiebert goes on to show that the storied framework of Israel, bearing the concepts of sin, sacrifice, salvation, and Messiah, is the narrative precursor for God's final revelation in Christ, concluding, "Had Christ come at the time of Abraham, the people would not have had the fundamental categories and worldview to understand his self-revelation."[20] If, then, the power of Israel's story so establishes the biblical worldview that the Christ event would not make sense apart from the preceding narrative, it is crucial that one presents the Christ event's implications to new audiences by rehearsing the same worldview-shaping narrative into which it fits.[21]

For one interested in communicating the biblical concept of atonement to a Muslim audience, then, the OBN can provide a means of distinguishing a Christian use of *kaffara* from that of the Qur'an. Despite the fact that the Qur'an lays claim to much of the same history as the Christians and Jews, this project will show that the qur'anic worldview diverges substantially from the biblical worldview, and that the concept of atonement is a central point at which this divergence might be recognized. The initial answer, then, to the question of why it is so difficult to explain Christian atonement to Muslims is that there are lexical,

---

In a similar vein, see the five-act-play model for Christian theology and life by Wright, *People of God*, 140–41.

19. Hiebert, *Transforming Worldviews*, 266.

20. Hiebert, *Transforming Worldviews*, 266.

21. Throughout, "Christ event" refers to the historical death, resurrection, and ascension of Jesus.

narrative, and worldview-level conflicts between the two systems of faith which coalesce at the concept of atonement.

Returning to the central concern of this project, then, one might ask again, "Does the book of Hebrews provide a narrative-driven, contextually appropriate section of Scripture by which to challenge the Qur'an's claim to continuity with prior revelation and also to explain a biblical perspective on atonement in Christ to those influenced by the Qur'an?" The following chapters will address this question, arguing an affirmative answer, and demonstrating that Hebrews overcomes lexical, narrative, and ritual barriers to communication, and finally proposing a model by which to utilize the message of Hebrews and to communicate a biblical position to Muslims in contextually appropriate manner.

Literature Review

Prior to beginning the argument, however, it is important to consider the concerns that have driven other arguments for how to engage Muslims contextually with the gospel. Surveying other offerings will both situate the current argument within the literature and prepare the reader for chapter six's concluding thoughts which will address many of the concerns of alternative methodologies. While it would prove inadvisable to attempt to investigate every piece of scholarly and popular literature that suggests a way forward in Muslim evangelism, there are several authors who have done the difficult-yet-invaluable work of categorizing approaches to contextualization.[22]

Unfortunately, despite several attempts at categorization, the discussion regarding various approaches to contextualized ministry among Muslims has neither agreed upon a single, universal taxonomy, nor utilized the same categorical labels in the same ways.[23] For this reason,

22. Some examples of such categorization of contextualization approaches include Hesselgrave and Rommen, *Contextualization*; Bevans, *Models of Contextual Theology*; Moreau, *Contextualization in World Missions*. For examples used in this project of Muslim-ministry contextualization categorizations, see Travis, "Must All Muslims?," 411–15; Terry, "Approaches," 314–19; Schlorff, *Missiological Models*.

23. Consider the distinction between Schlorff's use of "dialogical" vocabulary and Terry's use of the same. See Schlorff, *Missiological Models*, 23, whose dialogical model rejects attempts to encourage the conversion of people from one faith to another, opting instead for the creation of a diverse "community of communities." On the other hand, Terry, "Approaches," 316, uses dialogical to refer to the work of those who are culturally sensitive, engaged in listening and speaking, yet who are still committed to conversionism.

the following section will provide a synthesis of two such taxonomies: Steven Bevans's more general *Models of Contextual Theology* and Sam Schlorff's Muslim-ministry focused offering, *Missiological Models in Ministry to Muslims*.[24] The resulting simplified taxonomy highlights three basic evangelical approaches, grouping them by shared concerns, starting points, postures, and methods.

By restricting this taxonomy to evangelical approaches, this paper intends to follow the basic definition of evangelical offered by David Bebbington. Bebbington's so-called quadrilateral defines evangelicals as those who uphold the authority of the Bible, find salvation in the cross of Jesus the Messiah, are active in expressing the gospel and its implications, and who are committed to conversionism.[25] Such restriction does not suggest that non-evangelical missiologists do not offer significant contributions, but merely serves to narrow the scope of this project to distinctions within evangelicalism.

Stephen Bevans

As indicated above, Stephen Bevans is an influential writer who has proposed a taxonomy for categorizing six different approaches to doing contextual theology in the widely-read book *Models of Contextual Theology*. Bevans opens his book jarringly, stating, "There is no such thing as 'theology'; there is only contextual theology."[26] Working from this thesis, Bevans goes on within the book to suggest that there are six basic models for doing contextual theology (see Table 1.1).[27] Three of Bevans's models find expression in evangelical circles, broadly speaking: the synthetic model, the translation model, and the counter-cultural model.

---

24. Bevans' *Models*, xvi, went through nine printings in a decade. Its second edition, revised and expanded, is in its seventeenth printing. Schlorff, *Missiological Models*, xiii. Schlorff's book focuses on work among Muslims, though his categories overlap and occasionally depart from Bevans's distinctions. Thus, Bevans will be used due to his impact on missiology, and Schlorff will be consulted for his Muslim focus.

25. Bebbington, *Evangelicalism*, 2–3.

26. Bevans, *Models*, 3.

27. Bevans, *Models*, 31–33.

TABLE 1.1
Bevans' Six Models of Contextual Theology[28]

Model	Method	Strengths	Weaknesses
Translation Model View of Scripture: Supracultural & Complete	Know the context and insert the gospel into it	Takes Christian message seriously; recognizes contextual ambiguity; high view of Scripture	Naïve notions of culture and gospel; propositional notion of revelation
Anthropological model View of Scripture: Culturally conditioned & incomplete	Know the culture and pull the gospel out of it	Takes context seriously; provides fresh perspectives of Christianity; starts with where people are	Prey to cultural romanticism; insufficiently critical of culture; equates context and Scripture as equally authoritative
Praxis Model View of Scripture: Culturally conditioned & incomplete	Unending spiral of practice-reflection-practice	Strong epistemological foundation; provides an "alternative vision"	Close connection with Marxism; potentially dangerous overemphasis on human effort
Synthetic Model View of Scripture: Culturally conditioned & incomplete	Conversation with all partners in order to complete that which is lacking in both culture and Scripture/tradition	Attitude of dialogue; emphasizes the ongoing process of contextual theology	Danger of "selling out" and being "wishy-washy"; potentially syncretistic
Transcendental Model View of Scripture: Culturally conditioned & incomplete	Sympathy and antipathy; make room for experience and encounter	Emphasizes theology as activity; recognizes the contextual nature of all theology	Too abstract and ideal to be practical; false claim to universality
Counter-cultural Model View of Scripture: Complete though human understanding thereof is not	Use Christian story as a lens to interpret, critique, and challenge context	Strong engagement of context matched with fidelity to the gospel; high view of Scripture; basis in critical realist epistemology	Danger of being anti-cultural, sectarian, and mono-cultural

According to Bevans, the counter-cultural model is the most conservative. It takes a high view of Scripture, believing its message to be supracultural, and challenging to all who exist in the world of fallen

28. Adapted from Bevans, *Models*, 141–43.

cultures.²⁹ The approach taken by those of this persuasion is not, however, the combative, debate-like style suggested by Sam Schlorff's most conservative categories.³⁰ Instead, it is a Bible-driven approach to sharing the biblical metanarrative, expecting that the biblical story will confront all cultures.³¹

The second conservative category provided by Bevans is the translation model. Proponents of this model hold to a high view of Scripture, believing it to be complete in and of itself. However, in distinction with the posture of counter-cultural practitioners, they also hold a positive view of culture.³² Where the counter-cultural model seeks to radically challenge culture, the translation model expects to be able to deposit the kernel of biblical, propositional truth into the husk of a culture.³³

The third of Bevans's models to fit under the evangelical umbrella is the synthetic model. Bevans warns that this model is sometimes accused of being "wishy-washy" or of "selling out" to the culture because synthetic models see Scripture as incomplete apart from cultural appropriation.³⁴ While Bevans' warning must be heeded by evangelicals wary of compromising biblical fidelity due to cultural accommodation, the final chapter presents a model that takes a similar tack to the synthetic approach, modifying what David Clark refers to as a dialogical approach,

---

29. Bevans, *Models*, 31.

30. Schlorff, *Missiological Models*, 10–14. See Schlorff's nineteenth-century polemic and direct approach models.

31. Bevans, *Models*, 143, claims that the counter-cultural model uses the "Christian story as [a] clue to history; [to] use the story as [a] lens to interpret, critique, and challenge context."

32. Bevans, *Models*, 141.

33. Bevans, *Models*, 37–40. Both Bevans and Schlorff make use of a category of models they call "translation." Both cite Charles Kraft's distinction between dynamic equivalence in translation and formal correspondence as a key aspect of the translation model. Bevans, while recognizing the ongoing debate within evangelical circles regarding the content or essence of the kernel of gospel truth, leans toward a relatively conservative expression of Christian truth in the kernel of various world cultures. For Schlorff, however, translation models have drifted away from propositional claims toward flexible expression of basically congruent ideas. His perspective on the dangers of the translation model causes him to argue against its position within conservative missiology, placing it instead in a more liberal, synthetic category. See Schlorff, *Missiological Models*, 26, 124–32.

34. Bevans, *Models*, 94–95.

and militates against the cultural pressures to conform by arguing for a biblical rather than cultural starting point for intercultural theology and contextualization.[35]

These three categories, including their assumptions regarding Scripture and culture, find expression in contemporary evangelical missions. However, as Sam Schlorff's study brings to light, there is both overlap and divergence between the general categories offered by Bevans and the models employed in mission to Muslims. A brief overview of Schlorff's work will highlight similarities and differences between his and Bevans's work.

Sam Schlorff

Sam Schlorff, a long-time missionary to Muslims, has written what David Lundy calls a *pièce de resistance* surveying twentieth-century approaches to Muslim ministry.[36] While Bevans's work focuses more broadly on contextual theology writ large, Schlorff's book is concerned specifically with approaches to Muslim ministry. Table 1.2 provides a summary chart of Schlorff's categories, showing both strengths and weaknesses of each. As with Bevans, several of the categories that Schlorff includes in his taxonomy fall outside of the bounds of evangelicalism as defined above. The following chart allows the reader to see the various models considered by Schlorff so as to highlight those that might be considered evangelical and which are outside of the concerns of this project.

---

35. See Clark, *To Know*, 113–14.
36. Lundy, foreword to *Missiological Models*, xi.

TABLE 1.2

Schlorff's Seven Models of Ministry to Muslims[2]

Model	Method	Strengths	Weaknesses
Nineteenth-Century Imperial Model	Demolition of the house of Islam and the erection of Christianity in its place	Recognizes the discontinuity between Christianity and Islam; holds a high view of Scripture and exclusivity of the gospel	Discrepancies and contradictions; building on supposed "truths" of Islam to present the gospel; inattentive to Islamic culture
Direct Approach Model	Radical displacement of Islam	High view of Scripture and exclusivity of the gospel; corrective of the imperial model's destructive tendencies in favor of constructive gospel presentation	Islamic culture is not given serious attention
Fulfillment Model	Fulfillment through the gospel of the deepest needs of the Muslim which are unsatisfied by Islam	Culturally sensitive approach to sharing the gospel with Muslims; abandons the totally negative evaluation of Islam	Intrinsically relativistic and syncretistic; undermines the authority of Scripture and the exclusivity of the gospel message
Dialectical Model	Transformation of both Christianity and Islam into conformity with "the Christian revelation"	Recognizes the discontinuity between Christianity and Islam; insightful interaction with Islam	Tends to be based more on dialecticism/existentialism than on the biblical evaluation of man; views dialectic as a principle of truth
Dialogical Model	Creation of a synthesis of spiritualities, bringing all faiths into a "community of communities"	Originally borne of the biblically justifiable idea of dialogue; takes Islam seriously	Relativism, syncretism, and a loss of biblical authority
Translation/Dynamic Equivalence Model	Emergence of a "people movement to Christ" within the Islamic community	Serious attention to and concern with Muslim culture	Assumes Islamic culture to be a neutral vehicle; begins with Islamic rather than biblical categories and attempts to fill them with Christian meaning
Betrothal Model	Bring Muslims into the kingdom of God through faith in Christ; discipleship and community formation	Acknowledges the discontinuity between Christianity and Islam, the Qur'an and the Bible; begins with the Bible	Underdeveloped ecclesiology; lack of suggested biblical material

37. Adapted from Schlorff, *Missiological Models*.

For example, as defined by Schlorff, dialogical models fall outside of the bounds of this paper's evangelical concern. Schlorff notes that proponents of this approach deny the uniqueness of the gospel, reject a high, authoritative view of the Bible, and aim to create a pluralistic religious community rather than holding to conversionism.[38] Thus this category will not be considered below.

Regarding methods which espouse a high view of biblical authority, Schlorff's imperial and direct approach models see the purpose of Christian engagement with Islam as a battle for truth. Schlorff considers the polemics of the nineteenth century to coalesce rather seamlessly with the direct approach models of the twentieth century, though perhaps with more of an apologetic tenor than polemic.[39] Neither model exhibits much awareness of Islamic cultural concerns, thus neither approach has a direct corollary in Bevans' chart.

Turning to Schlorff's fulfillment, translation, and dialectical models, one finds overlap with Bevans's synthetic models. In fact, in terms of each model's hermeneutical approach, Schlorff defines these three categories as being synthetic mixtures of cultural and biblical authority.[40] Practitioners of the fulfillment model see Islam as a partial apprehension of truth which requires Christian revelation to fulfill and complete what it lacks.[41] Similarly, though more expansively, Schlorff's dialectic model proposes that Christian revelation offers corrective and affirmation to both Christianity and Islam.[42] Per Schlorff, proponents of the dialectical model maintain that the goal of Christian witness is to unveil how Christian revelation fulfills Christianity and Islam, with both systems being imperfect expressions of truth.[43] As defined by Schlorff, the translational model also employs a synthetic hermeneutic, seeking to utilize Islamic vocabulary while filling it with Christian meaning such that the result is

38. Schlorff, *Missiological Models*, 23–24.

39. Schlorff, *Missiological Models*, 13–14.

40. Schlorff, *Missiological Models*, 124–25. notes that on a hermeneutical level, most of his categories represent synthesis hermeneutics that either intentionally or inadvertently attribute some level of authoritative truth to the texts, religious practices, and culture of Islamic societies.

41. Schlorff, *Missiological Models*, 16–17, summarizes the hermeneutic of fulfillment models saying, "The Bible and Qur'an are interpreted in such a way as to bring the biblical and qur'anic perspectives more or less together (a hermeneutic of synthesis)."

42. Schlorff, *Missiological Models*, 16.

43. Schlorff, *Missiological Models*, 18.

an in-culture movement of Muslims to Christ.[44] Thus, per Schlorff's definitions, these three categories exhibit significant overlap with Bevans's synthetic model.

Finally, the model for which Schlorff argues, the betrothal model, straddles Bevans's translation and counter-cultural models. It is comparable to Bevans's translation model in that it aims to respect Islamic culture and meaning, extending Christian truth in comprehensible and non-ambiguous form. This requires understanding Islam and qur'anic vocabulary on its own terms, thus respecting the culture and its forms.[45] On the other hand, it takes a similar posture to the counter-cultural model by seeing culture and context as being non-neutral. Furthermore, the betrothal model utilizes analytic hermeneutics over and against the synthetic hermeneutic discussed above, which overlaps with Bevans's assessment of the counter-cultural model.[46] Schlorff describes analytical hermeneutics as those approaches which prioritize the texts of the Bible and Qur'an as they stand rather than attempting to redefine terms with different meaning than what they exert within their context.[47]

While Bevans and Schlorff both provide helpful insight into the field of contextual theology and missiological approaches to ministry among Muslims, this brief survey demonstrates that there is both significant overlap and distinction between their classifications. Likewise, both offerings have focused on missiological approaches of the twentieth century. To provide both fresh nomenclature and an updated set of references for the twenty-first century, the following section will offer a simplified taxonomy of approaches to Muslims for use within this project.

A Simplified Taxonomy

As can be seen in Schlorff's classification of models of Muslim ministry, there are commonalities between his and Bevans's work, yet there are also

---

44. Schlorff, *Missiological Models*, 26.

45. Schlorff, *Missiological Models*, 158.

46. Bevans, *Models*, 126. It should be noted, however, that Bevans' counter-cultural model is much more overtly focused on the narrative-driven presentation of biblical teaching and Schlorff's betrothal model is more concerned with kingdom teaching, being less obviously concerned to highlight the narrative shape of the gospel.

47. Schlorff, *Missiological Models*, 147, explicitly states, "the forms and religious structures of Islam cannot be considered 'a neutral vehicle' in the contextual process, as the proponents of dynamic equivalence [translation models] would have us believe."

places of ambiguity and some of Schlorff's models overlap with different categories as defined by Bevans.

Likewise, where Bevans includes the OBN-focused approach of the counter-cultural model, Schlorff's classification does not offer an exact corollary. For that reason, this book will consider the points of overlap between Bevans and Schlorff and attempt a simplified synthesis of evangelical models based on their relative concerns, themes, starting points, and methods (see Table 1.3).

The purpose for this simplified synthesis is not to challenge either Bevans or Schlorff's insight, but rather to avoid the confusion of using vocabulary that is already freighted with potentially divergent meaning. Likewise, the focus of this particular classification of methods is the underlying concerns and postures of various practitioners. This will allow the argument made in this paper to be assessed against the concerns of contending options in order to determine whether or not it is a satisfactory starting point for explaining Christian atonement to those who have inherited a qur'anic worldview.

As seen in Table 1.3, the three categories of approach which emerge from a fusion of Bevans and Schlorff are: combative models, conversational models, and OBN models. The following section will illustrate these three broad categories by a brief look at a selection of influential twenty-first-century practitioners who represent each category. Following the treatment of each model, a summary will highlight the concerns, themes, methods, and starting points of each approach. Finally, a brief critical analysis of all three broad methods will highlight strengths and weaknesses of each model.

TABLE 1.3
Fusion of Bevans and Schlorff

MODEL FUSION[48]	BEVANS	SCHLORFF	START POINT
Combative Models Concern: Defending truth; doing battle with falsehood Theme: Warfare Method: Debate & confrontation	Translation Model (supracultural message of Scripture) Counter-cultural Model (attitude toward culture)	Nineteenth Century Polemic Model Direct Engagement Model Betrothal Model (propositional & ideological)	Sender culture propositions and understanding Emphasis on reason and logic, often from a Western standpoint
Conversational Models Concern: Culturally appropriate gospel expression Theme: Dialogue Method: Hearing and discovering the religious other's perspective	Synthetic Model Anthropological Model Transcendental Model Translation Model (view of culture)	Fulfillment Model Dialectical Model Dialogical Model Translation/ Dynamic Equivalence Model	Receptor culture and understanding Emphasis on the cultural expression and embodiment of truth
Overarching Biblical Narrative Models Concern: Biblically-based formation of worldview prior to cultural expression Theme: Worldview Method: Storytelling	Counter-cultural Model (storied form of gospel presentation)	Betrothal Model (kingdom-focused approach)	Biblical narrative and worldview Emphasis on the worldview-shaping narrative of the Bible

48. For the purposes of this book, this fusion of categories has been formed from the surveys provided by Bevans and Schlorff. While there are points of overlap between Bevans's and Schlorff's taxonomies, this project seeks to simplify the surveys, to highlight the strengths and weaknesses present in the models on offer, to assess some of the most popular approaches to Muslim ministry that have emerged since Schlorff's work, and to screen out models that would be unacceptable to conservative evangelical missiologists and practitioners.

Combative Models

Schlorff and others have recognized that much of the Muslim ministry of the nineteenth century took a polemical approach to Islam. This approach, bearing little fruit and causing much disdain for the practitioners, has largely gone out of fashion.[49] However, even though most of the academic discussion in the early twenty-first century focuses on more nuanced contextualized approaches, one readily finds contemporary examples of those who approach Islam in the posture of combat.

Examples of such approaches often take the form of point-by-point debate or polemic approach to the religious other. As Schlorff indicates, such approaches are marked by a desire to expose the presumed cultural and logical inferiority of Islam.[50] The following section will consider some of the most influential advocates of this posture in order to highlight their concern to uphold biblical truth and demolish non-biblical truth claims made by Islam.

Norman Geisler and Abdul Saleeb

Perhaps one of the most circulated books in this category is the systematic treatment of Islamic claims against Christianity and Christian contentions against Islam found in Norman Geisler and Abdul Saleeb's book, *Answering Islam*.[51] Now in the fifth printing of its second edition, *Answering Islam* is widely read as a guide for Christians engaging Islam, having been cited in over one hundred publications as a resource purporting to explain and expose Islamic deficiency in light of Christian claims and theology.[52] The introduction to the second edition clearly identifies the authors' posture towards Islam as one of conflict, stating, "Like many other battles in history, we believe that the pen is sharper than the sword. The real war will be won with words, not weapons. The success of Christianity over Islam as a world religion rises or falls on the

---

49. See Schlorff, *Missiological Models*, 11–14; Terry, "Approaches," 314; Parshall, "Rethinking the Gospel," 117–18.

50. Schlorff, *Missiological Models*, 4.

51. Geisler and Saleeb, *Answering Islam*, 7, note in the preface to the second edition of their book that it had sold more than 42,000 copies.

52. See the 101 entries listed as having cited *Answering Islam* located by Google Scholar.

battlefield of ideas."⁵³ The stated purpose, then, of Geisler and Saleeb's work is to go to intellectual battle against Islam.

A cursory glance at the table of contents reveals the particular points of engagement with Islam roughly parallels the categories of Christian Systematic Theology employed by Geisler elsewhere.⁵⁴ This allows direct comparison between the two faiths, albeit from a categorical mold already formed by Christian thought and theology.

Michael Licona

Geisler and Saleeb are not alone in their combative approach. In 2006, Michael Licona wrote a book entitled *Paul Meets Muhammad*, staging a hypothetical debate between Paul and Muhammad. The topic of this debate is the historical resurrection of Christ.⁵⁵ In his introduction, Licona posits that, since the resurrection is Christianity's foundation, "the objective of this book is to assist Muslims and Christians in understanding the discussion and in making an informed assessment of the evidence, the arguments, and the conclusions on the resurrection of Jesus that each faith promotes."⁵⁶

Licona's projection of Paul goes about this task by making an argument for the resurrection based on logic, extra-biblical testimony, and historically trustworthy biblical material.⁵⁷ Thus, while Licona's work is unique in its presentation, it is also an example of Christian-Muslim

---

53. Geisler and Saleeb, *Answering Islam*, 8.

54. Geisler and Saleeb, *Answering Islam*, 5–6. The first part of the book covers Islamic theology using categories of monotheism (Doctrine of God), creation and man (Doctrine of Creation and Humanity), prophets (Doctrine of History/Revelation), Muhammad, the Qur'an (Doctrine of Revelation), and end times and salvation (Doctrine of Eschatology and Soteriology). Part two provides a Christian response to these Islamic categories, and is followed by part three that reinforces the Christian position over and against Islamic polemic against Christianity. For similarity in categorical treatment of Islam, see Geisler, *Systematic Theology*, whose categories here are "Bible," "God," "Creation," "Sin," "Salvation," "Church," and "Last Things."

55. Licona, *Paul Meets Muhammad*.

56. Licona, *Paul Meets Muhammad*, 13.

57. Licona, *Paul Meets Muhammad*, 28, writes, "My case for the resurrection of Jesus will be based on three facts for which I will present strong evidence. This evidence consists of logical arguments, nonbiblical testimony, and biblical testimony for which a robust case for historicity can be made. Indeed, my three facts can be supported and accepted by the professional historian."

engagement that is firmly rooted in the combative camp, going to intellectual battle against Islam.

It is noteworthy that, like other practitioners of the combative model, Licona's work highlights the importance of the Christ event—particularly the resurrection—for the Christian faith. In 1 Corinthians 15:14–19, Paul provides biblical precedent for this claim, demonstrating that Christian hope hangs on Christ's resurrection. Recognizing the truth of Paul's claim, Licona also falls in line with other combative approaches, placing the historical resurrection of Jesus at the core of his argument.

Nabeel Qureshi

Not only can one find contemporary support for the use of combative methods, but there are also recent examples of those for whom an encounter with the claims of Western Christian theology couched in the terms of formal logic have proven an effective means used by the Spirit in their conversion. Nabeel Qureshi is an author whose books, both of which are *The New York Times* bestsellers, detail his own journey through such logical, cognitive arguments from devout Muslim to committed Christian.[58]

Since logical, rational, and historical arguments for Christianity convinced Qureshi of the truth of the biblical message, he advocates for this type of method as he shares his own journey, making his case for the Christian gospel.[59] His stated purpose is "to equip you with facts and knowledge, showing the strength of the case for the gospel in contrast with the case for Islam."[60] Qureshi goes on to identify the death, resurrection, and claim to divinity of Jesus as the foundational pillars of the Christian confession. Likewise, in arguing for the historicity of these pillars, Qureshi acknowledges that the historical case for Muhammad's life and teaching is weak.[61] While both of Qureshi's books are presented as accounts of his personal experience, the clearly stated purpose is to equip

---

58. In fact, Michael Licona and his methodology were influential in Qureshi's life as he converted to Christianity. See Qureshi, *Seeking Allah*, 15.

59. See Qureshi, *No God but One*; Qureshi, *Finding Jesus*.

60. Qureshi, *Seeking Allah*, 17.

61. Qureshi, *Seeking Allah*, 18.

Christians with the ability to demonstrate the veracity of the gospel over and against those who would argue for Islam as the ultimate truth.[62]

Summary of Combative Models

The authors mentioned above are but a few twenty-first-century examples of a class of approach to Islam labeled as the combative model.[63] Such approaches usually begin with Western Christian theological premises and focus on points of divergence between Christian and Muslim theological propositions. Arguments are formed on biblical, logical, philosophical, and historical data and often take the posture of debate. Combative models concern themselves with the intellectual defeat of Islamic claims and a defense of biblical truth.

Other, perhaps more prolific, contemporary models of Muslim engagement diverge from the combative model by seeking instead to highlight the similarities and points of overlap between the faiths to encourage communication. Advocates of non-confrontational models seek to utilize commonalities to promote understanding and to encourage Christians to walk with Muslims as far as possible until the two paths diverge irreconcilably. Such practitioners are often drawn to a form of the second category of approaches: conversational models. The following section will highlight some of the influential approaches to Islamic engagement that fall under the umbrella of conversational models.

---

62. Qureshi, *Seeking Allah*, 17–18; Qureshi, *No God but One*, 13, writes of both works that, "[*Seeking Allah*] is the heart of my story. . . . [*No God but One*] is the mind of my story, examining the religions and their claims."

63. Other notable contemporary advocates of similar approaches include: Shamoun, "Where is the Blood?," whose article is an instance of the overarching approach of the answering-islam.org approach. His argument regarding the Day of Atonement, however, is of particular interest to the current project and will be referenced throughout; Also, Gabriel, *Jesus and Muhammad*; Tennent, *Christianity*; Madrigal, *Explaining the Trinity*. One of the most fair examples of this approach is Kateregga and Shenk, *A Muslim and a Christian*, who highlight the distinctives of both faiths, but the book is formatted in two parts so as to allow both Christian or Muslim concerns to be addressed in their own terms prior to inviting the opposing side's response.

Conversational Models

As seen in the classifications provided by Bevans and Schlorff, many of the distinctions in models of contextualized ministry derive from the practitioner's perception of the cultural context's relative truth value.[64] Bevans contends that there exist at least two basic poles of theological orientation which determine the trajectory of subsequent models of ministry: creation-centered orientations and redemption-centered orientations.[65] Creation-centered orientations expect to find God revealing himself within culture and creation.[66] Human experience and culture are basically good and potentially revelatory. Conversely, redemption-centered orientations view culture and human experience skeptically as tainted by sin and in need of either replacement or radical transformation.[67]

For evangelical missiologists, then, conversation models might best be thought of as those approaches which aim to find a middle way of dialogue between culture and supraculture, between experience and special revelation. Conversational models in ministry to Muslims intend to accommodate as much Islamic culture as possible without slipping into syncretism. Expressions of this accommodation, however, vary widely. Before surveying the highlighted practitioners of this model, it is necessary to clarify the general position of the dialogue partners who are the focus of this project. For this reason, a brief history of contextualization and an overview of the C1–C6 spectrum will help to narrow the field and highlight the general concern of conversation models by avoiding the particular nuances of the ongoing conflicts within evangelical missiology.

Contextualization and the C1–C6 Spectrum

Finding the appropriate balance between the poles of Bevans's two basic theological orientations has been a point of conflict for much of the contemporary discussion in mission to Muslims. Debate focuses on the appropriate degree to which one might clothe the gospel message in cultural garb in order to make it appealing, communicable, and meaningful

---

64. See Schlorff, *Missiological Models*, 124–25;
65. Bevans, *Models*, 21.
66. Bevans, *Models*, 21.
67. Bevans, *Models*, 21.

without endorsing anti-biblical concepts.⁶⁸ Particularly in the last half-century, the word "contextualization" has been widely used to describe this process of making the message of Scripture contextually comprehensible.⁶⁹ Though most evangelical missiologists unite around the expressed goal of meaningful communication of the unchanging word of God to changing cultural contexts, consensus regarding a common definition of contextualization has proven elusive.⁷⁰

Wanting for a commonly held definition for contextualization, John Travis has developed a spectrum of contextual approaches to describe and distinguish various methods of ministry to Muslims.⁷¹ Since its publication, it has become the field-standard way of referring to various approaches, serving to frame and shape the form of the debate itself.⁷² The

---

68. Tennent, "Followers of Jesus," 101, writes, "There has been considerable discussion in recent years concerning various proposals that might help the church to more effectively communicate the gospel to Muslims who continue to be the most resistant groups to the Christian message."

69. The word contextualization was introduced into missiological parlance by the Theological Education Fund, *Ministry*; Bevans, *Models*, 185–201. This lexical debut, attributed to Shoki Coe, is highlighted by Hesselgrave and Rommen, *Contextualization*, 28.

70. Hesselgrave and Rommen, *Contextualization*, 33–34, include definitions from Byang H. Kato: "[Contextualization is] making concepts or ideals relevant in a given situation." Bruce J. Nicholls: "[Contextualization is] the translation of the unchanging content of the Gospel of the kingdom into verbal form meaningful to the peoples in their separate culture and within their particular existential situations." George W. Peters: "Contextualization properly applied means to discover *the legitimate implications* of the gospel in a given situation. It goes deeper than application. Application I can make or need not make without doing injustice to the text. Implication is *demanded* by a proper exegesis of the text."

71. Travis's scale first appeared in 1998. Travis, "C1 to C6 Spectrum," 407–8. See also Travis's argument for C5 in Travis, "Must All Muslims?," 411–15. Debates are ongoing over the appropriate citation of the Qur'an; use of qur'anic terminology and names; whether or not former Muslims should refer to themselves as Muslim followers of *'isa* (the qur'anic name for Jesus); how to decide if a follower of Christ should participate in Islamic religious ritual (prayers, fasting, pilgrimage, alms); and whether or not a Christ-follower can say the Islamic *shahada* ("There is no god but God, and Muhammad is His messenger/prophet"). See, also, the debate over whether or not Christians and Muslims are identifying the same referent when they use the word, *Allah* as considered by Volf, *Allah*; likewise, see George, *Is the Father of Jesus the God of Muhammad?* Another C5 advocate is Massey, "Misunderstanding C5." For a case study, see Woodberry, "Contextualization," 171–86.

72. See Tennent, "Followers of Jesus," 101. Tennent cites the impact of Travis's spectrum, saying, "The most well-known summary of the spectrum of Muslim background

spectrum breaks down into six parts. On one end, C1 models import Western practices, forms, language, and ministry into a new context with little alteration. On the other end of the spectrum, C6 models involve secret groups of Christ-followers who maintain Islamic identity and remain hidden in the Muslim community.[73]

Contemporary controversy focuses on C5 models and their willingness to maintain Muslim identity, observe Islamic religious ritual, and uphold the authority of the Qur'an and Muhammad.[74] Some C5 advocates have even suggested that Arabic Bible translations should use an alternative to "Son(s) of God" as divine familial terminology (DFT) is offensive to Muslims.[75] While these conversations are of critical importance within the realm of Muslim ministry, C5 strategies fall outside of the intended boundaries of this project due to the potential compromise of biblical authority such practices represent.[76] The following section will survey three C4 proponents by briefly considering their approaches to contextualized ministry among Muslims.

Phil Parshall

Within the often-divisive discussions regarding appropriate Muslim contextualization, one advocate of the conversational model that has attempted to speak challengingly to all parties is Phil Parshall. While advocating for caution against the embrace of C5 contextualization and the promotion of so-called insider movements,[77] Parshall also suggests that

---

believers (known as MBBs) found in the Islamic world was published by John Travis in 19[98] and has become the standard reference point for discussing contextualization in the Islamic context." Also, Williams, "Revisiting," 335, notes, "This spectrum has helped to steer all subsequent discussion and discourse."

73. Travis, "C1 to C6 Spectrum," 407–8.

74. Williams, "Revisiting," 339.

75. For those who argue for flexibility in translation of Son(s) of God, see Brown, "Translating Biblical Term," 135–45, and "Why Muslims." For those who argue against changing the familial language of the Bible, see Hausfeld, "Necessity," 210–29.

76. I acknowledge the fact that this discussion is much more nuanced than this book has time or space to address. However, for those interested in a more robust argument regarding the risk posed to biblical authority by advocates of C5 models, see Tennent, "Followers of Jesus"; Hausfeld, "Necessity"; Williams, "Revisiting."

77. Parshall, "Danger! New Directions in Contextualization," 404–10. Parshall shows that insider movements (IM) are variously defined, but they tend to be forms of radical contextualization that promote the total retention of the Muslim identity and

there needs to be more sensitivity to potential works of God by way of C5 methodology among those of the C4 persuasion.[78] Parshall himself has a much longer missiological history than the C-spectrum, though, as with his many contemporaries, his recent writings have been drawn into and shaped by the spectrum's categories.

Throughout the body of his work, Parshall admits of his evangelical commitment to biblical authority and searches the Scriptures themselves for instances of contextualization, attempting to discover how far one might be biblically permitted to go in accommodating Islamic culture.[79] His findings, following most offerings on contextualization, focus on the use of non-Christian forms, texts, and customs to express Christian meaning. For example, he compares the Jerusalem Council's conclusions in Acts 15 with Paul's teaching on meat sacrificed to idols in 1 Corinthians 8 in order to show how Paul determined his teaching based on the cultural setting of his audience.[80]

---

at times can go so far as to endorse the Qur'an and Muhammad as a prophet. Some advocates of C5 methodology even recommend that Christian missionaries legally convert to Islam in order to be accepted within the *ummah* and to point Muslims to Jesus from within. See Parshall, *Muslim Evangelism*, 69–75. Parshall lauds the goals of the C-5 camp, though he notes that the same goals are held by C-4 advocates. He goes on, however, to list five areas of concern with C5 methodology: 1) Encouraging MBB's to permanently remain in the mosque; 2) Affirmation of the *shahada* that deems Muhammad to be Allah's prophet; 3) Use of the unqualified identifier, Muslim; 4) Misuse of biblical material to justify C5 approaches; 5) Replacement of "Son of God" with "*Isa Al-Masih.*"

78. Parshall, *Muslim Evangelism*, 75. After having expressed his concerns and also provided anecdotal evidence of expansive "Insider Movements" of Muslims to Christ, Parshall concludes, "I do not want to finish my life (now sixty-six years into it) as one known as a heresy hunter. Yes, I will continue (with greater sensitivity, I trust) to voice my concerns. But if I err toward imbalance, I want it to be on the side of love, affirmation, and lifting up my colleagues as better than myself."

79. See Parshall, *Muslim Evangelism*. For example, in the introduction to the revised edition of *Muslim Evangelism*, Parshall states his purpose for writing, saying, "As long as we do not engage in compromising the Bible, I feel that we are no worse off proceeding with careful and sensitive experimentation than we are by remaining content with methodology that has proven to be ineffective in bringing Muslims to our Lord." Additionally, while the original edition was published in 1981, the revised edition of 2003 has adopted C-spectrum vocabulary, reflecting the impact on his approach.

80. Parshall, *Muslim Evangelism*, 37–39. For the mixed groups of gentiles and former Jews addressed in Acts 15, Parshall notes that it appears that the gentiles agreed to abstain in order to avoid offense based on HB teaching. However, in Corinth, when writing to an exclusively gentile audience, Paul allows for more freedom of conscience

Ultimately, Parshall's methodology takes an insider's approach to knowing the culture in order to express Christian theology and practice in the garb of the culture so as to demonstrate that the supracultural message of the gospel is applicable and expressible to the receptor culture.[81] His suggestions require that the Christian communicator become familiar enough with the culture and the Bible so as to speak biblical truth in cultural language, and to suggest biblical forms that appear natural within the cultural setting. Where combative models tend to view the presentation of truth as being a supracultural and prophetic activity, conversational models engage the cultural nuances, expecting to be able to utilize the language, habits, and forms of the culture to express biblical truth.

Colin Chapman

Another proponent of the conversational model is Colin Chapman. His chapters in the book *Muslims and Christians on the Emmaus Road* give particular insight into his approach to contextualization for Muslims.[82] Through these essays, along with his influential book *Cross and Crescent*, Chapman's stated aim is "to see how far we can walk along the same road with the Muslim before we come to the fork where our paths diverge."[83] Thus, while combative models of Muslim ministry begin at points of departure, Chapman urges the Christian to begin with points of similarity.

Illustrating this, Chapman suggests that Christians can walk alongside of Muslims on seven common paths: God creates, is one, rules, reveals, loves, judges, and forgives.[84] Exploring such commonalities fosters relationship and dialogue. However, rather than leaving these seven

---

in the consumption of meat based on individual sensitivities. Parshall's conclusion, then, is that the receptor culture must play a formative role in how gospel implications are expressed.

81. Parshall, *Muslim Evangelism*, 45–46, concludes, "Contextualization must be carried out with emic methodology. Theological formulations should be made after coming to grips with emic concepts."

82. Chapman, "Rethinking the Gospel," 105–25; Chapman, "God Who Reveals," 127–47. While the aforementioned essays deal with contextualization directly, Chapman also has written a larger and more thorough investigation into Islam. See Chapman, *Cross and Crescent*.

83. Chapman, "God Who Reveals," 127.

84. Chapman, *Cross and Crescent*, 226.

concepts as superficial similarities, Chapman urges Christians to learn how Muslims understand each concept.[85] Viewing these concepts from within Islam allows the Christian to walk with the Muslim in solidarity until the point that the biblical concepts diverge, thus offering a challenge to the Muslim worldview precisely at the point that biblical teaching departs from Islamic understanding.[86]

Ultimately, Chapman suggests that a conversational posture, combined with an inside understanding of Islamic teaching and culture, allows the Christian to say to the Muslim, "We understand what *you* mean when you say Jesus is the Word of God or a Word of God. Will you allow us to explain what *we* understand by the title?"[87] Thus, Chapman's contextual approach involves a conversation between Islamic culture and biblical material in terms and thought patterns derived from a Muslim perspective.

Nabeel Jabbour

A third advocate of conversational models is Nabeel Jabbour. Jabbour, a Middle Easterner himself, provides unique insight into the Middle Eastern culture that is largely shaped by Islamic contours. While perhaps not as prolific a writer on contextualization as Parshall or Chapmann, Jabbour's insider perspective into the cultural fabric of the Arab world provides unique suggestions for moving forward in ministry among Muslims.[88]

Like Parshall and Chapman, Jabbour is aware that Christian missionaries from the West are tempted to import theology and forms from their home culture. Warning against this temptation, Jabbour challenges

---

85. See Chapman's discussion of how defining a prophet precludes a simple one-for-one comparison of the biblical and Islamic concept of prophethood. Chapman, "Rethinking the Gospel," 110.

86. Chapman, "Rethinking the Gospel," 121, shows how walking the road as far as possible with Muslims before diverging actually allows for a stronger critique of Islam, saying, "If Cragg's critics feel that he goes too far in his attempt to understand Islam from within, they cannot fail to notice the sharpness of the challenge which he addresses to Islam."

87. Chapman, "God Who Reveals," 135.

88. Three of Jabbour's most relevant works that include contextualization principles are, Jabbour, *Crescent*; Jabbour, "Relational Evangelism"; Jabbour, "Islamic Fundamentalism."

such missionaries asking, "When we consider the mission field in Muslim countries, do we start with blueprints of western models and assume that we will communicate?" The challenge is to look at Islam . . . as [a phenomenon] and dare to study [it] without prejudice."[89] Jabbour's urging of an objective assessment of Islam pushes the missionary to consider that there may be elements of biblical teaching that are already reflected in Middle Eastern culture, but which are foreign to Westerners.[90] Thus, while both Parshall's and Chapman's approaches focus on the importance of presenting the Christian message in culturally sensitive ways, Jabbour's contribution to the conversational model highlights the importance of the culturally sensitive presentation of the messenger.[91]

Summary of the Conversation Model

While each of the authors above have contributed to the contextualization discussion a great deal more than could possibly be summarized in such limited space, what has been seen is sufficient to suggest that they share a common concern: a culturally appropriate expression of the gospel which retains as much of the Muslim culture as possible. This comes, as highlighted above, from a theological orientation that believes that there is at least some of the Islamic culture that is redeemable and should be used to pass along the gospel among Muslim people. Likewise, there are pragmatic concerns which recognize that, the fewer cultural idiosyncrasies to accommodate, the more likely a message might be passed along throughout a community. Therefore, practitioners often take the

---

89. Jabbour, "Islamic Fundamentalism," 86.

90. For example, when Jabbour narrates a story of a Muslim teenager who comes to him asking to study the Bible, his refusal to meet with the young man until he has secured his father's permission is initially jarring to a Western-trained missionary. Yet, as Jabbour highlights, the Bible itself calls on believers to honor their parents. If Jabbour had neglected to first encourage the young man to honor his father by seeking his permission to read Scripture he would have missed out on both the opportunity to frontload Christian obedience into this young man's life and also on the opportunity to meet openly, having earned the father's blessing through a respectful approach. Jabbour, "Relational Evangelism," 156.

91. See Jabbour, *Crescent*, 22–117. The first part of Jabbour's book is a composite narrative of various ways that one might honor cultural expectations to earn a hearing once one has established a position of respect; two further illustrations are given in Jabbour, "Relational Evangelism," 153–56.

receptor culture as the starting point for their work, posturing themselves as learners in dialogue with a different way of seeing the world.

Overarching Biblical Narrative Models

Where the previous two models start in some sense with culture, the OBN model purports to begin with worldview. These approaches recognize, whether explicitly or implicitly, the truth of Paul Hiebert's claim that Israel's narrative forms and shapes the biblical worldview which prepares the reader for the Christ event. While there are admittedly fewer examples of this approach among Muslims than the other two models, the importance of considering the biblical worldview for this current project warrants a separate treatment of such offerings. In some ways, the OBN model bears similarity to both prior models while avoiding coherence with either. This approach parallels with the combative approach in that it upholds biblical truth as supreme and ultimately supracultural. Like the conversational approach, though, it takes cultural context seriously, encouraging the expression of the biblical worldview in culturally suitable forms that may differ from the missionary's. The following section will briefly consider three proponents of the OBN model.

Steve Smith and Ying Kai – "C2C"

Steve Smith and co-author Ying Kai have provided a major contribution to the formation of a model for seeing church planting movements (CPM) birthed through the book *T4T: A Discipleship Re-Revolution*. Through this book, Smith and Kai have had a great deal of influence on the strategy of many frontier missions organizations. Within *T4T*, Smith and Kai advocate for what they call a "Creation to Christ (C2C)" story set that tells the gospel using stories from the HB to lead up to the Christ event.[92]

Since Smith and Kai are interested in reaching both literate and illiterate peoples, they devise a story set that can be told in a relatively short period of time that provides summary of the whole story of the Bible using colloquial terminology. Thus, one tells C2C using neither biblical references nor biblical language. C2C offers a start towards forming

---

92. Smith and Kai, *T4T*, include this C2C story set as the appendix to their book.

a biblical worldview, though as a brief overview, it lacks precision and detail.

Trevor McIllwain – "Building on Firm Foundations"

Another author who has seen the value of telling the whole biblical story in the process of making disciples is Trevor McIllwain. Having spent significant time working among unreached peoples with the New Tribes Missions agency, McIllwain developed a five-volume set of chronological bible storying (CBS) materials for church planting. This project attempts to tell the story of the Bible chronologically, so as to highlight the development of redemption history as it prepares the reader for Christ. Practitioners use the first volume in evangelism, with lessons stretching from Genesis to the ascension. The remaining four volumes delve deeper into the material from Genesis to the ascension, and include a selection of other New Testament books for new believers.[93]

McIllwain's offering is a helpful long-term companion to something like C2C. His project is significantly more detailed and holistic than C2C as it aims to provide a curriculum for sustained investigation of Scripture. This is illustrated by the fact that first volume, intended as an evangelistic tool, is over five hundred pages and comprises seventy lessons.[94]

Theodore Curry – "Mission to Muslims"

The final advocate of OBN approach to ministry to Muslims is Theodore Curry, whose helpful article appears in the edited volume *Theology and the Practice of Mission*. In his chapter, "Mission to Muslims," Curry emphasizes the merit of the OBN structure, saying, "If one is to properly comprehend the Bible's teaching on the triune nature of God, the incarnation, the atonement, the church, eschatology, or ethics, these must be understood within the context of their organic relationship to the story

---

93. Volume 2 is 539 pages, including seventy lessons for evangelism using the chronological story from Genesis to Revelation. Volume 3 treats the same content in 226 pages, though presented for new believers in sixteen lessons. Volumes 4–6 address Acts, Romans, Ephesians, 1 Corinthians, 1 Timothy, and Titus. McIllwain, "Bible Teaching for Church Planting."

94. McIllwain, "Building on Firm Foundations."

narrated in the Bible and its redemptive theme."⁹⁵ Curry goes on to state, "Any presentation of the gospel message to Muslims must begin by laying out a framework for the proper interpretation of the Bible's comprehensive narrative: creation-fall-redemption, restoration."⁹⁶ This narrative framing of the biblical meaning of concepts is especially important when communicating with Muslims who, at times, have been exposed to similar concepts and vocabulary, yet which have alternate meaning within the Qur'an.

Curry not only endorses the OBN approach to Muslim ministry, but also cautions against a polemic approach that focuses on that which is inconsistent in Islam, writing,

> Even if this type of approach were effective in creating a critical attitude towards Islam, this is not the ultimate goal. The goal is the proclamation of the gospel though a faithful telling of the grand biblical narrative. It alone has the power to subvert the story told by Islam and convey the life-giving message of the gospel. And the best way to achieve that is to allow the Bible to have narrative control in any discussion with Muslims. This ensures that they understand God's message and can respond to his Son.⁹⁷

Thus for Curry, and also for this book, the goal of engagement with Muslims is not to destroy Islam as a system. Rather it is to uphold the beauty of the gospel of King Jesus.

While Curry does not give explicit suggestions as to where one should start with the biblical narrative, his essay might serve as a fitting prelude to the current book. Curry offers a different starting point than contemporary approaches to evangelism with Muslims which typically begin with abstracted theological principles, such as the Trinity, the incarnation, and Jesus' eternal existence as the pre-incarnate Word of God.⁹⁸ Concurring with Curry, I see the central role of the biblical story in providing narrative-driven meaning for concepts that appear to be shared with Islam.

---

95. Curry, "Mission to Muslims," 222.
96. Curry, "Mission to Muslims," 234.
97. Curry, "Mission to Muslims," 237.
98. Curry, "Mission to Muslims," 224.

Summary of the OBN Model

The three practitioners above represent a final category of approach to mission among Muslims considered herein who recognize that the biblical narrative shapes and forms a biblical worldview in its audience. Therefore, OBN models concern themselves with the formation of a biblical worldview in their audience as a prior step to considering cultural expression of biblical truth. The posture taken is that of a storyteller for whom the biblical story provides both the starting point and content for the encounter.

Critical Analysis of the Three Models

Having summarized three broad approaches to ministry to Muslims within the evangelical world, it is now important to critically assess the concerns, strengths, and weaknesses exhibited by each approach (see Table 1.4). Chapter 6 will provide a final analysis of how using the book of Hebrews addresses the concerns, avoids some of the weaknesses, and capitalizes on the strengths of each of these models. Therefore, this section will merely raise the issues of concern that emerge from each approach prior to explaining the method and limitations of the current project.

TABLE 1.4
Assessment and Proponents of Contemporary Offerings

MODEL	PROPONENTS	STRENGTHS	WEAKNESSES
Combative Models Starting Point: Sender culture Theme: Warfare Concern: Gospel truth	Geisler and Saleeb *Answering Islam* Michael Licona *Paul Meets Muhammad* Nabeel Qureshi *No God but One*	– High view of Scripture – Exclusivist soteriology – Provides a logical response to Islamic polemic	– Islamic culture is not considered – Arguments are formed by Western logic and reason – Focus on propositions to the neglect of the story in which propositions fit
Conversational Models Starting Point: Receptor culture Theme: Dialogue Concern: Culturally appropriate gospel expression	Phil Parshall *Muslim Evangelism* Colin Chapman *Cross and Crescent* Nabeel Jabbour *The Crescent through the Eyes of the Cross*	– Takes Islamic culture seriously – Open to secular disciplines as aids to ministry – Demonstrates cultural humility	– Can become syncretistic – Often focuses on the expression of faith rather than the message – Occasionally allows culture to take priority over Scripture (e.g., familial language controversy)
Overarching Biblical Narrative Models Starting Point: Biblical narrative Theme: Worldview Concern: biblically based formation of worldview prior to cultural expression	Smith and Kai "Creation to Christ" Trevor McIllwain *Firm Foundations* Theodore Curry "Mission to Muslims"	– Allows the biblical narrative to shape the message and worldview – Highlights the importance of the whole canon of Scripture – Prepares the listener to see why the Christ event is central to the story	– Selective stories told by the sender can still impose cultural perspectives – The telling of the story is dependent upon the sender

Core Criticisms

First, in terms of biblical fidelity, all of the models mentioned above recognize the Bible as being authoritative. However, because these models argue for various presentations of the Bible's message rather than arguing for a place in the Bible to begin allowing the Bible to speak for itself, they inevitably extend a theological message that has been formed outside of the context.

For example, combative models rely on extracted and systematized theological propositions argued against Islam. Such extraction and systematization inevitably takes the shape of the culture that is asking its own questions of the text and arranging the answers with related material. Conversational models encourage practitioners to listen to the context and to walk as far as possible along a shared path with a Muslim conversation partner prior to introducing distinctive perspectives that result in the parting of ways. Such an approach, however, fosters a willingness to see superficial similarity in teaching while apparent similarities may truly be diametrically opposed within the context of the non-biblical narrative.[99] Likewise, OBN models rearrange the biblical text to create a linear, chronological narrative. In so doing, one is not merely telling the story of the Bible, but is theologically explaining the events in a sequential fashion. Such arrangement and selection of biblical material highlights material that contributes to the author's understanding of the primary biblical message while omitting seemingly secondary material.

Second, conversational and OBN models are right to recognize that the approach of systematization and logical analysis, while appropriate and appreciated in Western culture, may not prove helpful in engagement with those of Eastern origins.[100] They discern the multicultural potential

---

99. Chapter 4 will demonstrate that this danger arises between Islam and Christianity at the point of atonement. Although both faiths use the same word often translated "atonement," closer inspection reveals that the word functions differently in the narrative and theology of the Bible and the Qur'an. Thus, by extracting a concept that is apparently "shared" from its narrative setting, a Christian communicator embracing the fact that Islam celebrates atonement imposes his or her own assumptions on the meaning of the word in an effort to walk farther down a shared road.

100. One might take, for example, the summary paragraph of Geisler and Saleeb's chapter on the Qur'an: "The Qur'an claims to be the Word of God, but it does not prove to be the Word of God. It has claims without supporting credentials. None of the arguments offered by its apologists is convincing. Each contains fallacies. Of course one can continue to believe in the divine origin of the Qur'an without evidence to support it. But those who seek a reasonable faith will have to look elsewhere." This

within the Bible's message and aim to both communicate and express the gospel in ways that will not flatten the cultural contours of the receptor culture. This affords new believers the opportunity to exhibit the effects of the gospel most appropriately within their cultural setting, a feature absent from the concerns of the combative method.

Finally, contextualization discussions tend to be about how far one might go rather than where one might begin in presenting the gospel.[101] Part of this tendency may be attributed to the C-spectrum of contextualization assessment itself. Travis's scale has postured the discussion in terms of the various manifestations of faith that are encouraged to emerge from reception of the gospel message.[102]

Since the C-spectrum categories themselves speak of external expressions of newfound faith or missionary approach, the conversation which follows focuses more on the appropriateness of using qur'anic vocabulary and citation when sharing the gospel, how new believers from a Muslim background might self-identify, and how local socio-religious customs may be retained without falling into syncretism within the new community of faith in Christ.

In other words, most contextualization concentrates on what can be done to make the biblical message understandable and expressible, rather than on what content in the Bible already exists in categories suited to a new culture's reception. Few of the offerings discussed above suggest where to start in the Bible when sharing the gospel or trying to explain

---

paragraph uses logical terminology (claims, argument, fallacies, support, reasonable) in order to assess the truth and veracity of Islam. In terms of Middle Eastern, Islamic, and qur'anic approaches to argument and logic, however, Gwynne, *Logic, Rhetoric*, xv, notes that argument "is a multivalent term in English: when translated by the Arabic word *jadal*, it more commonly indicates 'debate' . . . The qur'anic models are often obscured, however, by the preoccupation with forensics, that is, by the shift of focus from patterns of proof to techniques for the defeat of adversaries." Thus, while Gwynne's work investigates the formal logical and rhetorical integrity of the Qur'an, her work likewise recognizes the more common impulse within Islamic writings "to prove the superiority of the Qur'an over Greek logic" (xiv).

101. Douglas, "Ongoing Strategy Debate," 70.

102. Travis, "C1 to C6 Spectrum," 407–8; Regarding the formative impact the C-spectrum has had on contextualization discussion, see Williams, "Revisiting," 335. Williams, a missionary to Muslims in Southeast Asia for more than twenty years writes, "For more than a decade, evangelicals have framed contextualization strategies for ministry to Muslims in terms of the so-called 'C1–C6 spectrum.' The devising of this Spectrum has helped to steer all subsequent discussion and discourse."

Christian atonement to a Muslim.[103] This particular omission within the literature is the gap that this monograph intends to fill by arguing that the book of Hebrews can provide appropriate biblical content for explaining Christian atonement to Muslims.

The Crux of the Problem

Returning to the stated purpose of this project, one finds that none of the models above offers a satisfactory argument for where one might begin in Scripture to explain a biblical view of atonement to a Muslim audience. Yet, as the writers of Lausanne Occasional Paper 13 stated in 1981, "If the gospel was first given to us in an Eastern context, it ought to be possible for us to get behind the Greco-Roman patterns of thought through which we have interpreted it, and express it once again in ways that make more sense to the Eastern mind."[104] Recognizing this fact, it may be that many understandings of the gospel and atonement in the West are already contextualized forms of an originally Eastern concept. If so, one should expect to find passages of Scripture that already bear the marks of Eastern cultures and thus communicate powerfully to those whose worldview has been shaped by the Semitic contours of the Qur'an. One recent author has in fact argued that this is the first step toward proper contextualization.

Jackson Wu and Exegetical Contextualization

In 2016, Jackson Wu, a missiologist and missionary of over twenty years in an Asian context, published *One Gospel for All Nations*, in which he argues that contextualization begins not at cultural expression of the gospel, but by reading the Bible with fresh eyes. Wu claims convincingly, "Contextualizing begins whenever we read the Bible from the perspective of a given context. Contextualization is not primarily something we *do to* the gospel. Broadly stated, it is the mind's perception of and response to the gospel."[105] With this in mind, Wu helpfully distinguishes what he labels "cultural contextualization" from what he calls "exegetical

---

103. See footnotes 2, 3, and 4 above for references to exceptions to this rule.

104. Report of the 1981 Pattaya Consultation, *Christian Witness to Muslims*, 13–16. As cited by Chapman, "Rethinking the Gospel," 107.

105. Wu, *One Gospel*, 13.

contextualization."[106] While arguing that both forms are important to proper contextual theology, Wu's distinction between these two forms of contextualization begins to grasp the nettle for which this book is reaching.

Over the last fifty years, work among Muslims has predominantly occupied itself with "cultural contextualization" of the gospel. While such concerns are important and must be continually considered, this project will confine itself to the first step in evangelical contextualization as highlighted by Wu: the selection of Scripture appropriate to a context. Following Wu's insight, the following chapters will investigate the book of Hebrews through the eyes of one who is well-versed in the Qur'an's message, noting points of common ground and also direct challenges to the qur'anic worldview.

Method and Limitations

The Qur'an announces itself as the final revelation from God to mankind regarding religion and it claims to have perfected the monotheistic religions which have preceded it.[107] More specifically, and variously throughout its pages, the Qur'an also purports to complete and fulfill the prior revelation of the Torah and gospel.[108] This claim encourages the current project to proceed methodologically by way of an exegetical approach to the Bible and the Qur'an. Since this book concerns itself with communicating a biblical view of atonement to those steeped in the teaching of the Qur'an, chapter 2 will begin in the Torah. This will establish the biblical origins of the concept of atonement as seen through ancient Israel's reception of the ritual, narratively set in the book of Exodus, at the foot of Mount Sinai and explained in detail in Leviticus 16–17. Following this investigation of the ritual, the undergirding worldview formed through this narrative will be elucidated utilizing N. T. Wright's

---

106. Wu, *One Gospel*, 13, writes, "*Exegetical contextualization* refers to one's interpretation of Scripture from a cultural perspective. It means locating the cultural context within the biblical text." And of cultural contextualization, Wu writes, "*Cultural contextualization* refers to the interpretation of culture using a scriptural perspective. It nestles the biblical text within a contemporary cultural context. Hence, one looks at a culture and identifies various concepts that already exist in the Bible."

107. Cuypers, *Banquet*, 242.

108. See Qur'an 5:3.

worldview questions, as employed in his multi-volume work on the historical origins of Christianity.[109]

Chapter 3 will then proceed to discuss the manner in which the author of the book of Hebrews uses the Christ event to demonstrate the fulfillment of the concept of atonement and indeed the Day of Atonement ritual. For believers in Christ who read the message of Hebrews, then, it is apparent that the HB foreshadows and predicts the events of Christ's incarnation, death, resurrection, and ascension and the ritual of the Day of Atonement was always want for Christ's blood and priesthood even as ancient Israel observed it. Again, Wright's worldview questions, applied to the book of Hebrews and its treatment of Yom Kippur will provide a window by which to see the similarities between ancient Israel's worldview and the worldview that emerges post-Christ event.

Chapter 4 will turn to the Qur'an in an effort to answer the question, "How does the Qur'an deal with prior religious ritual as it claims to be the final revelation of perfected religion?" In tracing the trajectory of many Orientalist scholars, some missiologists have concluded that, since the Qur'an makes this claim to completion of Judaism and Christianity, but neither fulfills the Day of Atonement nor discusses atonement in biblical terms, it is therefore deficient in content and in error in its claim to completion.[110] Those following this path make the counterclaim that, since the Qur'an does not treat the Day of Atonement, it must be faulty and therefore Islam falls with it. However, this chapter contends that the Qur'an makes this claim from a very different understanding of what fulfillment is, as compared to the fulfillment claimed by Christ. If it can be shown that the Qur'an's worldview allows it to logically maintain this claim without having to treat the individual details of prior revelation, then such an accusation of error may be hasty.

Chapter 5 argues that the book of Hebrews' treatment of the Day of Atonement in light of the Christ event provides a more satisfying narrative

---

109. See the six worldview questions employed by Wright, *Paul and Faithfulness*, 26–27.

110. See Shamoun, "Where is Blood?"; Zwemer, "Atonement." Regarding the issue of the idea of atonement shared across the three faiths, the verb *kaffara* (كَفَّرَ) appears fourteen times in the Qur'an along with four instances of the noun *kaffāra* (كَفَّارَة). This is the same Arabic word/root that is used in the Arabic Bible to translate the Hebrew word כִּפֶּר (Lev 16:11) and the Greek word ἱλάσκομαι (Heb 2:17). However, contrary to the argument of Shamoun and others, it will be demonstrated that the word functions differently in the Bible than it does in the Qur'an and cannot be said to be a cognate.

explanation of Christianity's continuation of Judaism than the Qur'an makes for Islam's continuation of biblical revelation. In other words, the distinction between the Bible and the Qur'an, or Christianity and Islam, is not one of competing or missing rituals, but rather one of competing narratives and worldviews. Following Ninian Smart's phenomenological approach to comparative religions, this chapter will contrast biblical atonement with qur'anic atonement and will delve beneath the lexical and conceptual similarities and into the narrative and worldview that support them in the biblical and qur'anic systems.

Finally, prior to concluding the study, chapter 6 will offer a model by which a Christian missiologist might exploit the communicative power of the biblical narrative packed into the message of Hebrews to explain biblical atonement to an audience steeped in the worldview of the Qur'an. Utilizing the biblical-theological narrative approach of N. T. Wright and Kevin VanHoozer and coupling it with the cross-cultural insight of Paul Hiebert, chapter 6 will argue that one might utilize a trialogical model for cross cultural contextual theology to highlight the points of divergence between the qur'anic and biblical worldviews.

Among the recognized limitations of this project is the fact that by the time of the writing of the book of Hebrews, and certainly by the time of the compiling of the Qur'an, the ritual of the Day of Atonement had undergone significant adaptation from its original prescription found in Leviticus. Second Temple Judaism, rabbinic Judaism, Jewish communities in the diaspora, and post-70 CE Jewish practice all include different nuances in the keeping of the Day of Atonement rituals.[111] However, despite the fact that various Jewish groups expressed the Day of Atonement rituals differently, it is apparent throughout the book of Hebrews that the author is referring to the prescriptions given in Leviticus as the type of which the Christ event is the anti-type. Thus, this book will focus on the HB prescriptions for the observance of Yom Kippur as found primarily in Leviticus without treating the derivations which emerge in later forms of Judaism.

Likewise, one will notice a lack of significant attention given to the formative corpus of traditions in Islam known as the *Sunnah*. This would certainly be a major omission if one were seeking to understand the claim that Islam makes to fulfill prior revelation. Instead, however, this project

---

111. Heike and Nicklas, *Day of Atonement*.

intends to deal merely with the Qur'an on its own terms for at least two reasons.

First, following the work of several emerging scholars of Islam, specifically that of Gabriel Said Reynolds, it is well-recognized that the *Sunnah* cannot be admitted as historical data.[112] The *Sunnah* certainly has an impact on contemporary expressions of Islam, but it also distorts the text of the Qur'an by applying later concerns to the earlier message, fitting it with a politicized frame for which it is ill-suited, and attaching sectarian concerns to its interpretation.[113] Thus, the *Sunnah* will be referenced merely as a supplement to the Qur'an.

Second, and perhaps more important, all sects of Islam agree on the fact that the Qur'an is an Islamic source of authority, given by Allah, and perfect in its expression. Therefore, the findings and the suggestions offered herein have a much wider application than if one pursued a specific and sectarian style of exegesis or a particular school of jurisprudence.[114] For these two reasons, it is helpful to focus nearly exclusive attention on the Qur'an's claims over and against the later derivations of various schools of thought.

Finally, the target audience consists of Western-educated English speakers. This is because of the cultural distance that often exists between those trained in the West and those raised in the Middle East. Since this book aims to prepare Western Christians for engagement with Muslims raised under the influence of the Qur'an—a decidedly Semitic document—this study limits its focus to materials offered in English for engagement with Muslims.

Conclusion

Ultimately, this project seeks to elucidate the role of blood, sacrifice, and atonement in the Qur'an. Since the Qur'an purports to be connected to prior revelation contained in the Bible, investigation of blood, sacrifice, and atonement should begin with its origins in early Hebrew history. Blood, sacrifice, and atonement continue to play a role in Christian teaching. Each aspect features—though distinctly—in the Qur'an as well. To restate the proposed thesis and purpose, then, this monograph intends

---

112. See Part 2 in Reynolds, *Emergence of Islam*, 83–168.
113. Reynolds, *Emergence of Islam*, 92.
114. Philips, *Evolution of Fiqh*.

to argue that the book of Hebrews, and particularly the attention given to the manner in which the Christ event fulfills the Day of Atonement ritual, can be used to expose divergent worldviews between the Bible and Qur'an, challenging the manner in which the Qur'an makes its claim to continue previous revelation. Therefore, the book of Hebrews is a helpful place in Scripture to begin in explaining a biblical view of atonement to Muslims and those informed by the Qur'an.

As seen above, other approaches to Muslim ministry have aligned themselves with specific concerns, either biblical or cultural. Some, concerned to defend biblical truth, neglect cultural nuances which result in arguing for Westernized theological constructs in a philosophical and logical style that is culturally dislocated in the Middle East. Others, sensitive to cultural concerns, have focused more on the external expression of faith as opposed to where in the Bible one might find culturally communicative material that is both understandable to the Muslim and challenging to the qur'anic worldview. Yet others have recognized the manner in which the OBN forms a biblical worldview without squelching cultural expression, yet they have woven together their own sets of stories rather than suggesting that there might already be a place in Scripture that accommodates the cultural features of those steeped in the Qur'an's message while challenging the Qur'an's message with the biblical picture of atonement through the Christ event.

The use of Hebrews does not guarantee effective communication with Muslims, much less their conversion to a biblical view of atonement. Likewise, there are many valid contextualization questions that this project will not address, and which will require a great deal of prayer, thought, and wisdom on the part of emerging churches within groups of those formerly conditioned by the Qur'an. In the end, the narrative of the Bible will inform the meaning of the words, and the worldview will provide the distinction in the categories, such that a dialogue between a Christian and a Muslim might not remain on the level of propositions, claims, and doctrines. Instead, the conflict will arise at the worldview level where one might more appropriately compare the teachings of Islam and Christianity.

Furthermore, while the historical resurrection of Christ is clearly an important point of Christian doctrine and a central point of divergence from Islamic teaching, the fact of the resurrection, and indeed the whole Christ event, carries much more weight if it is preceded by the Old Testament narrative which prepares the reader for Christ's sacrificial death and life-restoring resurrection. Colin Chapman recognizes the problem of Christ's sacrificial death for Muslims should be answered not merely with a Christian positive assertion of the event, but with the foregoing logic which predicts and interprets this death. Chapman emphasizes this saying, "The greatest challenge for us is to find ways of helping Muslims to see the deeper logic which demands that the Messiah *must* suffer before entering his glory."[115] In other words, rather than giving opposing answers to the question "Did Jesus die on the cross and rise again?," a Muslim and Christian engaged in a discussion under the teaching of Hebrews might be led to ask, "Does the story of the Bible, or the story of the Qur'an make more sense of the account of the Christ event?" While Hebrews begins with reference to the creation, the story precedes Hebrews and Hebrews depends on the story to make its case.

---

115. Chapman, *Cross and Crescent*, 210.

2

Blood, Story, and Worldview
The Day of Atonement in Leviticus

As mentioned in the previous chapter, the Qur'an lays claim to many of the same historical persons and events described in the HB, tracing Islam's history through Abraham and all the way back to Adam. Furthermore, the Qur'an repeatedly asserts itself as the final revelation from God which in some way fulfills and completes the message of the previously revealed heavenly books: the *tawrah* (Torah), *zabur* (Psalms), and *injil* (gospel).[1] Since Islam claims to inherit much of ancient Israel's history and since atonement will be shown to play a central role in that history, one must address the question, "How does the Qur'an understand itself to inherit the concept of atonement as developed in the HB and NT?"

In fact, it is not only the Qur'an, but all three so-called Abrahamic religions of Judaism, Christianity, and Islam which maintain that the historical narrative presented in the HB is essential to each faith's religious belief and expression, communicating divine revelation to humanity. Judaism relies on Scripture, the Pentateuch in particular, as a way of remembering the promises of God and the identity Israel bears as his

---

1. Kaskas and Hungerford, *Qur'an*, 71 (Qur'an 5:44–48). Within this section confirming the *injil* and the *tawrah*, verse 48a says, "We sent you the Book, setting forth truth, confirming what is available of earlier revelations and with final authority over them." As a matter of convention, this monograph will use the English word "God" to translate the word *allah* (الله). This choice does not intend to ignore nor to delegitimize the nuanced and ongoing discussion as to whether or not, as one book title states the issue, "The Father of Jesus is the God of Muhammad," but rather to recognize that Arabic-speaking Jews, Christians, and Muslims have all employed this same word in reference to the deity whom they worship.

chosen people.² The New Testament—specifically through the book of Hebrews—states clearly that Jesus is the true image of that which was merely a shadow presented in the prophets, law, and rituals of the HB.³ Likewise, Islam claims that Muhammad is the "seal of the prophets" and offers in the Qur'an the final dispensation of divine revelation.⁴ Although each of these Abrahamic faiths interprets the HB narrative distinctly, they share characters, concepts, and stories that inform their worship and provide historical foundation for their religious claims.

One such concept that appears in the sacred texts of each of the three Abrahamic faiths is atonement. Therefore, as the following chapters will demonstrate, since Christianity and Islam both claim to properly continue along the historical arc begun in the Pentateuch, atonement can serve the present project as a point of comparison to assess each faith's claims to continuity. Rather than merely comparing instances of atonement language within the three Abrahamic faiths, however, this book follows the method of Ninian Smart, professor of comparative religions at the University of California. Smart argues that comparative religious study must consider the whole system of stories, rituals, and doctrines of each faith to hear each voice speak for itself on any given topic.⁵ Therefore, even when different faith systems exhibit lexical similarity or apparent conceptual overlap, one must allow each faith to define and use words and concepts for itself from within its own system and literature in order to pass beyond mere superficial comparison. In other words, to avoid

---

2. Redditt, "Leviticus," 53, shows that Scripture, the Pentateuch especially, is a central aspect of Judaism, especially after the destruction of the temple, when "rabbis emphasized prayer and substituted the study of the sacrificial laws for performing the ritual."

3. Heb 1:1–2; 10:1–18.

4. See Asad, *Message of the Qur'an*, Qur'an 33:40. ما كَانَ مُحَمَّدٌ أَبَا أَحَدٍ مِن رِجَالِكُم وَلَٰكِن رَّسُولَ اللَّهِ وَخَاتَمَ النَّبِيِّينَ ۗ وَكَانَ اللَّهُ بِكُلِّ شَيْءٍ عَلِيمًا—[And know, O believers, that] Muhammad is not the father of any one of your men, but is God's Apostle and the Seal of all Prophets. And God has indeed full knowledge of everything." This verse is traditionally considered by the *tafasir* (Islamic commentaries) as meaning that Muhammad and Islam were sent to complete Judaism and Christianity, particularly the *tawrah* as given to Moses and the *Injil* as given to Jesus. This verse is connected to Qur'an 5:48, which identifies the presence of earlier revelation given to the Jews and Christians that is fulfilled in Islam. On this Asad comments, "Because of the universal applicability and textual incorruptibility of its teachings—as well as of the fact that the Prophet Muhammad is 'the seal of all prophets'—the Qur'an represents the culminating point of all revelation and offers the final, perfect way to spiritual fulfilment."

5. Smart, *Dimensions of Sacred*, 70.

importing biblical understanding of atonement into qur'anic employ of the concept, this project will investigate atonement and its attendant narratives and rituals in the HB, in Hebrews, and finally in the Qur'an prior to venturing an answer regarding the qur'anic claim to succession.

In so doing, however, one not only compares concepts across faith systems, but one also begins to uncover the foundations of each faith's underlying, implicit worldview. As biblical scholar N. T. Wright argues, one's worldview shapes and is shaped by the story each culture tells. One's worldview provides the answers to basic questions of human existence, and gives meaning to the symbols of expression exhibited as both artifacts and events.[6] Therefore, when one investigates a doctrine, the story that carries the doctrine, and the rituals by which the doctrine is performed, one consequently engages the elements of worldview.

While worldview, as understood within the present work, functions discretely, affecting one's understanding of reality without often receiving direct engagement, Wright argues, "like the foundations of a house, [worldviews] can themselves be dug out and inspected."[7] Following Wright, and utilizing his six worldview questions as tools of excavation, this project will address what each faith means when it uses the word atonement in order to uncover the different worldviews supporting the Bible and the Qur'an. The present chapter, beginning with the origins of the concept of atonement in ancient Israel, argues that the Day of Atonement, as recorded in Leviticus, provides insight into not only the doctrine, ritual performance, and the narrative in which atonement is positioned, but it also exposes the foundations of the worldview espoused in Leviticus, which informs later tradition.

Atonement, *kipper* (כִּפֶּר), and Leviticus

Prior to investigating the Day of Atonement as a ritual, it will be instructive to consider the concept of atonement itself. In the HB atonement is the process given to Israel to deal with the problems of the guilt that is associated with sin and the impurity that accompanies ritual defilement. The following section leans on the work of several recent scholars, among them Jay Sklar and Jacob Milgrom, who have contributed to contemporary understanding of atonement in the HB. Sklar especially has

---

6. Wright, *People of God*, 122–24.
7. Wright, *People of God*, 117.

demonstrated that atonement engages both sin and impurity by a single process founded on YHWH's willingness to accept sacrificial blood as an agent of "ransom-purgation."[8] A brief investigation of the Hebrew word *kipper* (כִּפֶּר) as featured in the priestly literature of the HB will elucidate the undergirding logic of the process and provide context for the performance of the Day of Atonement ritual and effects.

The Verb "To Atone"

Through a survey of scholarly opinion regarding the Hebrew verb *kipper* in the HB, Jay Sklar concludes, "There is basic agreement that כִּפֶּר refers to sin being dealt with in such a way that the broken relationship between the LORD and the sinner is mended."[9] Addressing how this mended relationship occurs, however, Sklar also finds that English translators disagree as to how one should express the effects of *kipper*.[10] This disagreement occurs because the verb is used throughout the priestly literature of the HB both to effect cleansing in situations of impurity and also on occasions where a "ransom" is paid resulting in forgiveness of a debt or sin.[11] While "forgiveness" language seems appropriate to describe

---

8. Sklar, *Sin, Impurity*, 187. Sklar summarizes the results of his meticulous argument, saying, "In sum, inadvertent sin and major impurity both require sacrifice for atonement. Since both inadvertent sin and major impurity endanger (requiring ransom) and pollute (requiring purgation), sacrificial atonement must both ransom and cleanse. The verb used to describe this dual event is the verb כִּפֶּר and the power of the כִּפֶּר-rite to accomplish both is due to the lifeblood of the animal."

9. Sklar, *Sin, Impurity*, 2.

10. Sklar, *Sin, Impurity*, 1–8, whose introduction notes, "Traditionally, כִּפֶּר has been translated in the priestly literature with renderings such as 'to atone/make atonement' or 'to expiate/make expiation.' While these renderings have generally been agreed upon, there has been a diversity of opinion as to the exact nature of this atonement," Sklar, *Sin, Impurity*, 2. Sklar goes on to show, however, that atonement in contexts of sin can be understood as forgiveness, but in contexts of impurity where no sin or wrongdoing has been committed, forgiveness language is problematic. To this point, Sklar cites, Lavine, *In the Presence*, (*kipper* I) 61, (*kipper* II) 115, as a proponent of the idea that *kipper* can take two different forms. *kipper* I pertains to cleansing from impurity, while *kipper* II refers to ransoming a life from the effects of sin.

11. Sklar, *Sin, Impurity*, 1, explains, "In contexts of sin, this atonement results in forgiveness. In contexts of impurity, it is an atoning sacrifice that is required, and in both instances the priest is said to make atonement for the offerer: וְכִפֶּר עָלָיו הַכֹּהֵן."

the effects of atonement in contexts of sin, it strikes an awkward chord if used in amoral situations, such as impurity caused by childbirth.[12]

Seeking further understanding of *kipper* and its effects, some scholars have adopted renderings of *kipper* derived from similar word groups within related languages.[13] Thus some find clarity in the Akkadian word *kuppuru*, which means "to wipe clean."[14] Others use the Arabic word *kaffara*, meaning "to cover," to shed light on the Hebrew verb.[15] Yet others suggest that the Hebrew word might have two separate meanings depending on the context.[16]

Contra these renderings, however, Jay Sklar's exhaustive, synchronic study of *kipper* within the priestly literature reveals that atonement should be understood in all contexts to effect both ransom and cleansing.[17] Furthermore, sacrificial blood serves as the logical linchpin holding

---

12. Lev 12:1–8. In this passage, a woman is declared unclean after giving birth and must bring a one-year-old lamb and a pigeon or a turtledove to the tent of meeting so that the priest might make atonement (כִּפֶּר) for her.

13. See Sklar, *Sin*, 45n2. Prior to Sklar's study, many scholars in search of the meaning of כִּפֶּר went to neighboring languages for insight. As Sklar notes, however, this methodological procedure goes against the grain of contemporary linguistic theory: "This methodology has since been severely critiqued, and modern linguists hold the diachronic perspective to be largely secondary to that of the synchronic."

14. Lavine, *In the Presence*, 56, states, "An alternative interpretation of the verb *kipper* is supplied by the cognate evidence of Akkadian, where the D-stem of *kaparu*, *kuppuru*, has the sense: 'to wipe off', hence, 'to purify.'"

15. Wensinck, Heffening, and Leiv-Provencal, *First Encyclopaedia*, 1148. The encyclopedia takes the qur'anic use of *kaffara* as being equivalent to the Hebrew *kappara*. For an Islamic scholar who makes this same assertion, see Cuypers, *Banquet*, 360, who explains, "The term 'expiation,' *kaffāra*, which is repeated three times in the same passage (89c, h; 95f) and which we have already met in v. 45 (compensation in the case of the law of retaliation not being applied) appears to be derived directly from the Hebrew *kappārā*."

16. Wenham, *Book of Leviticus*, 59, writes, "It was pointed out in the introduction that *to make atonement* (*kipper*) has two different meanings in Hebrew, 'to wipe clean' or 'to pay a ransom.'" See also Lavine, *In the Presence*, 61, 115.

17. Sklar, *Sin, Impurity*, 182, concludes, "In either context [sin or impurity], however, it was seen that the end point of sin and impurity is the same: both endanger (requiring ransom) and both pollute (requiring purgation). As a result, it is not simply כִּפֶּר that is needed in some instances and purgation that is needed in others, but כִּפֶּר-purgation that is needed in both. In short, due to the similar ending points of sin and impurity, even when the emphasis is upon ransom (כִּפֶּר), it is a purifying ransom that is in view, and even when the emphasis is upon purgation, it is a ransoming-purgation in view. The verb that describes this dual event is כִּפֶּר and the ability of the כִּפֶּר-rite to accomplish this dual event is due to the blood of the sacrifice which both ransoms

together these dual functions of atonement in the priestly literature of the HB.[18] Thus, in both contexts of sin and defilement, substitutionary sacrifice and blood manipulation are of central import to the process of making atonement.[19]

A survey of the relationship between atonement, purification, forgiveness, and blood highlights the logical connections within the process. While, with Sklar, this chapter argues that atonement effects both ransom from sin and purgation of impurity as a single act, it is helpful to consider the logic behind atonement as purification and as ransom individually in order to highlight the role that blood plays as a conceptual linchpin, effecting both results.

Atonement and Purification

While many treatments of atonement focus on the remedy for sin-guilt, Old Testament commentator and theologian Jacob Milgrom has argued cogently that atonement removes impurity. Through two significant commentaries on Leviticus, Milgrom has demonstrated that Leviticus focuses not merely on the eradication of sins, but even more centrally with the removal of sin's attendant impurity which infects the sanctum of God.[20] Milgrom's work shows that as Israel's sins accumulate throughout the year, defilement of the camp encroaches inward, toward the center: the holy place of YHWH's dwelling. Thus, sin's polluting power threatens

---

and purifies."

18. Sklar, *Sin, Impurity*, 163.

19. Wenham, *Book of Leviticus*, 62, comments on the idea of an animal taking the worshipper's place vicariously, stating, "Both fit in well with sacrifices making atonement, i.e., the animal serving as a ransom for the life of man. One may regard the animal either as dying in the worshipper's place as his substitute, or as receiving the death penalty because of the sin transferred to it by the laying on of hands." Regarding the contentious issue of substitution in atonement theology, see Gathercole, *Defending Substitution*, 28. Having addressed several contemporary perspectives to the contrary, Gathercole defends the idea of substitutionary atonement, saying, "A response that one might make to any such challenges is that biblical exegesis simply demands substitution; therefore it cannot be avoided. . . . there is actually very good evidence for seeing substitutionary atonement as intrinsic to the biblical presentation of how God has reconciled the world to himself in Christ."

20. Milgrom, *Leviticus*, 162. See also, Milgrom, *Leviticus 1–16*, and Milgrom, *Leviticus 17–22*, and Milgrom, *Leviticus 23–27*.

to cause the abiding presence of YHWH to withdraw from the camp.[21] However, when the high priest presents the blood of atonement, blood provides the corporate remedy for such impurity.[22]

Biblically, one finds Leviticus 17:11–14 stating this clearly, as YHWH explicitly says that the life of the animal is in its blood, and that YHWH gives this life-blood to Israel in order that she might make atonement. Thus, Milgrom argues that blood draws its purifying power from its function as a symbol of life. As such a symbol, when presented before God, the purity of life drives out the defilement and impurity of death, which is the penalty for sin. However, focusing on the role of life in sacrifice goes against the grain of much Western scholarship. According to theologian Christian Eberhart, such scholarship has traditionally claimed "that the killing of an animal or a living being is the basis of the sacrificial ritual."[23] Thus, one of the main contributions of Milgrom's work is to challenge the exclusive focus on death involved in sacrifice, and to consider the importance of life symbolized through the presentation of the blood before YHWH.[24]

Summarizing the underpinning logic by which purification is effected through the Yom Kippur ritual, then, Milgrom concludes, "[Blood] as life is what purges the sanctuary. It nullifies, overpowers, and absorbs the Israelites' impurities that adhere to the sanctuary, thereby allowing the divine presence to remain and Israel to survive."[25] The tabernacle,

---

21. Milgrom, *Leviticus*, 15, whose insight provides a needed corrective to the myopic approach of those who see Yom Kippur as a ritual that merely effects the forgiveness of sin, overreaches his data. In fact, Milgom goes so far as to retranslate *yom hakkippurim* (The Hebrew name from which we get Yom Kippur, or the Day of Atonement) as "The Day of Purgation."

22. To this point, see also Leithart, *Delivered from Elements*, 114, who likens Yom Kippur to an annual release of impurity, saying, "Yahweh's very presence in Israel was a danger, and as the sins, rebellions and impurities mounted on the priest and in Yahweh's house, the danger intensified. Without a mechanism for decompression, it would rapidly become intolerable. Yahweh graciously provided a pressure valve in the complex ritual of *yom hakkippurim*, the Day of Coverings (Lev 16)."

23. Eberhart, "Characteristics," 39.

24. See also Moffitt, *Atonement and Logic*, 219, who takes this point further, showing that understanding blood-as-life avoids the abhorrent idea that sacrifice as a symbol of death—the ultimate defilement in biblical terms—enters into the presence of God.

25. See Milgrom, *Leviticus 1–16*, 711–12; see also, Sklar, *Sin, Impurity*, 184, who notes, "Inadvertent sins do not only endanger, they also pollute. . . . The requirement of the purification offering in Leviticus 4 and 5 thus suggested that these sins have

the camp, and the people themselves require some means of purging impurity from their midst so that YHWH might abide. For Israel, the covenant people distinguished by the presence of YHWH in their midst, this purifying function is of central importance and will be further discussed below. Prior to that, however, one must acknowledge that sin not only defiles, but it also incurs debt. Thus, to deal with both of sin's effects, atonement must also provide a means of "ransom."

Atonement and Ransom

While Milgrom is right to call attention to atonement's function in expelling impurity, Jay Sklar's book, *Sin, Impurity, Sacrifice, Atonement*, draws on Milgrom's insight rehearsed above while also demonstrating that blood-as-life provides a "ransom." In order to argue this point, Sklar demonstrates exegetically that the Hebrew word *kipper* is related to and effected by the presentation of a "ransom" or *koper* in instances of sin throughout the priestly literature of the HB.[26] He is, however, cautious about the implications of using "ransom" as the English rendering of the Hebrew word *koper*. Thus, Sklar more precisely defines this "ransom" as an ethically justified, mitigated penalty accepted by an offended party which cancels a debt and reconciles the offender and offended.[27]

Ultimately, based on his research on sin in the HB, Sklar argues that the result of sin is the forfeiture of the sinner's life. However, Sklar's treatment of atonement reveals that, in many cases, this death penalty may be avoided by payment of a "ransom" or *koper*. One well-known illustration of *koper* comes from Exodus 21:28–32, wherein a neglectful owner of an aggressive ox bears responsibility when the ox gores a neighbor. In this situation, because the owner neglected to control this ox, known to be aggressive, the owner falls under punishment along with the ox. The owner

---

resulted in the contamination of the sanctuary." See also Wenham, *Book of Leviticus*, 233, who says, "By cleansing the sanctuary [the Day of Atonement rituals] permit the Holy God to dwell among an unholy people."

26. See chapter 2 of Sklar, *Sin, Impurity*, 44–79.

27. Sklar, *Sin, Impurity*, 78. Sklar defines *koper* as, "[A] legally or ethically legitimate payment which delivers a guilty party from a just punishment that is the right of the offended party to execute or have executed. The acceptance of this payment is entirely dependent upon the choice of the offended party, it is a lesser punishment than was originally expected, and its acceptance serves both to rescue the life off the guilty as well as to appease the offended party, thus restoring peace to the relationship."

is subject to death due to this negligence, however, hope of escape from this punishment exists by way of a potential *koper* arrangement with the bereaved family.

Sklar summarizes this situation, saying, "The life of the ox-owner has been forfeited through their wrong into the hands of the family of the slain and their only hope of deliverance is for that family to choose to place a כֹּפֶר on them."[28] Thus, one sees that the offended party can extend mercy to the offender, choosing to receive a mitigated penalty and free the accused, restoring relationship and cancelling the debt.

Returning to Sklar's argument that a *koper* arrangement is part of the process of the *kipper* ritual, one sees that God plays the role of the offended party in instances of sin, while the sinner is the offender under the penalty of death. Because God willingly accepts the blood of the sacrifice as a mitigated and substitutionary penalty in place of the forfeited life of the sinner, however, this "ransom" forgives or expiates sin and restores the relationship between worshipper and God. Again, as blood serves as a symbol of life, YHWH receives the sacrificial blood of atonement as a mitigated, substitute payment of restitution in place of the forfeited life of the sinner.

Particularly within the Yom Kippur ritual, Sklar demonstrates how this "ransom" works in making atonement. Behind the veil of the holy place and over the *kipporet* (the covering of the ark of the covenant, sometimes called "the mercy seat") as the high priest presents the life blood of the sacrificial animal, YHWH receives it as a "ransom" for the life of the offerer, following the explicit explanation of Leviticus 17:11.[29] Therefore, as has been seen in both Milgrom and Sklar, the role of blood in making atonement is integrally related to both purification and forgiveness. Blood-as-life, then, is the key to understanding the dual-function of atonement as an act of ransom and purging.

Summary: Atonement and Blood

Summarizing the survey above, then, atonement involves a cluster of elements including sacrifice, forgiveness, and cleansing. Leviticus 17:11–14

---

28. Sklar, *Sin, Impurity*, 51.

29. Sklar, *Sin, Impurity*, 181, offers a rendering of the Hebrew of Lev 17:11 as follows: "For the life of the flesh is in the blood, and I myself have bestowed it upon you on the altar to ransom your lives, for it is the blood that ransoms by means of/as the life."

highlights the role of blood as a conceptual linchpin, holding these various elements together. This passage serves as the logical center for atonement within the priestly literature, wherein YHWH commits to both provide and accept sacrificial blood as a representation of life. The presentation of this blood, as a symbol of life granted to sinners and the impure by YHWH, results in the expulsion of uncleanness and serves as a vicarious substitute for the forfeited life of a sinner.[30] Therefore, as YHWH provides Israel with a means of making atonement, the blood-ritual allows one to use the word *kipper* in both situations of sin and impurity.

David Moffitt summarizes the logical congruence of the process of atonement succinctly. He writes,

> Blood/life stands at the center of the process that results in atonement, since the life in the blood is the agent that has the power to redeem and purify. Because blood has these properties, blood offering both ameliorates the punitive danger the people face *and* enables the divine presence to continue to dwell among the people in the tabernacle's inner sanctum.[31]

While Moffit's summary does well to feature the role of blood in making atonement, it also draws attention to the purpose of atonement as depicted in the HB: that the divine presence would continue to dwell among the people of Israel. At this point, having understood the effects and symbols of atonement, this project must also consider the role of atonement within the narrative of the HB in order to provide a more holistic understanding of how atonement affects ancient Israel's worldview.

Atonement and the Identity of Israel

As discussed above, in the HB, the Hebrew verb *kipper* (כִּפֶּר) occurs in situations of both sin and impurity.[32] Stated differently, both sin and impurity require atonement to escape the danger posed to one who is guilty of sin or who is ritually defiled in the presence of a just and holy God. The danger posed to Israel, as seen in Leviticus especially, is twofold. First, sin and impurity prohibit individuals from approaching the holiness and purity of YHWH. This prohibition is dramatically illustrated

---

30. Sklar, *Sin, Impurity*, 185. Sklar confirms that in the priestly literature the word *kipper* appears only in situations where a sacrifice and blood are involved.

31. Moffitt, *Atonement*, 265.

32. Ex. *Kipper* and sin, see Lev 16:11; ex. *Kipper* and impurity, see Lev 12:1–8.

by the story of Nadab and Abihu recorded in Leviticus 10:1–2. Here, two sons of Aaron dare to approach YHWH's tent with "unauthorized fire," and as they draw near, they are consumed by fire bursting from the tent of meeting and rejecting their uninvited approach. Later, in Leviticus 16:1–2, YHWH reminds Aaron of the danger of approaching the holy place without proper preparation, warning that even the high priest can only enter behind the veil once per year, after having followed the prescribed rituals of Yom Kippur.

Second, however, Israel's sins and impurities also threaten to pollute the camp. As this defilement encroaches upon the tabernacle, the threat increases that YHWH will remove his presence from the people. This second danger strikes at the heart of Israel as the covenant people. As the following section will illustrate, the presence of YHWH places a formative role in establishing Israel's self-understanding and in reminding her of her history through which YHWH's presence plays an ongoing role. Therefore, atonement as a means by which to retain YHWH's presence in her midst has major implications on Israel's ability to maintain her identity and to recall and reflect upon her narrative.

Atonement and the Presence of YHWH

For ancient Israel, the presence of YHWH serves as a definitive and distinguishing marker of her very existence as a people.[33] In Exodus 19:5, after the great Passover of Exodus 12, and after Moses led the people out of Egypt, YHWH makes a covenant with the people of Israel at Mount Sinai, establishing them as a holy nation and making them his "treasured possession among all the peoples."[34] Then, in Exodus 29:45–46, God declares his intention to dwell among his people, emphatically saying, "I will dwell among the people of Israel and will be their God. And they shall know that I am the LORD their God, who brought them out of Egypt that I might dwell among them. I am the LORD their God." Thus, Israel sees from the very beginning of her existence as the people of God that YHWH redeemed her from Egypt in order to dwell in her midst, setting her apart for himself.

33. Polen, "Leviticus and Hebrews," 215.

34. See Sarna, *Exodus*, 104, who comments on Exod 19:5–6, "This statement further defines the implications of being God's 'treasured people.' National sovereignty, here expressed by 'kingdom,' is indispensable for the proper fulfillment of Israel's mission."

Noting YHWH's presence to be a central tenet of Israel's identity, Old Testament scholar Christopher Wright comments, "It was to be God's covenantal presence in Israel that would mark them out as distinctive from the rest of the nations. . . . The very purpose of redemption was so that God should dwell among his people."[35] Yet, as Wright goes on to show, the impurity and impiety of Israel from the very beginning threatened the abiding presence of God. As Wright puts it, "The effect of sin and pollution was to render the holy profane and the clean unclean, [and] if left uncovered and unatoned for, [sins and impurities] would render Israel unfit for divine habitation."[36] That YHWH might remove his presence from the defiled camp is a threat to the very identity of Israel.

This threat is illustrated for Israel immediately upon receiving the covenant, within the narrative of Exodus by Israel's idolatry with the golden calf in Exodus 32. Finding the people worshipping an idol, Moses fears that God's holy presence will not abide this sinful people without intercession, declaring to the people, "You have sinned a great sin. And now I will go up to the LORD; perhaps I can make atonement for your sin."[37] Atonement, then, is the proposed solution to the threat posed by the sin of idolatry.

In Exodus 33:14–16, then, Moses ascends Mount Sinai to intercede for Israel, declaring that without the presence of God, the people of Israel would lose their distinctiveness and their identity. Old Testament scholar Douglas Stuart summarizes the identity-giving power of YHWH's presence, commenting, "It was God's presence with his people, and all that that implied, that made his people special—they did not have within themselves any particular intrinsic characteristics to 'distinguish' them. God's distinction was what they received derivatively but did not possess innately."[38] In other words, anything noteworthy about Israel is inherently related to her elected relationship with YHWH who has called them out and covenanted to be their God, dwelling in their midst. Consequently, anything that threatens to remove YHWH's presence from among the people strikes at the core of Israel's self-understanding. Atonement is the process given to Israel to restore and retain the relationship with YHWH signified by his abiding presence in their midst, and thereby to maintain Israel's identity as YHWH's people.

35. Wright, *Mission of God*, 334–35.
36. Wright, *Mission of God*, 337.
37. Exod 32:30.
38. Stuart, *Exodus*, 703.

Atonement and Memory

At the same time as YHWH's presence is essential to the identity of the people of Israel, it is also bound up with the history of Israel. To this point, in a book entitled *God and Earthly Power*, Gordon McConville detects a pattern in the OT of incidents in which sin threatens YHWH's proximity to humanity, such that he writes that OT history "is characterized by repeated ruptures and new beginnings."[39] For McConville, and for this book, the Day of Atonement provides the premier example of God's gracious provision of a ritualized means by which Israel might militate against such ruptures of the relationship with God and against threat of the removal of his presence from Israel.[40]

Having discussed the eviction from Eden and the flood narrative as evidence of a cycle of rupture and restoration in the relationship between God and humanity, McConville connects the preceding narrative with the Day of Atonement, which he identifies as a paradigmatic expression of the delicate relationship between God's presence among the people and his holiness that cannot abide sin.[41] In other words, the Day of Atonement assumes, recalls, and builds upon the narrative history that precedes it, offering an annual, ritualized celebration of God's gracious provision of a remedy for the repeated rupturing of the relationship between God and humanity.[42]

Unpacking this idea of the Day of Atonement as bound up with Israel's history, one finds that in the immediate context of the Sinai account where Moses eventually receives the prescription for the Day of Atonement ritual, Exodus 29:45–46 explicitly declares YHWH's intention to dwell among his people as their God who delivered them from Egypt. Thus, the Passover and Exodus are bound together with YHWH's purpose to dwell among his people. Then, following Moses' descent from

---

39. McConville, *God and Earthly Power*, 60.

40. McConville, *God and Earthly Power*, 60. McConville states, "The fine balance between the presence of God with Israel and his potential absence is nowhere better expressed than in the Day of Atonement rituals."

41. McConville, *God and Earthly Power*, 61.

42. McConville, *Being Human*, 111–12, develops this point regarding the mnemonic function of Israel's Scripture and ritual, writing that the OT is "within its own horizons, laden with memory, in such a way as to both preserve and to re-create [Israel's history]." McConville goes on to write, "Memories are carried by societies in both actions and texts. These function in different ways: actions tend to conserve memories and traditions by repetition, while texts allow for ongoing reflection on meanings."

Sinai to deliver the law and covenant to the people, he also establishes the priesthood and priestly rituals that will allow YHWH's presence to remain in the camp.[43] Finally, after the construction of the tabernacle, Exodus 40:34–38 records YHWH's arrival amidst his people. Not only does this account record his dwelling in the camp, but it also highlights his role in directing the people throughout their journeys. Thus, YHWH's presence both marks the culmination of the story of rescue and covenant recorded in Exodus, and also the beginning of Israel's journey toward the promised land.

Exodus, however, does not give explicit instructions for making atonement and retaining YHWH's presence. For such a detailed record of the priestly system through which atonement occurs, one must turn to Leviticus. Despite appearing as a non-narrative register of law and ritual, Leviticus and the priestly rituals it prescribes connect directly to the story from which they emerge.[44] As one reads and performs the rituals prescribed in Leviticus, one remembers and participates in the narrative of Israel.[45]

As indicated above, one such ritual, centrally recorded in ancient Israel's Scriptures, is the Day of Atonement referred to in Leviticus 16–17.[46] In reading this passage and performing this ritual, subsequent

43. In Exod 34:29, Moses descends from the mountain. Exod 34:32 states that Moses informed the people of everything that YHWH spoke to him on Sinai, and the rest of the book focuses on the preparation of the tabernacle (35–36), its instruments (37–39), and the consecration of the priesthood (40).

44. Sklar, *Leviticus*, 27, writes, "In order to understand Leviticus well, it is important to consider it in the context of the story that precedes it." On a larger scale, Barr, *Concept*, 356, says, "In general, although not all parts of the Bible are narrative, the narrative character of the story elements provides a better framework into which the non-narrative parts may be fitted than any framework based upon the non-narrative parts into which the story elements could be fitted." Therefore, proper attention to the manner in which apparently non-narrative portions of Scripture—such as Leviticus—feature within the story at large is important for a robust understanding of the Bible's message. I am indebted to Bartholomew and Goheen, "Story and Biblical Theology," 161, who highlight this quote.

45 For a helpful argument as to why even non-narrative portions of Scripture should be considered as having narrative value, see Newbigin, *Open Secret*, 81, who says, "In my conception all of the Bible counts as 'story.' A people's story is not necessarily purely narrative: materials of many kinds may be slotted into a narrative structure, and this is done in the Hebrew Bible. Thus legal materials are inserted and appear, almost entirely, as part of the Moses story."

46. McConville, *Being Human*, 123–24, comments, "The centrality of worship in the story and structure of the Pentateuch is highly significant. Joseph Blenkinsopp's analysis, in which Leviticus is the central panel of the five books, is an important foil

generations remember the significance of retaining YHWH's presence for the unfolding covenant story. While the instructions for performing the Day of Atonement as recorded in Leviticus are perhaps not written as the same type of narrative as one might find in Exodus, it presupposes, recalls, and rehearses the story of the Israel, speaking of her past, about the present, and toward her future.

Atonement and Yom Kippur (The Day of Atonement)

As the preceding section has detailed, Israel's sin and impurity require atonement in order for YHWH's presence to remain in her midst.[47] While individual sacrifices are prescribed for occasional atonement of individuals' sins and defilements throughout the HB, the Day of Atonement stands at the pinnacle of Israel's sacrificial cult as a corporate ceremony, atoning for the sanctuary and extending to the camp, annually offering forgiveness and cleansing to the people of Israel who faithfully observe the day.[48] Gordon McConville highlights the centrality of this day, writing, "When the high priest stands once a year in the tabernacle's holy of holies, this is, if only provisionally, a restoration of the close presence of God to humanity that was lost in Eden."[49] What distinguishes Yom Kippur from other prescribed sacrifices is that on this day, once per year, the high priest enters into the presence of YHWH behind the veil of the holy place.

Indeed, as indicated by Old Testament scholar Nahum Sarna, on Yom Kippur the four most sacred elements of Israel's cultic life coalesce to produce atonement: the most sacred individual (the high priest), the most sacred space (the holy of holies), the most sacred day (Yom Kippur), and the most sacred ritual (the sacrifices, rituals, and presentation

---

to the perception of them as the story of a progression toward land. The worship theme that unfolds in Exodus 25–40 and continues in Leviticus has a tabernacle at its center."

47. Milgrom, *Leviticus*, 9, notes, "The sanctuary symbolized the presence of God; impurity represented the wrongdoing of persons. If persons unremittingly polluted the sanctuary, they forced God out of his sanctuary and out of their lives."

48. To this point, Boda, *Severe Mercy*, 72, writes, "The moral violations of the Israelites introduced impurity to the sanctuary precincts and the rituals on the Day of Atonement were designed to remove these impurities from the sanctuary, and, by extension, the people."

49. McConville, *Being Human*, 124.

of the blood upon the *kipporet*, the "mercy seat").⁵⁰ In so doing the Day of Atonement creates, what Old Testament theologian Mark Boda calls "a theological-symbolic world" that emphasizes the danger that sin poses to defiled Israel juxtaposed with the merciful provision of YHWH.⁵¹ The following section will address the specific rites of Yom Kippur as prescribed in Leviticus 16–17 in order to consider this theological-symbolic world in preparation for assessing its effect upon Israel's worldview.

Yom Kippur: The Ritual Process

As the previous section has shown, sin and impurity require atonement in order to alleviate the danger they pose to Israel and her camp. In Leviticus 16, the precision required for proper performance of the Yom Kippur ritual highlights this tension between the danger of sinful and impure humanity improperly approaching YHWH's holiness and the necessity of YHWH dwelling in the midst of his people.⁵² In order to elucidate the theological-symbolic world that the Day of Atonement depicts in providing atonement for the people of Israel, the following section will investigate the various elements involved in observing the day. This will further highlight the manner in which the observance of the Day of Atonement recalls Israel's story, identity, and worldview.

Bathing and Linen Garments: Humility and Contrition

The Day of Atonement is a holy day, and while there is much to be celebrated through the forgiveness of sins and cleansing that it provides, it is referred to in Leviticus as a solemn day of affliction and Sabbath rest.⁵³ On this day, YHWH calls Israel to observe Yom Kippur as a holy convocation, remembering sin and acknowledging her impure condition before his holiness. Prior to making any of the sacrifices for the people, Moses commands Aaron to bathe himself and don the sacred linen clothing of the high priest.⁵⁴ This linen clothing, however, is not the elaborate

50. Sarna, *Exploring Exodus*, 205.
51. Boda, *Severe Mercy*, 73–74.
52. Lev 16:1–2. Aaron's sons are destroyed for bringing unauthorized fire before YHWH.
53. Lev 23:26–32; See Gelardini, "Hebrews," 122.
54. Lev 16:4.

garb of the high priest worn during other rites.⁵⁵ Instead it consists of plain linen garments, intended to reinforce "the abject state of the high priest in seeking expiation . . . [and] a contrite, reflective approach to the Most Holy Place."⁵⁶ The high priest is thus, from the outset of the ritual, cognizant of his own impurity and the need for humility in approaching YHWH.

A Bull: Sin Offering for the High Priest

After the priest has been purified by bathing he is to take a bull and offer it as a sin offering on behalf of himself and his household. In the same way as the high priest is to make himself ritually clean and present himself in purity, so too the animal for the sacrifice is to be pure and without blemish.⁵⁷ In Leviticus 22:33, this spotlessness is commanded for all of the sacrifices brought before YHWH, emphasizing the importance of purity and perfection.⁵⁸ While daily sacrifices were performed by the high priest on behalf of those bringing the offerings, in Leviticus 16 the high priest is called to first purify himself and to offer a sacrifice on behalf of himself and his household. In so doing, the high priest remembers and embodies the contrition that recognizes his own sinfulness and need of atonement at the outset of the Yom Kippur rite.⁵⁹

---

55. Wenham, *Book of Leviticus*, 230, notes, "Among his fellow men his dignity as the great mediator between man and God is unsurpassed, and his splendid clothes draw attention to the glory of his office. But in the presence of God even the high priest is stripped of all honor: he becomes simply the servant of the King of kings."

56. Rooker, *Leviticus*, 215. Some scholars suggest that the linen garments are indicative of the garb worn by the angelic hosts during their heavenly service, citing various HB references that seem to indicate what is worn by angels (see Ezek 9:2–3, 11; 10:2; Dan 10:5). See Willi Plein, "Some Remarks," 31; Milgrom, *Leviticus 1–16*, 1016. While this may be the case, the plain linen indicates humility whether worn by angels or priests.

57. Lev 22:17–33 provides YHWH's prescription for what types of animals are to be utilized. Leviticus 22:20 highlights spotlessness, stating, "You shall not offer anything that has a blemish."

58. Lev 22:33 requires spotless sacrifices because of YHWH's holiness. The passage reminds Israel that they are YHWH's people, rescued from Egypt and by whose presence they are made distinct.

59. According to the Mishna, the high priest prays for himself and his household, invoking the promise of Leviticus 16: "For on this day shall atonement be made for you to cleanse you from all your sins shall ye be clean before the Lord." Thus, before this promise might be spoken over the whole of Israel, Israel's representative must

Two Goats: Sin Offering and ʿăzāʾzēl

Once the high priest has been cleansed, the congregation is to bring two goats for which lots will be cast. One goat, determined by the lots, will be offered as a sin offering for the people, while the other, the high priest having confessed all of Israel's sins over it, will bear Israel's iniquities to the wilderness.[60] Scholars exert an extraordinary amount of effort to understand the meaning of the word ʿăzāʾzēl (עֲזָאזֵל), but the effort yields surprisingly little consensus.

Despite lack of consensus regarding the meaning of the living goat's name, Mark Rooker summarizes the apparent role of the two goats, writing, "In the Day of Atonement ceremony the first animal pictures the means for atonement, the shedding of blood in the sacrificial death. The scapegoat [עֲזָאזֵל] pictures the effect of atonement, the removal of guilt."[61] Similarly, Jay Sklar writes, "Sin [is] a lethal substance that had to be removed from the camp. . . . The lethal burden and penalty of the Israelites' sin was taken off their shoulders and placed on the goat, which bore it away and endured its consequences on their behalf."[62] Thus, despite a lack of consensus regarding translation, what can be said is that the ʿăzāʾzēl goat in the ritual serves as a symbolic vehicle, bearing the sins of the people and removing them from the camp. Thus, it is a visible depiction of a vicarious actor expunging sin from the camp.[63]

Blood: The *Kipper* Linchpin[64]

At the center of the ritual, as the high priest enters the holy place with a censer of coals and the sacrificial blood of the bull and the goat, Leviticus

---

recognize his own need for forgiveness, purification, and restoration of relationship with YHWH. Danby, *Mishna*, 165.

60. See Lev 16:20–22.
61. Rooker, *Leviticus*, 221.
62. Sklar, *Leviticus*, 212–13.

63. Rooker, *Leviticus*, 217, acknowledges the various opinions on the translation of עֲזָאזֵל, writing, "Regardless of the precise meaning of the term, the overall understanding of the passage is clear: the releasing of the goat indicated that the sins of the Israelites had been removed never to visit them again." Also Wenham, *Book of Leviticus*, 233–35, concludes that the role of the living goat is to remove sin from the camp.

64. This book recognizes that the author of Hebrews was almost certainly working with the LXX version of the Hebrew Bible (see Attridge, *Hebrews*, 23). However, the concept of כִּפֶּר and its related word group is exhibited through the rites associated

gives specific commands as to how he is to utilize the blood of the sacrifices to atone for the holy place, the tabernacle, the altar, and Israel herself. While Protestant scholarship has often focused on the importance of the slaughtering of the animal for the effecting of atonement, as detailed above, Milgrom and other recent commentators have shifted the focus away from the death of the animal and towards the power of the blood to effect purification.[65]

Indeed, it is clear that the blood manipulation component of the ritual of Yom Kippur takes center stage as the high priest is called to sprinkle the blood of the sin offerings around the mercy seat (to the east and in front) and then to anoint and sprinkle the altar with blood.[66] While the ʿăzāʾzēl goat bears Israel's sins and impurities out of the camp, it is the blood as a symbol of life that effects atonement. In fact, Leviticus 16:27 explicitly ties the making of atonement to the blood that is presented in the holy place.

Going beyond the declarative and prescriptive verses pertaining to blood in Leviticus 16, however, one also finds the rationale for blood's power in Leviticus 17:11: "For the life of the flesh is in the blood, and I myself have bestowed it to you upon the altar to ransom for your lives, for it is the blood that ransoms by means of/as the life."[67] As cited above,

---

with it, thus the use of Greek translation does not affect the dual nature of the ransom-cleansing function of the rite. The meaning of the ritual is not isolated at the lexical level, so Sklar's insights will remain appropriate for the following chapter's investigation; Moffitt, *Atonement*, 269, maintains Sklar's conclusions in addressing Hebrews itself.

65. See Eberhart, "Characteristics," 44. Eberhart rightly highlights the importance of blood manipulation in the process of making atonement, however, he does so to the detriment of the death of the animal, saying, "in the HB the slaughter of animals is rather insignificant." This claim is based on his etymological study of the Greek (θυσια) and Hebrew (קרבן, זבח) words used for offering/sacrifice that, as Eberhart argues, refer more to the means by which one draws near than the slaughter of a sacrificial animal. While the point stands that the effect of bringing an offering or a sacrifice is the progression towards God, and the means by which one approaches is the blood, not the death of an animal per se, the availability of the blood depends upon the slaughter of the animal. Thus, Eberhart is right to direct the reader's attention to the central role that blood plays, though it should not be concluded that the death of the animal is insignificant.

66. Lev 16:11–19.

67. Translation here is Sklar's, *Sin, Impurity*, 173–74. Having developed a convincing argument for either an essential or instrumental understanding the בְּ in בְּנֶפֶשׁ, Sklar concludes that this verse carries clear substitutionary implications, saying, "In this regard the life (נֶפֶשׁ) of the offerer is *ransomed* by means of the life (נֶפֶשׁ) of the animal, which is a payment that the offended party (the LORD) has agreed to (and indeed,

Jay Sklar's meticulous study of atonement in the priestly literature of the HB demonstrates that the power of the blood to effect atonement (both *koper* from the guilt of sin, and purgation of ritual impurity) is located in YHWH's willingness to provide and accept a substitutionary life by means of a prescribed ritual offering of animal blood.[68] As the holy place, implements of worship, and worshippers, then, come into contact with the blood, they are forgiven and purified by being brought into contact with what YHWH has given them as a ransom for their lives.[69]

Burnt Offering: A Pleasing Aroma

The final step in the Yom Kippur ritual is the immolation of the carcasses of both the sin offerings (the bull and the goat) and the burnt offering (the ram). Burnt offerings, already prescribed in the first chapter of Leviticus, produce a pleasing aroma to the Lord. Noting the presence of this concluding rite in all five types of priestly sacrificial rituals, Christian Eberhart argues, "rather than animal slaughter, it is the burning of at least some of the sacrificial material on the main and most holy altar which is the central ritual element of sacrifices."[70] Eberhart goes on to say, "The burning rite thus marks the final step . . . which is essentially a dynamic

---

provided), which is less than the penalty the offerer originally expected (viz. their own life), and which both rescues the offerer and restores peace to the relationship with the LORD." The blood, then, serves as a mitigation on behalf of the offerer. (Lev 17:11, כִּי נֶפֶשׁ הַבָּשָׂר בַּדָּם הִוא וַאֲנִי נְתַתִּיו לָכֶם עַל־הַמִּזְבֵּחַ לְכַפֵּר עַל־נַפְשֹׁתֵיכֶם כִּי־הַדָּם הוּא בַּנֶּפֶשׁ יְכַפֵּר׃)

68. Sklar, *Sin, Impurity*, 187, notes the difficulty in the English translation of כֹּפֶר, since the usual word "ransom" can imply that a payment is being paid to an offending party, as in the payment of a kidnapper. For that reason, the present work will prefer to leave the word untranslated, noting that a כֹּפֶר payment is a mitigated payment, paid to the offended party and accepted thereby in a reconciling of accounts and restoring of relationship. (See also Sklar, *Sin Impurity*, 77–79)

69. Sklar, *Sin Impurity*, 45–79. Sklar focuses in on Yom Kippur, through which YHWH is viewed as an offended party—by way of Israel's sin and defilement—who chooses to allow a כֹּפֶר payment (the lifeblood of the sacrificial animal) rather than the penalty due (the lifeblood of the offender). From the perspective of the offender, then, Sklar concludes, "While [כֹּפֶר] may serve to compensate the victim, this is only secondary to its function of redeeming the life of the guilty. . . . If the offended party does allow כֹּפֶר, then the guilty party would not perceive this as a penalty but as a gift: in the face of death, they are given life instead" (69). Then, despite the solemnity of the Yom Kippur fast, the day is to be received with joy and rejoicing due to the merciful willingness of YHWH to accept כֹּפֶר.

70. Eberhart, "Sacrificial Metaphors," 46, discusses חַטָּאת, זֶבַח שְׁלָמִים, מִנְחָה, עֹלָה, אָשָׁם.

movement through sacred space toward the center of holiness, thus as 'approach' (root קרב) to God. Transformed by the fire of the altar, the material offering given by a human individual or community is 'transported' to heaven in the ascending smoke."[71] Thus, Eberhart can conclude, "The purpose of the entire cult concept [is] approaching God."[72] This insight highlights the spatial elements involved in the ascending smoke of the immolated corpses, and reinforces the idea that the process of making atonement draws the community ever-nearer to YHWH's heavenly presence.

Each of the elements in the sacrificial process is quite different in nature, from the slaughter of an animal to the burning of its carcass and from the purifying bath of the high priest to the presentation of blood. As such distinct rites, the different elements of the Yom Kippur ritual have variously been identified as the most important aspect of the atoning process. Traditional evangelical scholarship has located atonement in the death of the animal.[73] Sklar and others have called attention to the ransoming and purifying effects of blood application.[74] Eberhart emphasizes immolation as the central ritual element of sacrificial offering.[75] While each of these advocates rightly indicates the importance of individual aspects of Yom Kippur, it may be that the quest to find the most important individual element of the ritual distracts from the importance of the process *in toto*, all of which is involved in the instructions for making of atonement.

---

71. Eberhart, "Sacrificial Metaphors," 47. While the smoke does rise, as if to heaven, it might be pressing the issue of spatial dynamics to see the rising smoke as indicating greater proximity to YHWH than the blood that is applied to the *kapporet*, which is considered to be the intersection of heaven and earth or the "center point of sacred space." See Polen, "Leviticus and Hebrews," 213–25, esp. 221.

72. Eberhart, "Sacrificial Metaphors," 62, comments on Hebrews' concern with the ability of sacrifice to grant access to God, though it is directly tied into Hebrews' interpretation of Leviticus. Likewise, see Backhaus, "How to Entertain Angels," 157.

73. Rooker, *Leviticus*, 218, writes, "The blood on the mercy seat indicated that Israel's sin was atoned for by a substitutionary death."

74. Sklar, *Sin, Impurity*, 181, builds on the work of Jacob Milgrom who convincingly argues for the role of blood in purging the tabernacle and instruments of worship of ritual impurity. See Milgrom, *Leviticus*, who overemphasizes the purgation aspect of Yom Kippur to the neglect of forgiveness. Sklar's offering strikes an appropriate balance where both forgiveness/ransom and purgation/cleansing are in view during Yom Kippur.

75. Eberhart, "Sacrificial Metaphors," 46.

Such a view of the entire process of Yom Kippur as the means of atonement finds warrant in the prevalent use of the verb *kipper* and its cognates. This atonement language occurs multiple times throughout the process of Yom Kippur from the offering of the bull on behalf of the high priest and his household (Lev 16:6, 11) to the sprinkling of the blood around the *kipporet* (Lev 16:16) and to the burnt offerings immolated for the high priest and for the people (Lev 16:24). The whole ritual process involves effecting atonement, thus it would be alien to the text to ask, "Which action within the ritual effects atonement?" Therefore, rather than arguing for an individual part of the process as the effective aspect, it is better to see the entire ritual, meticulously administered, as the means by which YHWH provides atonement. Furthermore, the ritual in its entirety as projected by the narrative of Leviticus 16, evokes Israel's history, identifies her place in God's story, and shapes the way she inhabits the world.

Since this ritual is evocative of Israel's story—the history to which the three Abrahamic faiths of Judaism, Christianity, and Islam lay claim—it is instructive to consider the effects of this ritual for Israel and readers of Israel's Scripture. Pertinent to this purpose, biblical scholar N. T. Wright argues that story, symbolic praxis, and worldview function together, concluding, "It is a truth insufficiently acknowledged that a sensible worldview equipped with appropriate symbolic praxis must be in want of a story. . . . Symbols and actions mean what they mean within a worldview."[76] Therefore, following Wright, if stories and symbols express and inform worldview, then a storied ritual such as the Day of Atonement can provide a window through which to view the underlying worldview of Israel.[77]

---

76. Wright, *Paul and Faithfulness*, 456.

77. Summarizing Wright's contribution, Moritz, "Reflecting," 184, writes, "For Wright . . . story and stories are major vehicles of worldviews—they even play a determining role in the formation of the latter."

TABLE 2.1

The Day of Atonement in Leviticus 16–17

COMPONENT	PROCEDURE	EFFECT
The high priest takes a purification bath and puts on Linen Garments Leviticus 16:4	The high priest bathes his body prior to donning the holy linen garments. These garments are not the daily garb of the high priest, but rather are plain clothes intended to emphasize the humble approach to the presence of YHWH.	The high priest recognizes his own imperfection and impurity and begins the ritual with contrition, humility, and seeking purification for himself.
A Bull presented as a Sin offering Leviticus 16:3, 6	The high priest slaughters the bull as a sin offering for himself and his household. He brings the blood of the bull into the holy place, sprinkling it seven times before the *kipporet*.	The high priest recognizes his own sin and makes atonement for himself before serving as a representative of the people.
Two goats: one goat as a sin offering & one goat as ʿăzāʾzēl Leviticus 16:5, 7–10, 15–22	The high priest slaughters the goat chosen by lot as a sin offering and brings the blood into the holy place. He sprinkles the blood of the goat before the *kipporet* as he did with the blood of the bull. Leaving the holy place, the high priest anoints the altar with the blood of the goat and the blood of the bull. The high priest then lays both hands upon the ʿăzāʾzēl goat, confesses Israel's sins over it, and sends it to the wilderness under the charge of one who is ready and waiting.	The high priest serves as a representative of the people of Israel before YHWH. Bringing atoning blood into the holy place and working outward toward the altar, the high priest atones for the sancta of the camp. By confessing Israel's sins over the ʿăzāʾzēl goat, the high priest lays Israel's transgressions on the goat that will be led outside of the camp, thus demonstrating the removal of Israel's iniquities.
Blood Manipulation and atonement Leviticus 16:14–19 & Leviticus 17:11–14	The high priest sprinkles the blood of the sacrifices before the *kipporet* and anoints the altar with the blood.	Blood as a symbol of life has the power to act as a "ransom" or *koper* (כֹּפֶר) for sinners and as a cleansing agent for those defiled by impurity. Sin and defilement are atoned for by blood-as-life.
Burnt offering Leviticus 16:24–25	The high priest offers two rams as burnt offerings. One ram is his offering, while the other ram is for the people.	Burnt offerings produce an aroma pleasing to the Lord, and the ascending smoke reminds the worshippers of the ultimate goal of sacrificial ritual, which is to draw near to the one that is in heaven.

The Worldview Evoked by Yom Kippur

In Western philosophy, the idea of worldview can be traced back to Immanuel Kant, who utilized the German word *"Weltanschauung"* to describe a person's outlook and the perspective by which one perceives the world.[78] While this concept features in various disciplines, it bears significant fruit when applied to hermeneutics, theology, contextualization and missiology.[79] Paul Hiebert, a Christian missiologist and anthropologist, defines worldview as "the foundational cognitive, affective, and evaluative assumptions and frameworks a group of people makes about the nature of reality that they use to order their lives."[80] He goes on to describe how "worldviews are not foundational ideas, feelings, and values, but 'worlds' that are inhabited."[81] Thus worldviews provide both a lens for understanding reality and also a model for behaving within that reality, and they do so in narrative fashion.[82]

---

78. Hiebert, *Transforming Worldviews*.

79. Hiebert, *Transforming Worldviews*, 13. Hiebert discusses varied uses of worldview, but focuses on the importance for worldview concepts that help "us understand the nature of our mission as Christians in the world."

80. Hiebert, *Transforming Worldviews*, 25–26.

81. Hiebert, *Transforming Worldviews*, 28. Hiebert cites Berger, *Sacred Canopy*, as using the phrase "sacred canopy" to refer to the manner in which a worldview provides a canopy under which one might establish individual and communal ways of living and sharing meaning.

82. While drawing on some of the valuable insights of post-modern thought regarding the power of narrative and its role in epistemology, many who would consider themselves evangelicals have been reticent to fully embrace the full-blown narrative theology that marked some mid-twentieth century theologians who relinquished the claim that the Bible tells true history in favor of simply following its story, regardless of its foundation in lived-history. (See Bartholomew and Goheen, "Story and Biblical Theology," 162–63, warning, "The threat lies in divorcing the Bible when seen as literature from its theological reality to which scripture bears witness. . . . In other words, we wish to assert a narrative realism in terms of the relationship between *this* story and our world and its creator.") This critique of so-called liberal streams of theology was clearly and helpfully made in a 1989 article by van Huyssteen, "Narrative Theology," 771, that cautions against the adoption of a pure narrative theology in that it leads to a non-realist epistemology. He writes, "The hermeneutical and epistemological problems created by the divergent trends in contemporary narrative theology is especially highlighted by Thiemann's 'pure' form of narrative theology when the irrational inclusion of God as the hard core of a theological paradigm reveals a retreat to an esoteric commitment which firmly bars the way of theology to the reality about which it proposes to make statements." He goes on to say, "Narrative, then, although an essential genre for communicating the Christian faith, by itself will not solve the epistemological problem

While various approaches to worldview analysis are available, this book will utilize a worldview assessment tool based around six basic questions whose answers derive from the narrative, symbol, and ritual of a culture or text. These questions are adopted from biblical scholar N. T. Wright's work wherein he claims, "Christian theology tells a story, and seeks to tell it coherently.... This story, as the fundamental articulation of the worldview, offers a set of answers to the [six] worldview questions."[83] When applied first to the worldview of the Israelites at the foot of Mount Sinai in Leviticus 16, these questions reveal that the practice of Yom

---

of the shaping of rationality in contemporary theology" (774). In conclusion, and in harmony with Wright's then-contemporary movement towards critical-realism, van Huyssteen recognizes the importance of narrative but is unwilling to relinquish the claim that true history actually matters and serves as a ground for Christian theology, concluding, "And as to the events in the life and death of Jesus: one can only generalise from parable to myth and from myth to fiction if it can be shown that historical questions are irrelevant to a full and proper religious understanding of the gospel narratives" (775). This article, published in 1989, is contemporary with Wright's *The New Testament and the People of God* (published in 1992), and serves as an early example of "critical realist" epistemological approaches to the narrative shape of Scripture. As noted above in the text, Wright espouses a critical realist approach to epistemology and Scripture, and in so doing draws from the merits of post-modern contributions to philosophy and theology while not relinquishing a realist posture towards knowledge and knowing. Likewise, Kevin Vanhoozer appeals to the narrative shape of doctrine and the ethical claims it makes on Christian living in his landmark work, *The Drama of Doctrine*, 18. He writes, "The drama of doctrine is rooted in Israel's history and is narrated with a high degree of literary sophistication so as to establish a worldview." Thus, the present book will proceed along the lines of both Wright and Vanhoozer's approach to narrative in Scripture and the relationship it has to worldview. Others to note the effects of narrative on worldview from an anthropological perspective would include Paul Hiebert, particularly in *Transforming Worldviews*, 265–66, who endorses narrative-driven worldview formation, saying, "To say there is no biblical worldview is to deny that there is an underlying unity to the biblical story.... The Old Testament is a record of the unfolding of a single cosmic story.... It was in this context of a worldview shaped over two millennia that God made his final revelation."

83. Wright, *People of God*, 132. Wright utilizes four worldview questions in *NTPG* (Who are we? Where are we? What is wrong? What is the solution?), he adds a fifth question in *Jesus and Victory*, 467: "What time is it?" and then adds a sixth in *Paul and Faithfulness*, 26–27: "Why?" Each of these questions will serve as a section heading for the following treatment of Lev 16. Chapter 3 will show how Hebrews' answers to the same questions demonstrate another of Wright's insights that storytelling can be a subversive and worldview-altering endeavor: "The subversive story comes close enough to the story already believed by the hearer for a spark to jump between them; and nothing will ever be quite the same again." Wright, *People of God*, 40.

Kippur is indicative, formative, and evocative of Israel's narrative and answers to the six worldview questions.

Who Are We?

Perhaps the most central concern of Yom Kippur, and indeed the entire sacrificial system, is the answer to Israel's question, "Who are we?" Amidst all the detail which attends the book of Leviticus is the central reminder that the Creator God, YHWH, has led his people out of bondage in Egypt, covenanted with them at Mount Sinai, and taken up residence in their midst in the desert tabernacle.[84] From this position as an elect people whose God dwells in their midst, Israel is also a people on the move, following the lead of YHWH toward the land and blessing YHWH has promised to them. The answer to Israel's question, "Who are we?" is inextricably linked to YHWH's covenanted presence in their midst.[85] A requirement of that presence is the sacrificial system—and, most centrally, the provision of Yom Kippur—which allows YHWH in his perfection to dwell in the midst of his people despite their imperfection. Thereby Israel maintains her identity while remaining cognizant that she is stained by sin and impurity and annually in need of YHWH's mercy extended to them through the Day of Atonement.

Where Are We?

Connected to the question of identity addressed above, the question "Where are we?" deals with the type of world the Israelites understood

---

84. See Lev 22:31–33; 25:38; 26:13. Throughout Leviticus the reminder is given that YHWH is the redeeming and rescuing God of the exodus from Egypt, thus Lev 26:44–45 says, "Yet for all that [disobedience resulting in curses and exile] when they are in the land of their enemies, I will not spurn them, nether will I abhor them so as to destroy them utterly and break my covenant with them, for I am the LORD their God. But I will for their sake remember the covenant with their forefathers, whom I brought out of the land of Egypt in the sight of the nations, that I might be their God: I am the LORD."

85. Exod 33:12–17. After the people's idolatry with the golden calf, Moses intercedes with God on behalf of the people contending, "If your presence will not go with me, do not bring us up from here. For how shall it be known that I have found favor in your sight, I and your people? Is it not in your going with us, so that we are distinct, I and your people, from every other people on the face of the earth?"

themselves to inhabit. This question is difficult to answer without reference to another question, "Where have we come from?" Having just witnessed the plagues which YHWH brought upon the Egyptians, the people of God at the foot of Mount Sinai have ample justification for understanding YHWH as the Creator who is in control of creation.[86]

Additionally, from a literary standpoint, Leviticus 16 begins with YHWH instructing Moses as to how to perform the annual Yom Kippur ritual. The name "YHWH" is the covenant name by which God sent Moses to deliver the people from Egypt. By utilizing this name, Leviticus invokes the particular history of Israel that reminds them of where they have been: in slavery in Egypt. The people can answer "Where are we?" at the foot of Mount Sinai in relation to where they have been, so as to say that they are no longer in slavery, but now *en route* to their own land.[87]

More directly involved in the Yom Kippur ritual itself, however, is the recognition that being in the holy place affords Israel opportunity to approach YHWH's glory.[88] On this day, through the representative high priest in the holy place, Israel enters back into the presence of YHWH, from which sin has expelled humanity since Eden.[89] Pervasive throughout the ritual, however, is the reminder that there is a protective and prohibitive barrier between all but the representative high priest and YHWH. This leads to the next question, "What is wrong?"

What is wrong?

The elaborate detail that marks the prescriptions for Yom Kippur and the meticulous manner by which the priests and worshippers must offer their

---

86. Exod 7–14. The ten plagues and the parting of the Red Sea demonstrate YHWH's repeated control over the natural world. Likewise, the tenth plague demonstrates YHWH's power over life itself through the death of the firstborn who were not covered by blood.

87. Milgrom, *Leviticus*, 6, notes, "Throughout Leviticus, Israel is camped at Sinai; in Numbers, Israel is preparing for, undertaking, and completing the journey through the wilderness."

88. Polen, "Leviticus and Hebrews," 221, writes, "At the very core of the system is the manifest divine presence, the Glory, which hovers in a cloud on the Ark-cover. Ultimately all rites are directed toward this presence."

89. McConville, *Being Human*, 124, writes, "When the high priest stands once a year in the . . . holy of holies, this is . . . a restoration of the close presence of God to humanity that was lost in Eden."

sacrifices are reinforced by the reminder of mortal danger for those who would approach YHWH improperly.[90] Indeed, throughout Leviticus, the reader is confronted with the terrible holiness and purity of YHWH held in tension with the necessity of his presence dwelling in the midst of Israel in order to maintain her identity.[91]

On one hand, Yom Kippur is a reminder of the danger that YHWH's presence poses to his people. Prior to the prescription of the Day of Atonement ritual, Leviticus records Nadab and Abihu's death as the result of their innovation in approaching YHWH and the tabernacle. In so doing, the literary structure of Leviticus reminds Yom Kippur participants of the consuming nature of YHWH's holiness and the impossibility of an improper, unauthorized approach.[92] After Nadab and Abihu's death, YHWH tells Moses in Leviticus 16:2, "Tell Aaron your brother not to come at any time into the holy place inside the veil, before the mercy seat that is on the ark, so that he may not die."

This story highlights central questions that would have presented themselves to embryonic Israel at the foot of Mount Sinai, and likewise, to the modern reader of Leviticus: "How in the world can the holy and pure King of the universe dwell among his sinful and impure people? How can he live here, in our very midst, without his holiness melting us in our sin and impurity?"[93] The directions given for Yom Kippur, then, cannot be removed from the reminder that YHWH's holiness and purity will not abide the impurity and sinfulness of humanity apart from YHWH's provision of atonement.

---

90. Lev 10:1–2; 16:1.

91. Leithart, *Delivered from Elements*, 114, writes, "Yahweh's very presence in Israel was a danger, and as the sins, rebellions and impurities mounted on the priest and in Yahweh's house, the danger intensified. Without a mechanism for decompression, it would rapidly become intolerable. . . . There rites provided an annual reboot for the sanctuary and an annual removal of impurity and reinvestiture of the high priest."

92. The reader is reminded of the events as recorded in Lev 10:1–2. This event is recorded immediately following Aaron's initial offering in Lev 9:8–24, which, having been offered "as YHWH commanded," was consumed by YHWH's fire. The contrast is apparent in Lev 10:1–2 where Nadab and Abihu's innovation is referred to as unauthorized or strange. Instead of their action being accepted by YHWH, they themselves are consumed by his fire in Lev 10:2.

93. Sklar, *Leviticus*, 27–28.

What is the Solution?

On the other hand, however, Yom Kippur features as the one day each year that Israel, through the high priest's representative action, is able to approach YHWH and reaffirm their identity in light of his presence among them.[94] Near the end of the prescription, in Leviticus 16:30, Israel is told emphatically, "For on this day shall atonement be made for you to cleanse you. You shall be clean before YHWH from all your sins."[95] Thus, Yom Kippur is a reminder that YHWH is willing and able to provide ritual access into his presence despite the sins the people have committed and impurities they have acquired throughout their daily lives. Following the ritual precisely as YHWH directs results in an annually renewed atonement—the forgiveness of sins and the purging of impurity.[96] Therein is found the solution—albeit an impermanent solution—to Israel's problem. On Yom Kippur the people of God are corporately granted access to the presence of YHWH through their representative, the high priest.

As noted above, Yom Kippur provides an annual reminder of YHWH's willingness to forgive and cleanse his people so that he might dwell in their midst without consuming them. The blood of the atoning sacrifices, annually given and accepted by YHWH as a כִּפֶּר-purgation, serves to ransom and restore Israel to their covenant God. The dual dilemma of sin and impurity, then, is managed through the temporary solution of the yearly, communal restoration effected by Yom Kippur. While this may not be considered a solution in the permanent sense of the word, it assures Israel that YHWH will provide a means by which his presence might continue with them year by year.

---

94. It is precisely YHWH's presence with his people that Moses identifies as Israel's distinctive mark of identity in Exod 33:16, saying, "Is it not in your going with us, so that we are distinct, I and your people, from every other people on the face of the earth?"

95. Sklar, *Leviticus*, 215, notes the manner in which this promise is highlighted by way of chiastic structure, writing, "Verses 29–31 form a chiasm, with verse 31 repeating the instructions of verse 29 in reverse order. At the chiasm's heart is verse 30, reiterating that this day's purpose was to *make atonement* for the Israelites and so *purify* (NIV cleanse) them *from all* their *sins*." Thus the author seeks to emphasize the dual nature of the כִּפֶּר-rites as being able to cleanse from impurity and forgive sin.

96. Sklar, *Sin, Impurity*, 139, writes, "כִּפֶּר refers both to the effecting of a כִּפֶּר-payment and to purgation. . . . it refers both to rescuing from punishment and to cleansing impurity."

If one follows this logic and considers the individual rites of Yom Kippur as a whole, Leviticus' teaching on atonement emerges as multifaceted. There are unavoidable elements of substitution inherent in the rite throughout, despite various contemporary scholarly attempts to reject such an idea.[97] The ʿăzāʾzēl goat expiates the sins of the community away vicariously.[98] The blood of the animal serves as a payment of *koper* on behalf of the offerer.[99] The presentation of sacrificial lifeblood in the holy of holies is representative of the lifeblood of the offerer.[100] While substitution can be rendered in a variety of ways—penal, representative, expiatory, and propitiatory—it cannot be categorically excised from the text.[101] Leviticus 16 understands atonement through the vicarious sacrificial process to effect expiation of sins through the ʿăzāʾzēl goat, purification of worshippers and tabernacle along with representation before YHWH through blood manipulation, and as a penal substitution

---

97. Gathercole, *Defending Substitution*, 17–18, writes, "When Christ died bearing our sins or guilt or punishment, he did so *in our place* and *instead of us*. . . . He did something, underwent something, so *we* did not—and never will—have to." Thus, Gathercole identifies the role of the scapegoat in the Yom Kippur ritual as being "clearly a substitute but not self-evidently a propitiatory one. The scapegoat eliminates contamination of sin but it is not—at least directly—a propitiation" (22). While Gathercole's work centers on New Testament treatment of atonement in Pauline writings, the point made in his introduction stands true of Leviticus as well: "Biblical exegesis simply demands substitution; therefore it cannot be avoided" (28).

98. Lev 16:22. See also Sklar, *Leviticus*, 216; Rooker, *Leviticus*, 217.

99. Sklar, *Leviticus*, 221, comments on the rationale for the use of blood in Lev 17:11, saying, "The animal's lifeblood was accepted as the ransom payment in place of the offeror's: it served as a mitigated penalty on the offeror's behalf, graciously accepted by the Lord (the offended party), in this way rescuing the offeror (the offending party) from due punishment and restoring peace to the relationship between the sinner and the Lord." This depicts a clear instance of penal-substitution and is contra the argument of Polen, "Leviticus and Hebrews," 217, who writes, "No doctrine of substitution is hinted at in P's sacrifices. The animal is not dying in place of, for the sins of, the human. . . . So we are left with blood as a covenantal sign, as a reminder of the kindship between God an Israel." While this comment rightly recognizes the covenantal elements of blood, it does not deal with the text's clear references to the vicarious nature of the sacrificial animals whose heads bear the sins of the offerors prior to their execution and whose offerors are forgiven and no longer bear their sins after the offering (Lev 4:15; 5:17–19; 16:21–though here this goat is not slaughtered, it is still referred to as a part of the sin offering in 16:5).

100. Moffitt, *Atonement*, 257.

101. Gathercole, *Defending Substitution*, 17–18; Green, "Kaleidoscopic View," 167.

whereby YHWH as the offended party accepts a כֹּפֶר-payment in order to restore relationship and settle accounts.[102]

What time is it?

The rhetorical audience of Leviticus 16 finds itself at a time of anticipation within the biblical narrative. Having just received the covenant, the law, and the priesthood, the newly formed people of God find themselves in the desert awaiting entrance into the land promised to Abraham. As such a wandering, landless people, they are dependent upon the faithfulness of YHWH to his covenant promises. Observing Yom Kippur provides an annual reminder of the fact that YHWH is faithful to provide atonement, so that he might live among his people and lead them to their land. While the time to enter the land has not yet arrived, as a promise given by the God in their midst, it is secure.

Why?

N. T. Wright's most recent volume in his series, *Christian Origins and the Question of God*, has added a sixth question to his previous list of five: Why? Wright views this question as a feeder into the prior questions. The question "Why did the people of Israel act this way?" leads into a description of who they believe themselves to be, what problems they believe themselves to face, what the solution is, etc. However, Wright also claims, "it is precisely at that point, in many different worldviews, a fuller answer may involve something we might call 'theology': some account or other of a god or gods, and particularly of their relation to the world and to humans."[103] Thus, as one asks this question of the Day of Atonement ritual, the answer provides both a summary and synthesis of the previous answers. Atonement is the process given to cleanse and forgive the

---

102. It is not clear that the Hebrew of Leviticus 16 teaches propitiation, though the author of Hebrews, reading the LXX, might be inclined to incorporate it by way of the Greek word ἱλάσκομαι, which allows Schreiner, "Penal Substitution View," 85, to say, "The verb for atonement is *kipper* in the Hebrew and *hilaskomai* in Greek. Careful study demonstrates that the latter verb has to do with the appeasement or the satisfaction of God's wrath."

103. Wright, *Paul and Faithfulness*, 27.

people such that the people's camp might be made a suitable habitation for YHWH.

Conclusion

As seen throughout this chapter, YHWH's holy presence is unable to abide Israel's sins and impurities. Yet, an existential tension arises for Israel at this point, because Israel is dependent upon YHWH's presence for their own identity. Israel is left to ask, "How can the holy presence of God relate to and dwell among a defiled and sinful people?" In response to this dilemma, the book of Leviticus provides the Day of Atonement as YHWH's prescribed resolution of the tension between these incompatible realities.

As shown above, though Leviticus appears as a non-narrative register of law and ritual, it is intimately connected to the larger story of Israel and should be understood by attending to the narrative backdrop. Indeed, as McConville writes regarding the role of the tabernacle, "[the completion of the tabernacle] represents the possibility of a continuing relationship between God and humanity notwithstanding the ongoing story of human sinfulness. . . . The fine balance between the presence of God with Israel and his potential absence is nowhere better expressed than in the Day of Atonement rituals."[104]

Thus, all of Israel's history and narrative trajectory that is wrapped up in the abiding presence of YHWH is evoked and recalled through Yom Kippur. The calling out of the people of God, from the covenant with Abraham[105] to the exodus from Egypt[106] to the giving of the law and the priesthood[107] is not merely for Israel's benefit, but in fact is theocentric: in Israel, God was creating a people for himself and in the covenant—including the promises, law, and priesthood—YHWH was

---

104. McConville, *God and Earthly Power*, 61.
105. Gen 17:7–8.
106. Exod 6:6–7.

107. Lev 22:31–33 records YHWH's command, saying, "So you shall keep my commandments and do them: I am the LORD. And you shall not profane my holy name, that I may be sanctified among the people of Israel. I am the LORD who sanctifies you, who brought you out of the land of Egypt to be your God: I am the LORD." According to Rooker, *Leviticus*, 280, the sanctification of the people, and the acknowledgement of YHWH as holy, takes place as YHWH dwells among his people.

pledging his faithfulness.¹⁰⁸ In other words, the central element of Israel's story—YHWH's dwelling in Israel's midst—is secured by the central element of her cult, Yom Kippur, thus Yom Kippur serves as the vehicle by which Israel's story might continue.¹⁰⁹

This ritual helps to form and maintain Israel's worldview as it recalls her history, speaks to the nature of her identity (an elect, covenant people among whom YHWH dwells), her problem (sin and impurity), the solution (YHWH's covenant faithfulness and merciful willingness to accept the Yom Kippur ritual as a temporary, annually renewed כִּפֶּר-purgation), and the direction she is heading (toward the promised land).

The Day of Atonement, and the concept of atonement itself, then, is not merely a ritual component of Israel's religious apparatus. Instead, it is a deeply seated rehearsal of her very identity, her story, and her hopes for the future. Therefore, for the purposes of this paper, it has been instructive to consider the HB teaching on atonement as a part of the foundational history that both Hebrews and the Qur'an purport to complete. Having done so, the next chapter turns to consider the Christian claim to continuation through the perspective of the author of Hebrews, who invites the reader to reconsider how to understand Israel's entire history by viewing Yom Kippur through the lens of the Christ event. Investigation of Hebrews' argument will reveal that the Christ event bends, but does not break, the arc of Israel's history begun in the Pentateuch. Retelling the story, however, results in alterations to the symbols and some aspects of the worldview fostered by this perspective on ancient Israel's history.

---

108. Polen, "Leviticus and Hebrews," 215, comments on Exod 29:46, striking on something that is centrally important to the identity of the people of God, writing, "The purpose of the Exodus from Egypt is not so that the Israelites could enter into the Promised Land, as many other biblical passages have it. Rather it is theocentric: so that God might abide with (לְשָׁכְנִי) Israel, as if God had arranged the entire Exodus drama so that he might find a home among his people." Thus, the whole narrative of Israel has pointed in the direction of YHWH dwelling among his people, and the Yom Kippur rites reveal how that might be in light of Israel's pollution and sin.

109. Rooker, *Leviticus*, 213, comments, "Leviticus 16 occupies the central position in the book (and of the Law as a whole), it is the consummation of the previous fifteen chapters and provides the spiritual energy and motivation to carry out the imperatives of Leviticus 17–27." Likewise, Polen, "Leviticus and Hebrews," 218, comments, "P's ritual and the theology it enacts are all about fostering and maintaining relationship between Israel and her God, creator of heaven and earth."

TABLE 2.2

Worldview Questions and Answers from Leviticus 16–17

QUESTION	ANSWER
Who are we?	The people whom YHWH rescued from slavery in Egypt. The people with whom YHWH has made a covenant. The people to whom YHWH has promised a land. The people whose uniqueness is demonstrated by YHWH's presence.
Where are we?	Between the exodus that has provided rescue and the land that is promised. Near the center of the universe, the holy place of YHWH. Except for the high priest's annual entry, however, Israel is separated from YHWH by the curtain that conceals the holy place.
What is wrong?	Sin and impurity endanger Israel in the presence of the holiness of YHWH. Sin and impurity threaten to expel the presence of YHWH from the camp.
What is the solution?	The Day of Atonement is given by YHWH as a ritual to manage sin and impurity for the camp once every year. Atonement effects temporary ransom and cleansing for sin and impurity.
What time is it?	A time of wandering and anticipation of entry into the promised land. A time to remember YHWH's covenant faithfulness, to repent of sin, and to hope for the fulfillment of his promises.
Why?	Israel's uniqueness is contingent upon YHWH's dwelling in her midst. YHWH exhibits his mercy by giving Israel the Day of Atonement ritual in order to provide a ransom and purification for the effects of her sin. YHWH remains in the camp because of the ransom-purgation effected by the Day of Atonement, and continues to lead Israel to the promised land, blessings, and fulfillment of his covenant promises.

3

Hebrews and Atonement

A Re-Envisioning of Israel's Narrative in the Light of Christ

THE STATED PURPOSE OF the present endeavor is to consider how Christianity and Islam take up the narrative begun in the previous chapter's exploration of Yom Kippur. As the preceding chapters demonstrate, both faith systems claim to complete that which has been revealed in the Torah. Therefore, since Yom Kippur is such a central component of ancient Israel's cultic celebration, one would expect to find rationale in Hebrews and the Qur'an for why Yom Kippur's atoning animal sacrifices are no longer practiced. In fact, even though atoning animal sacrifice features centrally in the Pentateuch as the God-given means by which to identify, distinguish, and make atonement for the people of God, neither the New Testament nor the Qur'an prescribe animal sacrifices for effecting atonement.

For Muslims, the Qur'an and Islamic tradition provide various explanations as to why Levitical sacrifices are not practiced within Islam. These explanations will be the subject of the following chapter. However, as the present chapter will demonstrate, in the New Testament, the book of Hebrews provides Christians with a description of how the Christ event fulfills Yom Kippur, the Levitical cult, and priesthood.[1] To that end,

---

1. This book uses the term "Christ event" as a convention to refer to the entirety of Jesus' ministry in history as the long-awaited Messiah. This includes the incarnation of the second person of the Trinity all the way to his ascension and promised return. It acknowledges that some use this terminology as a way of detaching the meaning of

this chapter will investigate the book of Hebrews in order to explain how it presents atonement through Jesus Christ despite the absence of efficacious and atoning animal sacrifice.

The book of Hebrews, however, is for scholars and exegetes an enigmatic book. Many have offered various perspectives on authorship, dating, purpose, and audience of the book of Hebrews, yet there is no unanimity among scholars.[2] One area of near-consensus has, however, emerged: the book presents the Christ event as the fulfillment of the Yom Kippur ritual.[3] For example, Hebrews scholar Gabriella Gelardini points out the clear connection between the Christ event and Yom Kippur in Hebrews, stating, "A deeper analysis of these chapters makes clear that Jesus functions here as the sin offering of Yom Kippur, by the means of which—so the author promises—he will attain atonement for his people."[4] Scholars remain divided, however, over how the author of Hebrews consequently conceives of the religious system within which Yom Kippur features.

Jesus's life and ministry from its historical grounding in order to preserve the dynamic, ongoing, and ever-developing nature of his ministry. See Macquarrie, *Jesus Christ*, 19. While not denying the importance of the ongoing impact of Christ and the need for preaching to extend its effects meaningfully to contemporary audiences, the term "Christ event" herein specifically refers to the events as they are recorded as history in the biblical material.

2. Authorship, audience, purpose, and date are all matters that have enjoyed no consensus among scholars. Regarding authorship, Attridge, *Hebrews*, 5, writes, "Like nature abhorring a vacuum, commentators have frequently been loathe to acquiesce in the anonymity of Hebrews. Some of the scenarios constructed around the various figures proposed are vivid and entertaining, but that so many are plausible means that none can ever be convincing. The beginning of sober exegesis is a recognition of the limits of historical knowledge and those limits preclude positive identification of the author." Regarding audience, Lane, *Hebrews 1–8*, liii, writes, "A reconstruction of the life situation that made Hebrews intelligible must be advanced tentatively as a working proposal. The evidence to be gathered from the document itself is ambiguous and open to divergent interpretations." Regarding date, Bruce, *Epistle to Hebrews*, xlii, writes, "In the absence of any clear evidence for the identity of the recipients or the author, the date of the epistle is also uncertain." Regarding purpose, see the widely varied proposals in the edited work of Gelardini, *Hebrews*.

3. See Gelardini, "Inauguration of Yom Kippur," 225–54; Attridge, *Hebrews*, 239.

4. Gelardini, "Hebrews, Ancient Synagogue," 122.

Supersession or New Covenantalism?

One of the most influential early commentators of the fourth century to propose that Hebrews refers to Christianity's eclipse of Judaism is John Chrysostom. Much Christian commentary, even into the modern period, has followed his lead, assuming Hebrews' message aims at Christians who are in danger of backsliding into Judaism.[5] For example, Hebrews commentator S. G. Wilson claims that the author "routinely and starkly contrasts Christianity and Judaism to the detriment of the latter."[6] Pointing to Hebrews 7:18, which indicates that the Levitical cult was weak and useless, commentators like Wilson assume the author of Hebrews is proposing Christian supersession over Judaism.[7] This proposal rests on the assumption that Christianity already exists as a separate category from Judaism for the author and audience of Hebrews.[8] This perspective, however, anachronistically reads a clear distinction between Jew and Christian that is foreign to Hebrews.[9] Such a distinction, in fact, distracts from the author's sustained dependence on the very sacrificial system within which Christ accomplishes his atoning work.[10]

---

5. See Synge, *Hebrews and Scriptures*, 44; citing this occasion for writing as a widely-held scholarly position, see Bernard, "Anti-Jewish Interpretations," cxxvii.

6. Wilson, *Related Strangers*, 117.

7. Bauckham et al., *Epistle to Hebrews*, 150–227. Five essays in this volume speak to the ongoing debate over the question, "Does the Book of Hebrews propose supersessionism?" These essays each include reference to an ongoing conversation that stretches back at least to the time of John Chrysostom.

8. Bernard, "Anti-Jewish Interpretations," 27, labors to turn the tide of scholarship away from anti-Jewish readings of Hebrews, yet her work reveals that since the time and writings of John Chrysostom, there has been a tendency to read anti-Jewish rhetoric into the Epistle.

9. Eisenbaum, "Locating Hebrews," 213–37, contends that, even with a late dating for Hebrews, many Christ-followers and Jewish communities may not have yet self-identified as clearly distinct and identifiable. Thus, reading anti-Jewish polemic into the text is a bias of later readers rather than the intent of the author.

10. Hooker, "'End' of Cult," 190–91, writes, "The idea that old practices were at best irrelevant, at worst incompatible with Christian belief, has not yet developed. . . . It was not the Christians who had concluded that confession in Jesus as Son of God was incompatible with Jewish beliefs, however, but the Jewish authorities. If the readers of Hebrews were being expelled from the synagogues or persecuted for their faith in Jesus as Messiah, they might well be tempted to abandon their new faith; but this was hardly a 'return' to something they had *left*."

Opposing this perspective, several scholars have recently rejected reading such a supersessionistic concern into this book.[11] In fact, if one reads Hebrews on its own, isolated from later Jewish-Christian categories, one does not find any reference to Christianity as a category distinct from Judaism.[12] To this point, addressing the question, "Does the book of Hebrews present a supersessionist theology?" Richard Hays writes,

> Read from a later Gentile Christian perspective—say in Chrysostom's fourth century Constantinople, or the liberal Protestant culture of nineteenth-century Germany—Hebrews seems obviously to be rejecting "Judaism." If, however, we stay within the text's own narrative world, such a claim may appear unwarranted, even puzzling. For that reason, it may be unhelpful to describe Hebrews' teaching as a form of "Christianity" over against "Judaism"; rather, it is better described as a form of Jewish sectarian "New Covenantalism."[13]

Hays's view of the matter leads him to reframe the question of the relationship between Christianity and Judaism as such: "How does the letter's new covenantalism engage and carry forward the heritage of Israel?"[14] This question fruitfully opens up Hebrews' conception of Israel's history beyond the anachronism of Christianity versus Judaism.

---

11. See Bernard, "Anti-Jewish Interpretations"; Anderson, "Who Are the Heirs?"; Eisenbaum, "Locating Hebrews."

12. Perhaps, conditioned by Paul's attack on Judaizers who abuse and misuse the law (Gal 5:1–15), adding to it and thus distorting it, Christian interpreters have read the book of Hebrews from a similar posture. While it is true that the author of Hebrews undoubtedly demonstrates Christ's sacrifice to be qualitatively better than the bulls, sheep, and goats offered by Aaron and his sons, his sacrifice is not "other" than that called for by the Levitical prescriptions. Commenting on later Pauline accusations against Judaizers, Hays, "No Lasting City," 165, writes, "At no point does Hebrews suggest that the law is legalistic, that it leads to self-righteousness, that its moral laws are in any way inadequate, or that its conception of God stands in need of correction." In fact, if one sees Hebrews as a criticism of the concept of the sacrificial system, the author's argument for Christ's fulfillment of the central sacrificial rite—Yom Kippur—falls to the same criticism. See also Wedderburn, "Sawing Off Branches," 409.

13. Hays, "No Lasting City," 155.

14. Hays, "No Lasting City," 155.

Hebrews, the Christ Event, and Israel's Story

Applying Hays's fertile way of thinking about the heritage of Israel carried forward by new covenantalism, this chapter argues that the author of Hebrews reconfigures Yom Kippur around Jesus Christ and, in so doing, advances Israel's story. For the author of Hebrews, it is precisely through Christ's Yom Kippur-shaped eternal atonement that Israel's history continues. Thus, the new covenantalism proposed in Hebrews intends to extend Israel's narrative, not to supersede it. Further, by claiming Christ's provision and expansion of Yom Kippur's atoning effects, the discourse of Hebrews reenvisions the narrative history that Yom Kippur evokes through the lens of Jesus Christ. In other words, for the author of Hebrews, the retelling of the Yom Kippur ritual in light of the Christ event is not merely a way of seeing the sacrificial cult fulfilled and atonement provided, but it also justifies a new way of extending and expanding Israel's story.[15]

As with Leviticus 16, N. T. Wright's worldview questions, answered through Hebrews, reveal that, as the author takes up Israel's story afresh and instructs readers on how they are to live as the people of God between the ascension and Christ's return, the biblical worldview reaches maturity. This chapter argues that the author's focus on Christ's fulfillment of Yom Kippur warrants the retelling and extension of Israel's story, resulting in the author's invitation to continue the narrative in Christ. Thus, as Hebrews explains the Christ event as the final Yom Kippur, it also explains the absence of atoning animal sacrifice in contemporary Christian practice, expands the biblical worldview, and provides a new-covenant way of extending the story of the people of God.

Hebrews, Yom Kippur, and Narrative Setting

As Christians have reflected on the meaning of the Christ event throughout the centuries, Christ's death as an atoning sacrifice has been a perennial locus of concentration.[16] The author of Hebrews is no exception,

---

15. Lev 16–17 provided the material for the previous chapter because, as this chapter will demonstrate, this is the text through which the author engages Yom Kippur, though the author of Hebrews was almost certainly using the LXX. See Hooker, "'End' of Cult," 189.

16. Young, "Christological Ideas," 46, contends, "It is frequently said that the early centuries showed no interest in formulating a doctrine of the Atonement, but this is a

demonstrating that the Christ event is atoning by virtue of its completion of the Day of Atonement ritual. Hebrews 9:7 makes the comparison between Yom Kippur and the Christ event explicit by referring to the high priest's annual entry into the holy place, though this explicit reference is part of the larger argument sustained throughout Hebrews 7–10.

The present section will consult the book of Hebrews in order to show that the author labors to demonstrate that Jesus's sinless life, cross, resurrection, and ascension serve as corollaries to both the high priest and the perfect sacrifice that feature in Leviticus 16.[17] Having addressed the similarities that result in completion of Yom Kippur, then, the following section will turn to the pivotal distinctive features of the Christ event that allow the author to retell and extend Israel's story. This chapter concludes with an investigation into what effects such an expanded narrative, retold through the Christ event, might have on the worldview of Hebrews' audience. This investigation will demonstrate how Hebrews sustains the claim to continue and complete the revelation contained in the Torah.

Completion and Fulfillment

As seen in the previous chapter, Yom Kippur provides ancient Israel with the one and only day each year on which the high priest could enter the holy place to represent the people before YHWH. As already noted, Hebrews is explicit in its reference to this day in Hebrews 9:7. Additionally, throughout Hebrews 9–10 the author claims that the Christ event finally and eternally obtains Yom Kippur's effects, referring to the tabernacle's cleansing (Heb 9:21), blood-wrought forgiveness of sins (Heb 9:22), and entrance into the holy place by way of Christ's own blood (Heb 9:12). For the author of Hebrews, all that Israel accomplished annually by observing Yom Kippur is attained eternally through the Christ event and its once-for-all atonement.

---

grossly misleading statement. The formulation of both Trinitarian and Christological definitions was directly caused by soteriological beliefs."

17. Moffitt, *Atonement*, 295, demonstrates convincingly, contrary to those who do not find the Christ's resurrection featured in Hebrews, that, "far from destroying the unity of the high-priestly Christology and soteriology developed by the author, the resurrection of Jesus' human body is a significant component in his explanation for *how* Jesus' offering effected atonement."

These effects obtain through Jesus's service as a high priest (Heb 8:1) who has presented his own body once for all as a sacrifice (Heb 10:10), has passed through death (Heb 2:14–15), and has entered into the holy place to present his own blood in the heavenly tabernacle (Heb 9:11–14). These features of Christ's ministry call to mind the activities of the high priest on Yom Kippur that were discussed in the previous chapter. Furthermore, and perhaps most succinctly, Hebrews 10:19–22 identifies the parallels the author intends to make between the Christ event and the Day of Atonement:

> Therefore brothers, since we have confidence to enter the holy places by the blood of Jesus, by the new and living way that he opened for us through the curtain, that is, through his flesh, and since we have a great high priest over the house of God, let us draw near with a true heart in full assurance of faith, with our hearts sprinkled clean from an evil conscience and our bodies washed with pure water.

Thus, for the author of Hebrews, Jesus as the eternal high priest not only entered the holy place, he opened the way for his followers to join him in drawing near to God. He not only completed the ritual requirements, but embodied the symbolic world such rituals evoked, both satisfying and extending the narrative within which such rituals exist.

Beyond completing the Day of Atonement, however, by recasting this annual celebration in the light of the Christ event the author of the book of Hebrews engages in a fresh retelling of Israel's history. What N. T. Wright claims of other New Testament authors applies also to Hebrews: "The whole story of God, Israel, and the world [are] now compressed into the story of Jesus."[18] Ultimately, Hebrews demonstrates that through the Christ event, new-covenant people are warranted to pick up and continue Israel's story without practicing animal sacrifice. Part of making this claim, however, requires an intentional look at what story the author of Hebrews is reading and retelling.

---

18. Wright, *People of God*, 79, acknowledges the fact that Paul's writings have been shown to retell "the whole story of God, Israel and the world as now compressed into the story of Jesus." However, Hebrews, likely a non-Pauline section of Scripture, might also be said to engage in exactly this same sort of redemption-historical hermeneutic, though with more of a focus on the Levitical cult.

Hebrews and Israel's Narrative

One of the features of the message of Hebrews that is most informative for the purposes of retelling Israel's narrative is the point in Israel's history that the author of Hebrews calls his audience to remember. Rather than referring to the temple or the people of God dwelling in the promised land, the setting for the author's engagement with Yom Kippur is the very inception of the ritual, at the foot of Mount Sinai and in the middle of the desert. This location is evident because, instead of writing of the Day of Atonement as performed in the Jerusalem temple in all its glory, the author consistently uses the word σκηνῆς ("tent") to refer to the tabernacle whose glory was bound up in the presence of YHWH in its midst.

Among the various references to the tent/tabernacle, Hebrews 8:2 provides a key example, saying of Christ the high priest that he is "A minister in the holy places, in the true tent (σκηνῆς) that the Lord set up, not man." As the discussion progresses, the author emphasizes that the tent and implements of worship are copies and shadows (ὑποδείγματι καὶ σκιᾷ) of the heavenly things (Heb 8:5). Likewise, Hebrews 9:1–2 connects the covenant and its regulations for worship to the building of the tent prior to making the claim in Hebrews 9:11–14 that Christ has entered in through the greater and more perfect tent. Thus, rather than using the temple in Jerusalem as a reference point, the author of Hebrews intends his readers to call to mind the first place of ancient Israel's priestly worship and atonement: the desert tabernacle.

Reinforcing this observation, Pamela Eisenbaum comments, "The author of Hebrews never actually uses the word 'temple.' He speaks only of the 'tabernacle,' which encased the presence of God and was carried by the Israelites in the wilderness."[19] By choosing to refer to the tent, the author interprets the first Day of Atonement as described in Leviticus 16 in light of Christ rather than expressions of Yom Kippur observed by his contemporaries. Not only does this focal point locate Israel in the desert, but it also signifies that the author of Hebrews intends to draw on the ritual as it is recorded in the Torah.[20] Thus the author focuses on Scripture with the desert wandering as the narrative backdrop, reminding the

---

19. Eisenbaum, "Locating Hebrews," 225.

20. Eisenbaum, "Locating Hebrews," 225. Eisenbaum reinforces this claim, concluding, "All the information conveyed in Hebrews about the cult derives from the biblical text, primarily Exodus and Leviticus."

reader of the exodus and covenant, the transient nature of the tabernacle, and the anticipation of the promised land yet in the future.

The author capitalizes on this summons to recall the time of wandering in Hebrews 3:7–15 and Hebrews 4:7–9, both of which use Psalm 25 to the recall the wilderness generation waiting to enter the promised land. This psalm functions in Hebrews 4:7–9 to highlight the fact that Joshua, in leading Israel into the promised land, did not complete the promise of providing rest: "For if Joshua had given them rest, God would not have spoken of another day later on. So then, there remains a Sabbath rest for the people of God." Hebrews 4:11, then, turns to the readers, urging that they might not fail to enter the rest that yet remains. By referring to the tabernacle and the time of wandering, the author of Hebrews intends his new-covenant readers to recognize that they are still sojourners wandering in search of a lasting city of their own (Heb 13:14).

Calling attention to the transient nature of the new people of God in Christ thus serves to situate the people chronologically near the Passover, the exodus, the giving of the law, the establishing of the covenant, and the promise of a future rest. In Egypt under pharaoh, Israel was in an embryonic stage of development as a covenant people. Through the exodus and at Sinai, YHWH redeemed his people and extended the Abrahamic promises to them (Exod 19:1–6).

As the previous chapter revealed, the identity of Israel is bound up in the presence of YHWH in her midst and inextricably tied to the formalization of her covenant relationship to YHWH at the foot of Sinai. The author of Hebrews, then, calls his readers to remember the Day of Atonement as it was first practiced in the tabernacle at Sinai, inviting the reader to reread Israel's history as told in Hebrews in the light of the Christ event. The points of distinction between Leviticus's Yom Kippur and the Christ event, however, allow the author to expand and extend this history most dramatically.

Informative Distinctions Between Hebrews and Yom Kippur

The author of Hebrews, having invited the reader to figuratively return to Sinai and to recall the story of Israel, exploits three central points of distinction between Yom Kippur and the Christ event to explain the differences in the new-covenant teaching on atonement. While the previous section showed that the effects of atonement all obtain through the Christ event, the author labors to show that these effects exceed that which could have been hoped for under the old covenant. In fact, these three points of distinction prove to be pregnant with meaning, not merely explaining atonement, but also giving birth to a whole new way of seeing Israel's story extended and expanded.

Melchizedekian Priesthood

One of the requirements for service in the priesthood is descent from the tribe of Levi. For the high priest, this Levitical descent must come specifically through the line of Aaron. This requirement appears in Exodus 28:4, where YHWH declares that Aaron and his sons are to serve as priests (Lev 8–10; Num 3:5–13; Heb 7:5). Likewise, the author of Hebrews acknowledges this as a potential problem for Christ as a high priest, stating in Hebrews 7:14, "It is evident that our Lord was descended from Judah, and in connection with that tribe Moses said nothing about priests." However, the author contends that Melchizedek serves as a precedent of one who served as a high priest by means of different credentials: God's oath and an indestructible life (Heb 7:15–28).[21]

The author relies on Psalm 110:4 to establish this precedent, as it says, "You are a priest forever after the order of Melchizedek." Capitalizing on the unnamed referent in Psalm 110:4, the author of Hebrews attributes this appointment to Jesus as the recipient of this oath (Heb 7:15–22). Like Melchizedek, then, Jesus is without a priestly lineage.[22] Though the author of Hebrews does not consider this to be a problem due to the fact that Jesus's priesthood begins by divine oath and his indestructible life secures it (Heb 7:16). In fact, New Testament commentator William Lane contends that by using the word ἀκαταλύτου ("indestructible"), Hebrews

---

21. Lane, *Hebrews 1–8*, 182, comments on Heb 7:13–17, noting, "No one from this tribe [Judah] had ever officiated at the altar. . . . It verified that the priesthood of Jesus does not depend on physical descent, but on a radically new arrangement." This radically new arrangement comes from the oath declared in Psalm 110:4b, and here (Heb 7:17) claimed by the author of Hebrews as referring to Jesus.

22. Lane, *Hebrews 1–8*, 182–84, draws on Gareth Cockerill's dissertation, *Melchizedek Christology*, 92–93, to show that, just as Melchizedek's lack of genealogy can be employed to provide a parallel to Christ's eternality, it can also indicate that he has no legal, genealogical right to serve at the altar of the tabernacle or temple.

indicates that this priesthood rests on the superior power of Jesus's life that has been demonstrated by way of overcoming the power of death.[23]

Resurrection and an Eternal Priesthood

It is at this point in the discourse that the author demonstrates the importance of Jesus' resurrection for the logic of his argument. Despite noting that many commentators regularly claim that it is Jesus's death and ascension that most commonly occupy the author's analogy, David Moffitt's monograph, *Atonement and the Logic of Resurrection in the Epistle to the Hebrews*, argues convincingly that resurrection is central to the author's understanding of Jesus's accomplishment.[24] In fact, for the author of Hebrews, Jesus's resurrection distinguishes him from the bulls and rams that must be offered year after year (Heb 10:3–4) and his seated position at the right hand of God signifies the completion of his task (Heb 10:12). His resurrection is therefore logically necessary as the hinge between the offering of his body (Heb 10:10) and his ascension to the right hand of God (Heb 10:12).

Additionally, Jesus's resurrection demonstrates his indestructible life (Heb 7:16), and confirms his inheritance of the oath of Psalm 110 along with the eternal priesthood promised therein (Heb 6:19–20; 7:20–28).[25] Therefore, rather than being embarrassed by Jesus's non-Levitical

---

23. Lane, *Hebrews 9–13*, 184, demonstrates that the word indestructible (ἀκαταλύτου) is intentionally chosen as it indicates his exposure to death, but by his resurrection, Jesus proves the power of his life to be superior.

24. Moffitt, *Atonement*, 295, concludes his lengthy articulation of the author's dependence on the bodily resurrection of Jesus stating, "The author's argument has not, as is generally assumed, ignored or denied the resurrection. . . . Far from destroying the unity of the high-priestly Christology and soteriology developed by the author, the resurrection of Jesus' human body is a significant component in his explanation for *how* Jesus' offering effected atonement." Likewise, Lane, *Hebrews 1–8*, 184, comments, "The characterization of 'power' in v 16 by the qualitative genitives ζωῆς ἀκαταλύτου, 'of indestructible life,' offers a striking definition of the meaning of the phrase εἰς τὸν αἰῶνα, "forever," in Ps 110:4, which is cited in v 17. It designates the eternity of the new priest from the perspective of his postresurrection existence."

25. Attridge, *Hebrew*, 202–3, notes that there is a lack of consensus as to whether Christ is endowed with the role of high priest after his resurrection, or whether it is a function of his eternal nature. However, Attridge recognizes that the author's attention is not focused on when this priesthood began, but rather that it is currently and forever instated.

lineage, the author of Hebrews capitalizes on this distinction in order to set apart Jesus's priesthood as one which might bring the old order to completion and instate a new order by his eternal presentation of his own blood (Heb 7:11–14).[26] This oath and eternal priesthood, however, are contingent upon the fact that he is no longer subject to death as were the Levitical priests, but by virtue of his resurrection, he lives and serves as a high priest forever (Heb 7:23–24).[27]

A New Priesthood and a New Covenant

While Jesus's resurrection establishes the author's argument that even though he is not from Levi, Jesus is an eternal high priest, the resurrection is not the only purpose that the author sees in this genealogical anomaly. It is also precisely at the point of Jesus's improper lineage that the author of Hebrews discusses the new covenant of Jeremiah 31:31–34. In Hebrews 8:8–12 the author records Jeremiah's promise that YHWH will make a new covenant with the house of Israel. This new covenant will be unlike the former covenant in that YHWH's law will be written on the hearts of his people (Jer 31:32–33). At the same time, the purpose of the new covenant remains the same: that God will call a people to himself (Jer 31:34).

Capitalizing on the promise of a new covenant, the author of Hebrews demonstrates that when there is a change in priesthood, there is a change in the law and covenant (Heb 7:12). Hebrews 8 continues on to argue that the Levitical system depended on high priests who received their station by the coincidence of their birth, and served at an altar that required an annual performance of Yom Kippur to effect atonement. Jesus, however, is an eternal minister appointed by the divine fiat in Psalm 110:4 and capable of presenting a once-for-all sacrifice (Heb 10:10).[28]

In fact, while the author is keen to show that Jesus completed the sacrifice of Yom Kippur, the fact that he does so as a priest of Melchizedekian order allows for the institution of a new law. Hebrews 7:12 contends for this very idea, saying, "For when there is a change in the

---

26. Moffitt, *Atonement*, 256, comments on Heb 10:5–10, showing, "Jesus' body ... is not the only thing identified by the author as constituting Jesus' offering. He also says that Jesus presented his blood and himself to God."

27. Moffitt, *Atonement*, 197–99.

28. Lane, *Hebrews 1–8*, 187.

priesthood, there is necessarily a change in the law as well."[29] In order for a new covenant and law to arise, however, the previous covenant and law must either be fulfilled or radically discarded. As the previous section indicated, the author of Hebrews argues that fulfillment has occurred in the Christ event.

Once for All

Finally, this section of the argument in Hebrews 7:26–28 concludes by showing that Jesus, as the eternal high priest of the new order, offered himself as a Yom Kippur sacrifice of the old order "once for all."[30] To this point, Lane comments, "The fact that Christ offered himself ἐφάπαξ, 'once and for all,' signifies the completeness of his sacrifice. In the NT, ἐφάπαξ is a technical term for the definitiveness and uniqueness of the death of Christ and the redemption it secured."[31] As a priest like Melchizedek, appointed by an oath, Jesus is able to offer a single sacrifice that secures an eternal salvation. His eternal priesthood, then, is superior in quality in every way, yet it performs the same functions as the impermanent Levitical priesthood prefigured. Therefore, in inaugurating the new covenant and priesthood, the Christ event meets and exceeds the requirements of the old covenant and priesthood.

Eternal Blood and a Single Sacrifice

Having addressed Jesus's priesthood in Hebrews 7:1–29, the author goes on to consider his sacrifice and the eternal presentation of Jesus's blood in Hebrews 10:11–12. There the author compares the Levitical priests' many and repeated offerings with Christ's single offering, writing, "Every high priest stands daily at his service offering repeatedly the same sacrifices, which can never take away sins. But when Christ had offered for all time a single sacrifice for sins, he sat down at the right hand of God." In other words, Jesus's single sacrifice for all time exposes the limitation of the previous system in that it required multiple, repeated, annual sacrifices.

---

29. Contra Attridge, *Hebrews*, 200, this is not an *ad hoc* argument, but rather a logical inference that comes from the author's claim that the OT law is based on the Levitical priesthood.

30. Heb 7:27.

31. Lane, *Hebrews 1–8*, 193.

Additionally, as seen in the previous chapter, Leviticus features five animals for the performance of Yom Kippur: a bull for the high priest's sin offering, two rams for a burnt offering, and two goats for the people's sin offering. One of the two goats is slaughtered and the other, the ʿăzāʾzēl goat, is led into the wilderness (Lev 16:5). In Hebrews' treatment, all of the component parts of the Day of Atonement are accounted for through the Christ event, though not all are required by Jesus's priesthood.

The High Priest's Sin Offering and Humility

One example of such a distinction within Hebrews' treatment of the Christ event is that Jesus as the high priest does not make a sacrifice to atone for himself and his household, though the Levitical high priests required it as a preparation for the day's intercession and mediation (Lev 16:6). In Hebrews 7:26–27, the author provides the rationale for the absence of the priest's sacrifice, saying that, because of Jesus's holiness and spotlessness, "He has no need, like those high priests, to offer sacrifices daily, first for his own sins and then for those of the people."[32] Therefore the bull that the high priest is called to sacrifice is unnecessary based upon the sinless and pure condition of Jesus.

Hebrews does, however, demonstrate that Jesus participated in part of the preparatory process by clothing himself in humility prior to serving as the high priest. As highlighted in the previous chapter, Leviticus 16:4 calls the high priest to prepare himself by wearing plain linen garments prior to entering the holy of holies. Explaining this, Gordon Wenham claims that these plain linen garments were symbolic of humility as the priest prepares to enter the presence of YHWH. Wenham comments,

> Among his fellow men [the high priest's] dignity as the great mediator between man and God is unsurpassed, and his splendid clothes draw attention to the glory of his office. But in the presence of God even the high priest is stripped of all honor: he becomes simply the servant of the King of kings.[33]

---

32. Lane, *Hebrews 1–8*, 194, notes that the author, though centrally concerned with Yom Kippur sacrifices, is willing to regard all sacrifices as atoning ones, thus, even though the high priest is not required to make daily sacrifice for his own sins and then for the sins of the people, "it would not have been hard to interpret the daily sacrifices in the light of the Day of Atonement."

33. Wenham, *Book of Leviticus*, 230.

This humility can be seen as part of Jesus's preparation in Hebrews 2:5–9. Here the author shows Jesus being made low for a time prior to being crowned with glory and honor. This humility in the face of the task of priesthood—representing the people before the presence of God—is retained both in Jesus's incarnation and his submission to the will of the Father as seen in Hebrews 10:9–10. Thus, while Jesus need not make atonement for his own sin prior to atoning for the sins of the people, he is yet marked by the humble approach Leviticus demands of the high priest.

The Remaining Four Sacrificial Animals

Looking beyond the sin offering, then, one notes that four sacrificial animals remain as prescribed in Leviticus 16—the slaughtered goat, the ʽăzāʾzēl goat, and the two rams of the burnt offering. This book follows Harold Attridge and others who conclude that throughout Hebrews the author allows the multiple animals of the Yom Kippur ritual to coalesce into a single sacrifice concept completed in Christ's self-sacrifice.[34] Along with denying the need for Christ to repeat his sacrifice, this conflation of several individual sacrifices is what the author intends in Hebrews 10:14, which says, "For by a single offering he has perfected those who are being sanctified." Likewise, Hebrews 13:11 speaks generically of the blood and immolation of sacrificial animals without specifying which sacrifices are being discussed, giving an indication that the author is not concerned to distinguish each animal sacrifice involved, but rather to sum up the sacrificial concept in Christ's death and resurrection.[35]

Taking a similar approach, Kelly Kapic contends that since the Old Testament sacrifices were merely shadows of the Christ event, that his sacrifice is sufficient to sum them all up. Kapic writes, "The animals' deaths were the type, and Christ's sacrifice was the object typified. . . . Old

---

34. Attridge, *Hebrews*, 397.

35. Attridge, *Hebrews*, 397, comments on generic sacrificial language in Heb, specifically citing Heb 13:11, saying, "The verse describes the tabernacle ritual with which the sacrifice of Christ will be compared. The description consists of a generalizing paraphrase of Leviticus 16:27, part of the ritual of Yom Kippur. Instead of specifying the calf and the goat sacrificed on that day, Hebrews simply refers to 'animals' (ζῴων)." Additionally, in Leviticus, three carcasses are burnt on the altar outside of the camp, and the ʽăzāʾzēl goat is sent out into the wilderness to bear away the sins of the people. It may be that Heb 13:10–12 envisions the three remaining sacrifices as being bound up in Jesus' crucifixion outside of the camp.

Testament sacrifices on their own did nothing, but they pointed beyond themselves to the fullness and finality of the death of Christ, and it is on this very point that the author of Hebrews builds his conception of the priesthood of Christ."[36] Thus, the author does not distinguish the sacrifices of Yom Kippur, viewing the sacrifice of Christ as sufficient to sum up the Day of Atonement ritual *in toto*.

Therefore, by establishing that the sacrificial animals of Yom Kippur offered on behalf of ancient Israel culminate in the single sacrifice of Jesus, the author of Hebrews capitalizes on Jesus's eternal priesthood as the sufficient basis for the coming of a new priesthood and covenant (Heb 7:18–22). At the same time, Jesus's eternal sacrifice provides the requisite blood by which to satisfy the demands of the old covenant in perpetuity (Heb 9:11–22). Finally, concluding this section in Hebrews 10:12–18, the author twice refers to Jesus's single sacrifice as being sufficient to inaugurate the new covenant of Jeremiah 31:31–34. In so doing, the author highlights the forgiveness of sins that the Christ event makes possible in completing the Day of Atonement ritual once and for all. Therefore, for the author of Hebrews, it is clear that the Christ event is the reality of which the Levitical prescriptions for Yom Kippur were merely the shadow. One more distinction remains to consider: that of the difference between the earthly tent and the heavenly tabernacle.

The Heavenly Tabernacle: τυπος, σκιὰ, and εἰκον

For the author of Hebrews, then, the Christ event has satisfied the requirements for a new priesthood and sacrifice through the complete and eternally valid observance of Yom Kippur, as indicated in Hebrews 10:12–14.[37] Likewise, Hebrews 8:5 explains, "[Levitical high priests] serve a copy and shadow (σκιὰ) of the heavenly things. For when Moses was about to erect the tent, he was instructed by God, saying, 'See that you make everything according to the pattern (τυπος) that was shown you on the mountain.'"

This idea of a shadow and its true form is explicitly linked to the body of Christ in Hebrews 10:1–10, which begins in Hebrews 10:1 by referencing the law as a shadow of the true image or form (Σκιὰν γὰρ ἔχων

---

36. Kapic, "Typology," 152–53.
37. Kapic, "Typology," 152–53.

ὁ νόμος τῶν μελλόντων ἀγαθῶν, οὐκ αὐτὴν τὴν εἰκόνα τῶν πραγμάτων) and then concludes by showing the sanctification that Christ's sacrificial body attains once for all in Hebrews 10:10. Thus the previous priesthood, sacrifices, and tabernacle function typologically as a shadow of an image (ἐικον) and pattern to which they point in Christ.[38] Where Israel's infidelity to the previous covenant brought about exile and punishment, this new covenant is guaranteed by Jesus's eternal service and eternal blood that is offered before God in the heavenly tabernacle, the pattern for the earthly tabernacle.

In concluding the book, then, the author of Hebrews summons those in Christ to join him outside of the camp. Since the earthly tabernacle is no longer the place of service for the true high priest, then the atonement effected by his service at the right hand of God renders the local, earthly tabernacle obsolete. No longer does the worshipper need to draw to the center of the camp, towards the holy place, to approach YHWH because the curtain has been removed (Heb 10:19–20).

Yet, this invitation to leave the camp is shocking to an audience used to drawing closer to the center of the camp to approach God, because now, in Christ, they are invited outwards, to join Jesus beyond the perimeter of the camp. No longer is the dwelling place of God restricted to the inner portions of the holy place, but Christ, in making permanent atonement, brings the presence of God out beyond the veil and even beyond the camp.

In all of these distinctions, the author of Hebrews repeatedly highlights the superiority of Jesus's priesthood and sacrifice and the new covenant that he inaugurates. However, despite the superiority of these new elements, they retain and extend the original design and intent. As such, the new priesthood and sacrifice are not to be seen as "other" than that which was promised and provided by way of the old covenant. Rather, the Christ event completes the former covenantal requirements in order to inaugurate the new covenant promised in Jeremiah 31:31–34, whereby God promises to write his law on the new hearts of his people.

---

38. Heb 8:5 speaks of the priests serving a shadow of the heavenly things, and the tabernacle is modeled after the pattern that God showed to Moses on Mount Sinai. Heb 10:1 extends this typological treatment to the whole Mosaic law itself. Commenting on Heb 10:1, Bruce, *Epistle to Hebrews*, 226, writes, "Our author is thinking more especially of the law prescribing matters of priesthood and sacrifice in relation to the wilderness tabernacle and the Jerusalem temple."

As the author of Hebrews draws Jeremiah's promise of a new covenant into the vision of what has occurred in Christ, the old covenant is satisfied in Christ's new, eternal priesthood and sacrifice, yet the old covenant's purpose of creating a means of being the people of God remains. Ultimately, the author suggests that Jesus can institute a new covenant and that Israel's sacrificial system has been "done away with"[39] because Jesus is eternally fulfilling the duties required under the old.[40]

Recognizing Yom Kippur as Israel's central ritual and the tabernacle itself to be σκια of which the Christ event is the ἐικον, the author invites his readers to revisit the whole of Israel's history with an eye to further typology.[41] In so doing, the author extends Israel's history through the lens of the Christ event into the present by way of an invitation to reconsider how the people of God might appropriately live in and view the world. This reality will be borne out more fully by inspecting the accumulated impact of the Christ event's fulfillment of Yom Kippur on the worldview of the people of God encountering the message of Hebrews.

---

39. Heb 10:9b. "He does away with the first in order to establish the second."

40. Lindars, *Theology of Letter*, 126, writes, "Jesus possesses a real priesthood.... He regards this as essential, because only the high priest is qualified to perform the blood-ritual in the Day of Atonement, which he takes as the standard of sacrifice for sins."

41. Lane, *Hebrews 1–8*, cxxiii, notes, "Typological interpretation plays a key role in the developing argument in Hebrews.... For the writer of Hebrews, the history of Israel is redemptive history, and the significance of an OT type resides in its particular relationship to the divine plan of salvation. His typological interpretation of the OT depends on the historical correspondences between the old and new orders of redemption."

TABLE 3.1

The Day of Atonement Comparison: Leviticus 16–17 and Hebrews

COMPONENT	LEVITICUS	HEBREWS
The high priest takes a purification bath and puts on linen garments Leviticus 16:4	AARONIC PRIEST HUMILITY IN APPAREL The high priest bathes his body prior to donning the holy linen garments. These garments are not the daily garb of the high priest, but rather are plain clothes intended to emphasize the humble approach to the presence of YHWH.	MELCHIZEDEKIAN PRIEST HUMILITY IN HIS HUMANITY The Son was made like his brothers in every respect (Heb 2:17) despite being the radiance of the glory of God and the exact imprint of his nature (Heb 1:3). He put on the robe of humanity in humility and became a high priest by virtue of divine oath like Melchizedek.
A bull presented as a sin offering Leviticus 16:3, 6	PRIEST'S SINS ATONED FOR The high priest slaughters the bull as a sin offering for himself and his household. He brings the blood of the bull into the holy place, sprinkling it seven times before the *kipporet*.	NO SINS FOR WHICH TO ATONE Jesus was without sin (Heb 4:15), so it was unnecessary for him to offer the bull of the sin offering for himself (Heb 7:27).
Two goats: one goat as a sin offering & one goat as *ʿăzāʾzēl* Leviticus 16:5, 7–10, 15–22 Two rams for burnt offerings: one for the priest & one for the people Leviticus 16:24–25	SACRIFICE AND EXHIBITION The high priest slaughters the goat chosen by lot as a sin offering and brings the blood into the holy place. He sprinkles the blood of the goat before the *kipporet* as he did with the blood of the bull. Leaving the holy place, the high priest anoints the altar with the blood of the goat and the blood of the bull. The high priest then lays both hands upon the *ʿăzāʾzēl* goat, confesses Israel's sins over it, and sends it to the wilderness under the charge of one who is ready and waiting. This exhibits the departure of sins from the camp. Finally, a bull is offered as a burnt offering.	SACRIFICE AND EXHIBITION Hebrews 10:12–14 claims, "But when Christ had offered for all time a single sacrifice for sins, he sat down at the right hand of God, waiting from that time until his enemies should be made a footstool for his feet. For by a single offering he has perfected for all time those who are being sanctified." Thus, for the author of Hebrews, Christ's self-sacrifice provides a single sacrifice brought by an eternal high priest that accounts for the remaining sacrificial animals prescribed for the Day of Atonement ritual in Leviticus 16.
Blood Manipulation and atonement Leviticus 16:14–19 & Leviticus 17:11–14	BLOOD IN THE HOLY OF HOLIES EFFECTS OF SIN MANAGED The high priest sprinkles the blood of the sacrifices before the *kipporet* and anoints the altar with the blood once every year on the Day of Atonement.	BLOOD IN HEAVEN EFFECTS OF SIN ERADICATED Jesus's eternal blood presented in the heavenly tabernacle as a symbol of life has the power to act perpetually as a *koper* (כֹּפֶר) for sinners and as a cleansing agent for those defiled.

The Worldview of Hebrews

As the previous chapter indicated, when one engages narrative, ritual, and symbol, one begins to gain access to an understanding of the implicit worldview that informs a community or an individual. Worldview, as considered here, is not an intentional, considered, and reasoned construct, but rather the fundamental, assumed categories by which people make sense of their world.[42] N. T. Wright and others employ the analogy of eyeglasses to this perspective on worldview, stating that a worldview is something like one's spectacles: one regularly looks through glasses, but rarely looks at them.[43] So it is with worldviews. These worldviews are often more caught than taught, and most commonly form by the telling of stories by which people record, order, organize, and understand their history, their present, and their expectations for the future.

Further explaining the role of narrative in forming worldview, N. T. Wright notes that it is not just the telling of stories that performs powerful acts of worldview shaping, but also the retelling of stories that can effect fundamental changes in the lens through which one might see life as a whole.[44] Thus, as the author of Hebrews views Yom Kippur through the lens of the Christ event, Israel's worldview undergoes an adjustment. While Christ introduces some fundamental expansion to Leviticus' depiction of Yom Kippur, one sees that the core of the worldview has much continuity with that of Israel at Mount Sinai. Discontinuity, however, is introduced in consideration of the expanded effects Christ's atonement. Wright's questions help to bear this claim out.

Who Are We?

This study began with recognition of the long history of a scholarly tendency to assume that Hebrews is written to Christians who were in danger of relapsing into Judaism. However, while the Christ event does affect the identity of the people of God in Hebrews, it does so by perfecting, expanding, and extending the same identity given to ancient Israel.[45]

---

42. Wright, *People of God*, 121.

43. Wright, *People of God*, 124–25. See also Hiebert, *Transforming Worldviews*, 15, who discusses worldview as "a set of assumptions that people make about the nature of things" that determines how people live their lives. As assumptions, these are usually not reasoned conclusions, but unspoken expectations and convictions.

44. Wright, *People of God*, 39.

45. Heb 11:39—12:2.

Hebrews does not suggest the presence of a new religion, as such, but instead a new way of being the people of God.

This new way of being the people of God is seen in the very first verses of the book of Hebrews that confront the reader with the author's use of first-person plural pronouns. Hebrews 1:1 states, "Long ago, at many times and in many ways, God spoke to our fathers by the prophets, but in these last days he has spoken to us by his Son." The use of third person plural pronouns "our" and "us" shows that the author stands among the audience, laying claim to the lineage of the prophets and patriarchs while receiving God's communication now through the Son.

Likewise, Hebrews 11 lists exemplars of faith from the story of Israel. With each reference to the forebears of Israel, the reader receives mnemonic stimulus to call to mind the stories that attend their lives and make up Israel's collective history. Abraham (Heb 11:8–12, 17–19), Isaac, Jacob, Esau, Joseph (Heb 11:20–22), and Moses (Heb 11:23–28) bring the reader from the promise of a people and worldwide blessing given to Abraham (Gen 12:1–3) to the Passover (Exod 12; Heb 11:28). Rahab, a gentile woman, calls to mind the approach to the promised land (Heb 11:31). David and Samuel recall the kingdom, dwelling in the promised land, and the role of the prophets (Heb 11:32). In just one chapter, the author evokes much of Israel's formative history.

As this section culminates, then, Hebrews 11:39—12:2 gathers up all of the old-covenant history that has just been recited and connects it to the new-covenant people by suggesting that the faithful of the old covenant are completed in the people of the new covenant.[46] Throughout this chapter, the author includes the audience within the arc of Israel's history, cult, and narrative in order to reveal that there is a single people of God, now apprehending in Christ what was previously unseen under the old covenant.[47]

Thus, the answer to the question "Who are we?" in Hebrews is not fundamentally distinct from the answer given at the foot of Mount Sinai.

---

46. However, as has already been established by the author's argument, the people of the new covenant are inextricably connected to the narrative and covenant of the ancient people of God, thus the perfection afforded in Christ for the new- and old-covenant people is mutually requisite.

47. Attridge, *Hebrews*, 356–57, highlights the fact that Jesus, as the author and perfecter (Heb 4:10; 12:2), is the source and object of faith, both for the saints of old, and for the new-covenant community. He writes, "The catalogue of chap. 11 had indeed suggested that it was the attainment of the divine promises in Christ and his followers that makes possible the ultimate salvation of the ancient people of God."

The author and audience are of the stock that were led out of Egypt in the exodus, who received the covenant, and who understood their identity based on YHWH's presence in their midst.[48] The covenant has been fulfilled, renewed, and extended through the Christ event, but YHWH is still the new-covenant Maker.[49]

Where Are We?

To the question, "Where are we?" the author of Hebrews suggests that the new-covenant people of God are again transient, anticipating the true promised land and city that is yet to come (Heb 4:6–11; 12:28; 13:14). Having situated the audience at the foot of Mount Sinai by recalling the Leviticus 16 requirements for Yom Kippur, Hebrews 12:18–24 reveals that new-covenant people no longer find themselves unable to approach YHWH's mountain, but instead have come to the true mountain, Mount Zion. Thus, as the people of God in Christ consider themselves again in the wilderness, having just experienced an exodus from the annual requirements of the old covenant, there is yet a reminder of whence they have come, and whence they are heading: a new rest, greater than what Joshua provided (Heb 4:8–11).

---

48. Regardless of the composition of the author's audience, this connection to the old-covenant people of God stands, if not on a genealogical level, then at least by way of faith-connection to Christ.

49. Jer 31:31–34 features centrally in Hebrews and reveals that YHWH had already declared that he would make a new-covenant. Hebrews' claim throughout is that the Christ event was both the completion of the old and the inauguration of the new, yet YHWH is responsible for establishing both; Nanos, "New or Renewed?," 184. One might go so far as to say that, for the author of Hebrews, the church—to utilize a clearly anachronistic category in order to highlight contemporary contentions—is not seen as the new Israel, but the people of God under the new covenant as renewed and expanded Israel. Nanos, building on Hays's "No Lasting City" essay, suggests that rather than seeing Heb 8:13 speaking of making something new as in πλαιοω, the concept of renewing is present in the author's conceptualization and use of Καινὴν. He writes, "What if this covenantalism is conceptualized and described as *continued* but *augmented* to be made *effective* in a *new way* or to a *new degree*, freshening up something worn-out (within the semantic domain of *kainos* versus *palaioō* in 8:13)?" Nanos, himself a Jew, extends this argument to suggest that modern-day Judaism and cultic practice might retain validity alongside of new-covenant people in Jesus. While this chapter disagrees with the conclusions of Nanos, as Hebrews itself is clearly intent on warning the audience not to neglect the great salvation provided by the Son through whom God has now communicated, the phrasing of renewed covenant captures the idea of completion of the old covenant and extension into the new covenant.

The author also expands the readers' understanding of cosmological origins. While the Israelites at Sinai would have understood themselves to be in a world created by YHWH, Hebrews 1:1–4 reveals that Jesus was involved in creating and sustaining the universe. The world itself owes its creation to the one who has, in the Christ event, made atonement for it. Those who have placed their faith in Christ, then, have not merely trusted another high priest, but rather one who is more fully understood as Creator of the world in which they dwell.

Finally, where the *kipporet* was viewed in Leviticus as the intersection of heaven and earth, separated from the populace by a curtain, the author of Hebrews claims that Jesus has extended an invitation to enter in to the holy place behind the curtain through his work.[50] Surprisingly, however, the author also extends another invitation in a different direction at the end of the book, saying in Hebrews 13:13, "Let us go to [Jesus] outside the camp and bear the reproach he endured." Previously, drawing near to YHWH required the worshipper to approach the tabernacle. Hebrews 9:8 reminds the audience that, through the presence of the veil barring entrance to the holy place, the Holy Spirit formerly testified that the way into YHWH's presence was yet closed.

Through the Christ event, however, Hebrews 10:20 declares that the way has been opened through the curtain of Jesus's flesh. While Hebrews' pneumatology is not as apparently developed as one finds in the Pauline corpus, in fact, it may be that this dual-invitation—to come behind the curtain of the holy place and to leave the camp to bear reproach with Jesus—is the key to pulling together the references to the Holy Spirit that are included in the message (Heb 2:4; 9:8, 14).[51] Now that Christ has opened the way into the holy place, the Holy Spirit can testify that the

50. Heb 10:19–23. See also Willi-Plein, "Some Remarks," 29, who writes, "The connection between earthly and heavenly sanctuary is not metaphorical, but may rather be described as 'real presence.' By amplification of reality the throne in heaven corresponds to the throne of the Cherubim with the *kapporet* as a propitiatory (ἱλαστήριον)."

51. Heb 2:4 speaks of gifts of the Holy Spirit; Heb 6:4 speaks warning against those who have shared in the Holy Spirit and yet fall away from faith; 9:8 says that the Holy Spirit indicates that the way into the holy place is not yet open; 9:14 speaks of the eternal Spirit being an aid to Christ's spotless offering of himself; 10:15 speaks of the Holy Spirit bearing witness to the people of God that there is a new covenant coming. While there is room for additional research on the role of the Spirit in Hebrews, if the Holy Spirit previously indicated that the holy place was inaccessible, when the way into the holy place is opened, the Holy Spirit may have a role in indicating this as well. Perhaps also pertinent to an investigation of Hebrews' pneumatology would be the suggestion of Wright, *Resurrection*, 736, who claims that when early believers referred to Christ as the "Son of God" it evoked his resurrection and included the sending of the Spirit.

way into the holy place is open, and that YHWH lives in their midst even outside of the camp.[52]

What Is Wrong?

While the fundamental problems of sin and impurity remain, Hebrews 10:11 reveals the truth hidden in plain sight regarding the problem with the Yom Kippur ritual and Israel's forgiveness and cleansing: the annual performance of the ritual indicates its impermanence and ineffectiveness. Likewise, Hebrews 10:5 calls to mind Psalms 40:6–8 to show that the blood of animal sacrifices is not pleasing to YHWH, nor can it remove sin. The author of Hebrews, then, is quick to show that, despite the annual performance of Yom Kippur, the problem of sin and impurity facing Israel remains unless there is a more permanent, eternal priest and sacrifice that might once and for all secure atonement.

Furthermore, the specific problem for the rhetorical audience that Hebrews hopes to address is evident within the parenetic portions of the book. For example, in Hebrews 12:25–29, the author urges the reader to heed the warning of the one speaking from heaven, and to receive the new-covenant kingdom that cannot be shaken. Therefore, having established that the Christ event has completed the old covenant and inaugurated the new, the author is concerned that his audience will remain under the old covenant, which, having been fulfilled, has also fulfilled its purpose in pointing ahead to Christ. Rather than anachronistically reading the distinct categories Christianity versus Judaism into Hebrews, preferring to see the author's renewed covenantal concerns allows the reader to remain fully indebted to the Israel-shaped history that is inherited and reconfigured under the Christ event. The problem for the author's audience is the temptation to neglect the great salvation that the Christ event has revealed the old covenant to be indicating.

---

52. Heb 6:4 warns those who would fall away that their faith in Christ has made them participants in the Holy Spirit. Heb 10:20 speaks of a new and living way opened through Christ's flesh to enter into the holy place. Heb 13:13 invites believers to join Jesus outside of the camp.

What Is the Solution?

The solution, for the author of Hebrews, remains focused on atonement.[53] However, while the author's explanation of atonement carries with it all of the effects expounded in Leviticus 16–17 above, Hebrews 9:22–28 reveals that the atonement offered by the Christ event exceeds that which was offered by Aaronic observance of Yom Kippur.[54] Viewed from a post-ascension perspective, William Lane explains the cultic ramifications of the Christ event, saying, "Christ's high priestly action is depicted as closely analogous to the ritual of expiation on the annual Day of Atonement. . . . The result of his cultic action was not the limited, recurrent redemption of the annual atonement ritual (9:9). He obtained 'eternal redemption.' Eschatological finality characterizes his ministration."[55] In other words, Christ's atonement satisfies the cultic requirements of Yom Kippur, effecting atonement of a similar kind, yet of a more extensive scope.

In fact, the author of Hebrews brilliantly reveals that Leviticus 16 could offer nothing more than an indicator of a coming solution—a shadow of the fullness to come—due to the annual repetition of the rite (Heb 8:5, 10:1).[56] The Christ event, seen as the embodiment of the shadow, offers complete, eternal forgiveness of sin and purgation of impurity based on the eternal blood ceaselessly presented by Jesus the great high priest before the throne of God.[57]

53. Heb 9:22–24. Here one sees the necessity for the activities of Yom Kippur performed on earth, to likewise be performed by Christ in the heavenly tabernacle, recording, "Indeed, under the law almost everything is purified with blood, and without the shedding of blood there is no forgiveness of sins. Thus it was necessary for the copies of the heavenly things themselves to be purified with better sacrifices than these. For Christ has entered, not into holy places made with hands, which are the copies of the true things, but into heaven itself, now to appear in the presence of God on our behalf." Therefore, Vanhoozer, "Atonement in Postmodernity," 382, says, "Hebrews 9–10 point to the shed blood of Christ as *effecting* what animal sacrifices only represent, namely, the removal or cancellation of sin from God's sight, and hence the purification of the sinner."

54. Lindars, *Hebrews*, 125, writes, "Hebrews brilliantly seizes the essentials of the Day of Atonement, and shows how the death of Jesus has all the necessary qualifications for atonement sacrifice."

55. Lane, *Hebrews 9–13*, 236.

56. Heb 8:5; 10:1. The author shows first that the tabernacle itself is a shadow of the heavenly tabernacle, then later that the sacrifices were a shadow whose fullness is found in Christ. Thus, referring to the use of σκιᾷ/Σκιὰν in both Heb 8:5 and 10:1, Bruce, *Epistle to Hebrews*, 226, can say, "'Shadow' is used not so much in the Platonic sense of a copy of the heavenly and eternal 'idea' as in the sense of foreshadowing."

57. Bruce, *Epistle to Hebrews*, 226, comments on Heb 10:1, writing, "'The good

While the quality of Christ's priesthood and sacrifice exceeds that of the Aaronic high priest and the animal sacrifice, so too the effects of what atonement achieves exceeds that of the prior system. In keeping with the concept of atonement provided by Yom Kippur, Hebrews speaks of Christ's offering of his substitutionary life, represented through the presentation of his blood, which expiates and forgives sin and also effects purification.[58]

What Time Is It?

While the Israelite community at the base of Sinai understood themselves to be awaiting the land of promise, Hebrews beckons the reader to return to that same expectation. However, pressing the audience to look beyond the land of Canaan, Hebrews points its readers to the heavenly Jerusalem that, rather than being conquered and subdued, will come down to earth when Christ returns to save those who eagerly await.[59] Thus, while the new covenant envisions again a time of sojourning, it also anticipates a greater and more certain promised land that will be manifest when "the Day" comes, bringing Christ's salvation with it in full (Heb 10:25).[60]

---

things to come' embrace the unrepeatable sacrifice of Christ and His present high-priestly ministry, which carry with them eternal redemption and uninhibited access to worship the living God. They are the only absolutely 'good' things because they comprise the 'perfection' which [sic] the old order was incapable of supplying."

58. See Heb 9:26. See Sklar, *Sin, Impurity*, 173, 181–82; Gathercole, *Defending Substitution*, 19–23, 28.

59. This point is made variously throughout the book. For example, Heb 9:28 reminds the audience that Jesus is coming again to save his people; 11:16 shows the exemplars of faith as looking to a heavenly city; 13:14 speaks of the people of God awaiting a city that is to come.

60. Speaking of eschatology in Hebrews, Hays, "No Lasting City," 166, comments, "Despite its conviction that Jesus has in fact completed his atoning work in the heavenly sanctuary [Hebrews] retains a remarkably open-ended eschatology that continues to look to the future for the consummation of salvation." See also Wright, *Ressurection*, 736, who considers the effect of the resurrection on the early believers as they witnessed in Jesus's resurrection a foretaste of what they had believed to be an eschatological hope: "[Early Christians] developed their theology by embracing one of the central Jewish beliefs of their day . . . and by understanding it all the more deeply in the light of what they believed had happened to Jesus. This is what made them a messianic group within Judaism." Thus the Christ event, with special attention to both Jeremiah's prophecy and Jesus's resurrection, brings eschatological categories into the present, while also keeping them at a distance in the book of Hebrews where "the day" is yet to come.

Additionally, and perhaps most importantly for the author, Hebrews 8 declares that the people of God in Christ find themselves in a new age, where they have received the new covenant of which God spoke in Jeremiah 31:31–34.[61] In this new age, the community is no longer dependent upon one of the Aaronic priestly class to represent them in drawing near to YHWH before the *kipporet*. Rather, Hebrews 10:15–22 establishes the fact that Christ's fulfillment of the old covenant and inauguration of the new has made a way for new-covenant people to draw near to the presence of God.[62] The author extends such an invitation in Hebrews 10:19–22, saying,

> Therefore, brothers, since we have confidence to enter the holy placed by the blood of Jesus, by the new and living way that he opened for us through the curtain, that is through his flesh, and since we have a great high priest over the house of God, let us draw near with a true heart in full assurance of faith, with our hearts sprinkled clean from an evil conscience and our bodies washed with pure water.

Thus, the answer to the question, "What time is it?" is answered by the several warning passages throughout the book, all of which can be summed up in by urging the reader that the time has come to draw near to YHWH, now through faith in Jesus.[63]

Why?

As the previous chapter demonstrated, the practice of Yom Kippur offered a window by which to see some of ancient Israel's answer to the question, "Why did ancient Israel perform the rites of the Day of Atonement?" as it pertains to her identity. Impurity and sin threatened to make Israel's

61. Lane, *Hebrews 1–8*, cxi, notes, "[The author] shares with primitive Christianity the understanding that the ministry of Jesus introduced the final phase of history."

62. Commenting on Jeremiah's importance to the author of Hebrews, Atrridge, *Hebrews*, 281, writes, "It is by virtue of Christ's interior or spiritual act of conformity to God's will that the covenant is initially inaugurated and sin effectively forgiven. At the same time, it is in virtue of the effective forgiveness of sin that an intimate covenantal relationship with God is made possible."

63. Attridge, *Hebrews*, 372, comments on Heb 12:18, noting the common refrain throughout Hebrews that uses the concept of "approach" to refer to a relationship with God, writing, "Both balanced portions of the comparison of Sinai and Zion begin with the verb 'approach' (προσεληλύθατε), which may derive from the reference to the Sinai experience in Deuteronomy, but also recalls Hebrews' common term for coming to a relationship with God."

camp unfit for YHWH's habitation, and thus threatened her very identity as a people. The Day of Atonement temporarily and annually managed the effects of sin and impurity. It was observed by ancient Israel because YHWH had called her to be his people, distinguished by his presence in her midst. Israel as the people of God observed the Day of Atonement to maintain that identity.

Likewise, for the author of Hebrews, the Christ event as a completion of the Day of Atonement ritual provides a window to the new-covenant answer given to the question, "Why did the Christ event occur?" In many ways, the question results in a similar answer. Hebrews makes it clear that the Christ event as the fulfillment of Yom Kippur allows the presence of God to remain in the midst of his people perpetually because of the once-for-all sacrifice of Jesus' body (Heb 10:10). Likewise, Hebrews 4:14–16 calls believers to draw near to the throne of grace with confidence, knowing that Christ as our eternal high priest intercedes for us and has entered into the holy places ahead of us.

Because the Christ event has completed the Day of Atonement requirements, Christ's single offering sanctifies (Heb 10:10) perfects (Heb 10:14), forgives (Heb 10:18), and cleanses the people of God in Christ (Heb 10:22). Therefore, the answer to the "Why?" question is given in Hebrews 10:19–22, where it says,

> Therefore, brothers, since we have confidence to enter the holy places by the blood of Jesus, by the new and living way that he opened for us through the curtain, that is through his flesh, and since we have a great high priest over the house of God, let us draw near with a true heart in full assurance of faith with our hearts sprinkled clean from an evil conscience and our bodies washed with pure water.

The answer Hebrews gives to the question, "Why did the Christ event occur?" is thus the same as it is for those looking at Yom Kippur as prescribed in Leviticus: this is the means by which one might draw near to the presence of God and by which one's identity as the new-covenant people of God might be maintained.

The distinction between Leviticus and Hebrews, however, comes from the question, "How do these events effect atonement?" The answer Hebrews gives is that the Christ event makes redemption perpetually possible and that the presence of God might be approached through drawing near to Jesus. As Hebrews 9:11–12 says,

> But when Christ appeared as a high priest of the good things that have come, then through the greater and more perfect tent (not made with hands, that is, not of this creation) he entered once for all into the holy places, not by the means of the blood of goats and calves but by means of his own blood, thus securing an eternal redemption.

Additionally, Hebrews 13:12–13 says, "So Jesus also suffered outside the gate in order to sanctify the people through his own blood. Therefore, let us go to him outside the camp and bear the reproach he endured." Where previously the worshipper was to approach God's presence by drawing ever-closer to the center of the camp, the author of Hebrews demonstrates that in Christ, the presence of God is released beyond the bounds of the camp, and the curtain of separation has been removed (Heb 9:8; 10:20).

While the old covenant managed sin annually, the new covenant deals with it perpetually. Jesus's role as both the eternal high priest and the one whose body and blood function as an eternal sacrifice (Heb 9:11–14) are now the means by which the new-covenant people of God might draw near to God's presence. Where Leviticus 16–17 provided ancient Israel with the temporary means to engage the tension between God's intention to dwell among his people and his people's sinfulness and impurity, Hebrews shows that the Christ event offers an eternal means to access the presence of God. Thus, for the author of Hebrews, God's merciful and gracious provision of an eternal atonement is why the Christ event happened as it did, fulfilling and completing the Levitical system that foreshadowed Jesus' eternal sacrifice and priesthood.

Worldview Summary

Having established that the Christ event is the means by which the sacrificial cult and, more centrally, the Yom Kippur ritual is being fulfilled in the heavenly realm, the author of Hebrews reveals that Christ's atonement fulfills and exceeds the Aaronic atonement. In so doing, the author reaches beyond Yom Kippur and begins to consider the typological nature of other elements of the Israelite story—touching the foundations of the Israelite worldview—demonstrating that, in the light of Christ, Israel's history reads differently. Therefore, the author summons the audience to return to Sinai and consider that, in Christ, there is yet a further exodus, tabernacle, and promised land for the Christ-following community to whom Hebrews is written.

TABLE 3.2
Worldview Questions and Answers Comparison: Leviticus 16–17 and Hebrews

QUESTION	LEVITICUS	HEBREWS
Who are we?	THE PEOPLE OF YHWH The people whom YHWH rescued from slavery in Egypt. The people with whom YHWH has made a covenant. The people to whom YHWH has promised a land. The people whose uniqueness is demonstrated by YHWH's presence.	THE PEOPLE OF YHWH IN CHRIST The descendants of the people whom YHWH rescued from slavery in Egypt. The people with whom YHWH has made a new covenant in Christ. The people who are still waiting for a lasting city that is to come. The people whose uniqueness is demonstrated by Jesus leading them into YHWH's presence..
Where are we?	AWAITING THE PROMISED LAND Between the exodus that has provided rescue and the land that is promised. Near the center of the universe, the holy place of YHWH. Except for the high priest's annual entry, however, Israel is separated from YHWH by the curtain that conceals the holy place.	AWAITING THE PROMISED CITY At the foot of Mount Zion, waiting for the lasting city that is to come. Outside the camp, following Jesus and offering a sacrifice of praise to God. Having passed through the true curtain of Jesus's flesh, believers stand in the holy place, the intersection of heaven and earth.
What is wrong?	SIN AND IMPURITY ENDANGER Sin and impurity endanger Israel in the presence of the holiness of YHWH. Sin and impurity threaten to expel the presence of YHWH from the camp.	OLD-COVENANT IMPERMANENCE Sin and impurity endanger humanity in the presence of the holiness of YHWH. The old covenant way of managing sin and impurity was impermanent.
What is the solution?	ANNUAL DAY OF ATONEMENT The Day of Atonement is given by YHWH as a ritual to manage sin and impurity for the camp once every year. Atonement effects temporary ransom and cleansing for sin and impurity.	PERPETUAL ATONEMENT IN CHRIST The Christ event provides the image of which the Day of Atonement was but a shadow. Jesus' eternal blood and sacrifice perpetually forgive, cleanse, and redeem.
What time is it?	BETWEEN EXODUS AND PROMISED LAND A time of wandering and anticipation of entry into the promised land. A time to remember YHWH's covenant faithfulness, to repent of sin, and to hope for the fulfillment of his promises.	BETWEEN ATONEMENT AND HEAVENLY JERUSALEM A time of sojourning without a city, awaiting the heavenly Jerusalem's descent. The time to draw near to God by drawing near to Jesus.
Why?	RETAIN YHWH'S PRESENCE Israel's uniqueness is contingent upon YHWH's dwelling in her midst. YHWH exhibits his mercy by giving Israel the Day of Atonement ritual in order to provide a ransom and purification for the effects of her sin. YHWH remains in the camp because of the ransom-purgation effected by the Day of Atonement, and continues to lead Israel to the promised land, blessings, and fulfillment of his covenant promises.	YHWH'S PERMANENT PRESENCE YHWH has provided in Jesus a means by which he might create a people for himself, and that he might dwell among them through the Holy Spirit (see Heb 6:4). The Christ event provides the image of which the Day of Atonement was a preparatory shadow, thus Jesus's priesthood and sacrifice offer a once-for-all solution to the problem of sin and impurity.

Summary of Atonement: Extension and Expansion

This study began with two distinct-though-related questions. The first question, "If Christians claim to continue the story begun in the Torah, how do they explain the absence of atoning animal sacrifice?," has been answered by way of Hebrews' attention to the Christ event's fulfillment and expansion of the atonement promised in the Yom Kippur ritual. No longer do the people of God in Christ rely on the blood of animals to fulfill the ritual, because the blood of Christ eternally satisfies the ritual's demands and provides an expanded and eternal atonement.

However, while the preceding treatment has demonstrated that Hebrews conceives of the Christ event as a completion and extension of the Hebrew Bible's presentation of atonement, one should also note that, for the author of Hebrews, the effects of atonement in Christ expand beyond the effects glimpsed in Leviticus. The following section will summarize four of the additional effects that the book of Hebrews perceives as the result of the Christ event.

Additional Atonement Motifs in Hebrews: Propitiation (ἱλάσκομαι)

Beyond those motifs common to Leviticus 16, other atonement motifs emerge throughout Hebrews. For example, despite some scholarly attempts to excise the concept of propitiation from biblical conceptions of the atonement, Hebrews clearly makes propitiation available through Christ's atonement. Along with the use of the word ἱλάσκομαι in Hebrews 2:17, the author specifically refers to God's wrath in reference to the generation of Israelites that was denied access to the promised land.[64] In Hebrews 3:11 and 4:3, the author quotes Psalm 95:11, saying, "As I swore in my wrath, 'They shall not enter my rest.'" Further clarifying the warning, the author goes on to ask rhetorically, "And with whom was he provoked for forty years? Was it not with those who sinned, whose

---

64. For a helpful survey of the discussion regarding propitiation (ἱλάσκομαι), see Akin, *1, 2, 3 John*, 260, who cites the work of Leon Morris (*Apostolic Preaching of the Cross*) as convincingly establishing that ἱλάσκομαι includes an appeasement of God's wrath, demonstrating that propitiation is a biblical category of atonement, over and against the work of Dodd (*Bible and the Greeks*). Regarding its presence in Hebrews' argument, the warning passages clearly refer to God's wrath (Heb 4:3b). Coupling this warning with the use of ἱλάσκομαι in Heb 2:17, propitiation is clearly an aspect of Christ's atonement in the writer's mind.

bodies fell in the wilderness? And to whom did he swear that they would not enter his rest, but to those who were disobedient?"[65] In evoking this propitiatory theme of the atonement, the author draws in more of Israel's story in order to frame the warning to the audience to pay careful attention to the great salvation at hand.

Additional Atonement Motifs in Hebrews: Christus Victor

Another atonement theme that is picked up is the victory over the curse, death, and the devil. In Hebrews 2:14–15, the author writes, "He himself likewise partook of the same things, that through death he might destroy the one who has the power of death, that is, the devil, and deliver all those who through fear of death were subject to slavery." Likewise, as Jesus is proven to be a worthy priest by the power of his indestructible life, one might again see the author's appeal to Christ's atonement as a victory over death and the grave.[66] In contemporary terminology, then, there is a clear element of the *Christus Victor* motif of the atonement present in Hebrews.[67]

Additional Atonement Motifs in Hebrews: Redemption

Furthermore, the author includes redemption as an image by which one might understand the nature of the atonement. The idea of YHWH redeeming his people from slavery in Egypt is highlighted in Deuteronomy's appeals to the exodus story, and latent in the performance of Yom Kippur as noted above.[68] However, the redemption theme is also picked up as an effect of Jesus's death in Hebrews 9:12, where the author says, "He entered once for all into the holy places, not by means of the blood of goats and calves, but by means of his own blood, thus securing eternal redemption." Thus the author of Hebrews connects Jesus's death to YHWH's act of redemption, though this redemption has an eternal nature.[69] Again, then, the author has moved beyond the scope of the Yom

---

65. Heb 3:17–18.
66. Heb 7:16.
67. Marshall, "Soteriology in Hebrews," 261.
68. Deut 7:7; 9:26; 13:15; 15:15.
69. Lane, *Hebrews 9–13*, 236, comments on the nature of redemption in Heb 9:12, saying, "The result of his cultic action was not the limited, recurrent redemption of

Kippur understanding of atonement and, in so doing, has invited a fresh understanding of how the new-covenant people of God might speak of Israel's history as their own.

Additional Atonement Motifs in Hebrews: Liberation

Attention to Hebrews' expanded understanding of atonement allows the reader to see yet another way in which the author engages in the extension of Israel's narrative into the present. Her identity secured through Christ's fulfillment of Yom Kippur, Israel is invited to reconsider the true terminus of her historical arc. If Yom Kippur as the central means by which Israel's identity was maintained could be shown to serve as a shadow pointing forward to something more substantial, the author seizes upon the idea that other elements of history could point to and beyond the Christ event as well.

Because of the atonement wrought by the Christ event, not only is forgiveness and cleansing on offer, but there emerges a promise of liberation from slavery to fear and victory over the power of death. This liberation is made explicit in Hebrews 2:14–15:

> Since therefore the children share in flesh and blood, he himself likewise partook of the same things, that through death he might destroy the one who has the power of death, that is, the devil, and deliver all those who through fear of death were subject to lifelong slavery.

Thus, in making an eternal atonement for his people, Jesus has defeated the one who held the power of death and led his people out of the shadow of fear that death formerly cast. In at least these four ways, then, the atonement provided by the Christ event expands beyond the effects recorded in Leviticus.

Conclusion

Beyond expanding the effects of atonement, the book of Hebrews' attention to the idea of eternal atonement in Christ provides at least an initial answer to the second question this chapter has been addressing, "How

---

the annual atonement ritual. He obtained 'eternal redemption.' Eschatological finality characterizes his ministration." One might be justified in seeing atonement as liberation in Hebrews as another valid motif.

does Hebrews' new covenantalism engage and carry forward the heritage of Israel?" While Hays's own answer to this question is substantially helpful, he falters in his conclusion that Hebrews is a "self-consuming artifact."[70] Having granted the validity of Wedderburn's claim that Hebrews undermines the effectiveness of Jesus's blood in the claim that the blood of animals cannot remove sin,[71] Hays suggests that the author intends to both negate and deconstruct itself and its readers in the process of following its logic, so that after one "climbs the argument's ladder," the ladder itself might be kicked away.[72] What has been argued in this study, however, is that the ladder of Israel's cult and history is not kicked away, but pulled up through the Christ event for further climbing.

By exposing the atonement available in Christ to be the atonement to which Israel's heritage always pointed, the author opens the door for a new way of viewing Israel's history. If Israel's identity, tied up in the observance of Yom Kippur, could be proven to be itself a shadow pointing toward something yet coming, then the narrative that helped to establish the identity might also be understood to point beyond itself.[73] Thus, having found the Christ event to provide the image of which Yom Kippur was the shadow, the author of Hebrews finds warrant to consider the typological nature of other parts of Israel's history.

Therefore, as YHWH called his people out from Egypt, so too the author of Hebrews calls the audience to come out from the camp to join Jesus in his suffering. Likewise, new-covenant readers are to strive to enter the still-future promised land and Sabbath Rest by way of faith in the eternal sacrifice and priesthood of Jesus. While much more might be said regarding the specific manner and ethics by which the author of Hebrews expects the new-covenant people of God to live, it is apparent that the arc of Israel's history is not broken, but rather bent through Christ and toward a new understanding of the *telos* to which that history points.

70. Hays, "No Lasting City," 168.

71. Wedderburn, "Sawing Off Branches," 409, concludes, "Hebrews seems to persist resolutely with cultic terminology even after it has, to all intents and purposes, dealt the cultic way of thought a *coup de grace*."

72. Hays, "No Lasting City," 169–70, utilizes this imagery, quoting from Wittgenstein's *Tractatus Logico-Philosophicus* to demonstrate what he intends by "self-consuming artifact." Hays notes that Hebrews is this sort of document, "meant to lead the reader beyond its own rhetoric and to an encounter with the Living God."

73. Hahn, "Covenant, Cult," 87. Likewise, Hays, "No Lasting City," 159, states, "The role of the sanctuary prescribed in the Torah was provisional in character, never intended to be other than a foreshadowing of the reality of Christ's priestly offering."

Having heard Hebrews' answer to the question posed by this book, it remains to ask, "How does the Qur'an explain the absence of sacrificial atonement while maintaining its claim to fulfill prior revelation?" Two divergent approaches to the Qur'an reveal divergent answers to this question, thus the following chapter will briefly survey both approaches prior to offering an accurate answer.

4

The Qur'an and Atonement

A Conspicuous Absence

ONE OF THE PRESUPPOSITIONS of this project is that both the New Testament and the Qur'an purport to complete and confirm the heavenly revelation recorded in the Torah. Thus, in order to argue that the book of Hebrews can be used to challenge the Qur'an's claim of continuity with prior revelation, the previous two chapters have established the teaching of the Torah regarding the Day of Atonement and the manner in which the book of Hebrews claims that the Christ event eternally completes and fulfills the requirements of Yom Kippur. This chapter, then, turns to address the Qur'an's treatment of the concept of atonement.

Prior to doing so, however, it is necessary to establish both where and how the Qur'an makes such claims to complete and confirm the revelation that precedes it. While the question of how the Qur'an completes prior revelation requires the further treatment and investigation given later in this chapter, this introductory section will briefly highlight key places where the claim occurs. Then, by investigating the Qur'an's treatment of sacrificial atonement, the body of this present chapter further considers how the Qur'an understands itself to confirm prior revelation.

The Qur'an's Claim of Continuity

As mentioned above, finding instances of the Qur'an's claim to continue and endorse prior revelation is not a difficult task. Throughout its pages, the Qur'an refers to the *tawrah* (Torah) and the *injil* (gospel) as genuine revelation from God. One of the first instances of such a claim appears in the second *Sura* of the Qur'an. *Surat al-Baqarah* (2):89[1] claims that the Qur'an as divine revelation confirms (مصدق) that which God has revealed previously in Judaism and Christianity through the prophets.[2] This idea appears again two verses later in *Surat al-Baqarah* (2):91 to repeat the claim that the Qur'an, as revelation given to Muhammad, confirms the truth of prior revelation.[3] Such verses provide the foundation for one of the presuppositions of Islamic theology that Islam coincides with what God has revealed to Moses, Jesus, and the "People of the Book."[4]

Similarly, the fifth *Sura*, *Surat al-Mai'da*, commends the revelation given to Jews and Christians in several places, not least of which is verse 68a, which says, "Say: 'Oh People of the Book! Ye have no ground to stand upon unless ye stand fast by the Law [*tawrah*] the gospel [*injil*] and all the

---

1. As a matter of convention, this paper will list the transliterated name of each *Sura* and then the corresponding *Sura* number in parentheses followed by a colon and the verse number. However, for expedience, in footnotes the reference will be limited to the *Sura* number and verse.

2. Qur'an 2:89: "And when there comes to them a Book from God, confirming what is with them—although from of old they had prayed for victory against those without Faith—when there comes to them that which they (should) have recognized, they refuse to believe in it but the curse of God is on those without Faith."

3. Qur'an 2:91: "When it is said to them, 'Believe in what God hath sent down,' they say, 'We believe in what was sent down to us': yet they reject all besides, even it if be truth confirming what is with them. Say: why then have ye slain the prophets of God in times gone by, if ye did believe."

4. Ali, *Qur'an: Text, Translation, and Commentary*, Qur'an 5:12-15. "People of the Book" is a qur'anic convention used to refer to those who have received divine revelation, particularly Jews and Christians. Likewise, see Griffith, *Bible in Arabic*. See also Reynolds, *Emergence of Islam*, 155, who notes, "The Qur'an seems to mean that Jews and Christians are 'People of the Book' because they are nations to whom God has *already* given revelation—a chapter of the heavenly 'book'—in the past." Furthermore, see the qur'anic claims recorded in Ali, Qur'an 2:136: "We believe in God, and the revelation given to us, and to Abraham, Isma'il, Isaac, Jacob, and the Tribes, and that given to Moses and Jesus, and that given to (all) Prophets from their Lord: We make no difference between one and another of them: and we bow to God (in Islam)." Commenting on this verse, Ali writes in footnote 135, "Their message (in essentials) was one, and that is the basis of Islam." See also Qur'an 5:44-50: In these verses the law of Moses and the gospel of Jesus are commended as having been given as "a guidance and an admonition" revealed by God, and the Qur'an was given "confirming the Scripture that came before it, and guarding it in safety." In a footnote explaining this point, Ali states, "The Qur'an comes with a twofold purpose: (1) to confirm the true and original Message, and (2) to guard it, or act as a check to its interpretation" (n759).

revelation that has come to you from your Lord."⁵ The fifth *Sura* proves particularly helpful for linking previous revelation with the Qur'an as the final line of *Surat al-Maiʾda* (5):3 records God saying, "This day I have perfected your religion for you, completed my favor upon you, and have chosen for you Islam as your religion."⁶ Thus, while recognizing the divine act of sending down revelation (نزل) to the Jews and Christians, the Qur'an further claims to be the summation and perfection of the original and sustained message of God to mankind.

Islamic Scholarship and Explanation of Continuity

Such an understanding of the Qur'an's posture toward the *tawrah* and *injil* is standard within Sunni literature. For example, expounding upon qur'anic endorsement of prior revelation, Islamic scholar Muhammad Kamal Ibrāhīm Ja'far writes,

> There are truths concerning history that are contained in Judaism and Christianity which are relevant to those ascertained by Islam. As is well known, Islam does not claim that it initiated what did not exist before. For the Qur'an informs us that God has instituted for us what he had previously given to Noah and Abraham and whoever followed them of the prophets.⁷

Going beyond this recognition of shared historical origins, the early Islamic apologist Ibn Qayyim al-Jawziyya asserts that Islam's advent is the only thing that validates the prior revelations of Judaism and Christianity.⁸ Islam is thus self-consciously intertwined with the teachings before it, claiming to be the final summation of all religion.

Additionally, *Surat al-Ahzab* (33):40 further reinforces this posture by referring to Muhammad as the "Seal of the Prophets."⁹ This title is the foundation for the prevailing Islamic understanding that God has

---

5. Ali, Qur'an 5:68: قُلْ يَا أَهْلَ الْكِتَابِ لَسْتُمْ عَلَىٰ شَيْءٍ حَتَّىٰ تُقِيمُوا التَّوْرَاةَ وَالْإِنْجِيلَ وَمَا أُنْزِلَ إِلَيْكُمْ مِنْ رَبِّكُمْ ۗ وَلَيَزِيدَنَّ كَثِيرًا مِنْهُمْ مَا أُنْزِلَ إِلَيْكَ مِنْ رَبِّكَ طُغْيَانًا وَكُفْرًا ۖ فَلَا تَأْسَ عَلَى الْقَوْمِ الْكَافِرِينَ. The fifth *Sura* also speaks positively about the *tawrah* and *injil* in verse 43, referring to the *tawrah* as "the plain command of God" (عِنْدَهُمُ التَّوْرَاةُ فِيهَا حُكْمُ اللَّهِ); verses 47 and 68 refer to the gospel as revelation from God (أَنْزَلَ اللَّهُ).

6. Ali, Qur'an 5:3b.

7. Ja'far, "Islam Looks," 174.

8. Accad, "Muhammad's Advent," 222.

9. Ali, Qur'an 33:40. "خَاتَمَ النَّبِيِّينَ".

revealed his will through three books given to prophets—the *tawrah* (the first five books of the Hebrew Bible), the *injil* (the gospel), and finally Muhammad's Qur'an.¹⁰ The Qur'an of the Islamic prophet Muhammad commends itself as a completion of previous revelation and a correction of that which has allegedly been distorted by subsequent Jewish and Christian tradition.¹¹

Thus, Islamic scholar Gabriel Said Reynolds sums up Islamic tradition on the matter of continuity, claiming that the Qur'an contends, "Muhammad did not found a new religion but rather preached anew the very religion that Abraham, Moses, and Jesus preached before him."¹² This brief survey of the Qur'an's teaching regarding its relationship to prior revelation suffices for the moment to recognize the qur'anic endorsement of the Torah and the gospel along with its claim to perfect and confirm their message. However, turning to the question of how the Qur'an understands itself to relate to prior revelation, the argument of this chapter is that the Qur'an's claim to continuity differs significantly from the narrative continuity exhibited throughout Hebrews.

Approaches to Understanding the Qur'an

Having seen that the Qur'an claims to continue previous revelation, then, it remains to discover what the Qur'an means by this claim. However, when one begins to investigate the meaning of the Qur'an, one quickly finds that one's presuppositions and approach to the study of the Qur'an radically alter the conclusions that one reaches. This chapter outlines

---

10. Accad, "Muhammad's Advent," 222–23. Perhaps the clearest qur'anic references to this concept are found in Qur'an 5:46-47 "(46) And in their footsteps We sent Jesus the son of Mary, confirming the Law that had come before him: We sent him the Gospel: therein was guidance and light and confirmation of the Law that had come before him: a guidance and an admonition to those who fear God. (47) Let the people of the Gospel judge by what God hath revealed therein. If any do fail to judge by (the light of) what God hath revealed, they are (no better than) those who rebel."; The Qur'an includes the Psalms of David as previously revealed Scripture. See Qur'an 4:163: "We have sent thee inspiration, as We sent it to Noah and the Messengers after him: we sent inspiration to Abraham, Isma'il, Isaac, Jacob and the Tribes, to Jesus, Job, Jonah, Aaron, and Solomon, and to David We gave the Psalms."

11. Accad, "Muhammad's Advent," 222–23. For a careful inspection of the qur'anic material regarding *tahrif*, or the idea of scriptural falsification, see Reynolds, "Qur'anic Accusation," 189–202.

12. Reynolds, *Emergence of Islam*, 28.

two approaches to the Qur'an—one traditional and one intertextual—to answer the question, "How does the Qur'an treat sacrificial atonement in its claim to complete prior revelation?" Both approaches provide answers to the question of continuation, and both of those answers provide a glimpse of the conflict between the biblical and qur'anic worldview at the point of understanding atonement.

The traditional approach, followed by both most Muslim and secular scholars, relies upon Islamic sources to understand the historical setting and consequent interpretation of the Qur'an. Some emerging scholars, however, argue that the Qur'an is a work of intertextuality, intentionally engaging biblical and extra biblical material. While most Muslims adhere to traditional accounts of Islamic history, this chapter contends that an intertextual approach bears more fruit for understanding the Qur'an's message regarding atonement and completion of biblical revelation. A brief history of the last two centuries of Islamic studies will provide the background for the following discussion, allowing the reader to apprehend the different conclusions born of the two approaches.

Varied Starting Points

Since the early seventh century CE, the three so-called Abrahamic faiths of Judaism, Christianity, and Islam have inhabited and hallowed some of the same lands in the Middle East. Geographical proximity and common ancestry have forced each faith to develop ways of articulating its own distinct theology and philosophy in relationship to the others. Many, driven by various motivations, have undertaken to study the common ground shared by these three traditions in order to understand the nuances of their earliest relationships to one another.[13] Jewish historians, Christian missionaries, Islamic apologists, secular scholars, and others have contributed to the overabundance of material on offer regarding the earliest stages of Jewish-Christian-Islamic interaction, despite the fact that relatively little conclusive and corroborated data exists from the first two centuries of traditional Islamic origins.[14] The dearth of conclu-

---

13. Roggema, *Three Rings*.

14. Reynolds, *Qur'an*, 1–36. Introducing his particular method of qur'anic study, Reynolds summarizes the majority approach to the Qur'an as improper, saying, "For the most part, scholars of the Qur'an accept the basic premise of the medieval Islamic sources that the Qur'an is to be explained in light of the life of the Prophet Muhammad. The life of the Prophet, meanwhile, is recorded in those sources with intricate

sive historical data makes it difficult to offer a retelling of early Islamic history and relationships with Christian and Jewish communities with confidence, though many have tried.[15]

What Did Muhammad Borrow?

One influential example of such an attempt in the field of comparative religion comes from Abraham Geiger, who is often credited as being the forefather of Jewish-Islamic study.[16] His mid-nineteenth-century essay, "What Did Muhammad Borrow from Judaism?," posits the idea that Muhammad, being engaged in dialogue with Jewish tribes living in Medina, drew heavily and directly on Jewish tradition in the composition of the Qur'an and that this borrowing set the theological trajectory of the religion that emerged.[17] Secular scholarship has largely continued pursuit of Geiger's line of thought, seeking out evidence of borrowing from Jewish and Christian sources in the composition of the Qur'an and Islamic traditions.[18] Other recent scholars, however, have radically challenged the Islamic tradition-dependent methodology of qur'anic study.[19]

---

detail. This detailed information, one might assume, should allow scholars to explain at least the literal meaning of the Qur'an without difficulty. But it does not." Reynolds goes on to demonstrate that the biographical material used to decipher the Qur'an is itself exegetical rather than historical, thus basing any conclusions on circular argument; Likewise, Ohlig, *Hidden Origins*, 8–9, opens this compilation by saying, "All the biographical 'information' [of Muhammad] we have can be found in two types of sources. The first consists of the biographical works of the early ninth and tenth centuries.... The second type of source consists of the six canonical collections of hadith, which date from the late ninth century.... Following the canons of historical-critical research, these reports, written approximately two hundred years after the fact, should be taken into consideration only with great reservations.... The first two 'Islamic' centuries lie in the shadows of history."

15. See Katsh, *Judaism in Islam*; Peters, *Judaism, Christianity*; Armstrong, *Muhammad*; Levenson, *Inheriting Abraham*; Reynolds, *Emergence of Islam*, 205. Concluding his introduction to Islamic studies and commenting on the difficulty of attaining certain knowledge of the historical setting during the rise of Islam, Reynolds admits that despite widespread attempts at recreation of the earliest days of the Islamic faith, "The question of Islam's emergence is far from settled."

16. Firestone, "Qur'an and Bible," 11.

17. Geiger, "What Did Muhammad Borrow?"

18. As examples of following Geiger's Orientalist approach, see Torrey, *Jewish Foundation*; Katsh, *Judaism in Islam*.

19. As examples of those who challenge the Orientalist approach by way of historical-critical scholarship, see Warraq, *Origins of Koran*; Reynolds, *Qur'an*; Small, *Textual*

In some emerging enclaves of qur'anic study, this challenge has shifted attention away from Islamic borrowing from Jewish sources and tradition, and towards investigation of potential Christian and biblical influence on the Qur'an.[20] Following the data produced by this research, some scholars have largely dismissed the Islamic telling of its own history.[21] For example, despite nearly unanimous consensus within Islamic scholarship to the contrary, some have concluded that Mecca and Medina are not the birthplace of the faith and even that the Islamic prophet Muhammad might never have existed in the manner in which tradition depicts him.[22] Much of this criticism of traditional history is derived from the absence of extra-Islamic corroboration of the historical claims found in the earliest purportedly historical renderings of Muhammad's life and ministry, which are themselves at least one hundred years removed from his death.[23]

What Muhammad Didn't Borrow

With all of the various perspectives on offer based on a relatively small amount of historically verifiable data, researching the intersection of Judaism, Christianity, and Islam at the earliest stages of the Islamic faith requires one to sort through volumes of biased information, caricature, speculation, and hot debate.[24] Additionally, due to the "sectarian milieu" present already in seventh and eigth century Arabia, one seeking to

---

Criticism; Ohlig, *Early Islam*.

20. Reynolds, *Emergence of Islam*, 153, notes, "The Qur'an's interest in taking Christians to task for their doctrines about Christ suggests that Islam emerged in an environment where theology and Christology were topics of general interest. Second, the Qur'an's frequent reference to biblical traditions (and the allusive nature of those references) suggests that Islam emerged in a context where biblical literature was well known (including later Christian works such as the *Protoevangelium of James*)."

21. Ohlig, *Early Islam*; Ohlig, *Hidden Origins*, 8–9.

22. Ohlig, *Hidden Origins*, 8–9; Ohlig, *Early Islam*, 12; Spencer, *Did Muhammad Exist?*

23 Ohlig, *Hidden Origins*, 8. As quoted above in footnote 14, Ohlig cites Ibn Hisham's biography of Muhammad's life, which was written prior to his death in 834 CE. However, Ibn Hisham's work purports to be a recreation of Ibn Ishaq's *sira*, which would have been written sometime prior to 768 CE. Thus, taking the most generous approach within the Islamic sources themselves, there remains a one-hundred-year gap between Muhammad's death and the writing of his biography.

24. Wasserstrom, *Between Muslim and Jew*, 157.

discern instances of Islamic borrowing must first ask the questions, "Which Judaism? Which Christianity? Which Islam?"[25] Finally, regardless of the historical connection between the three faiths, the term "borrowing" itself can be pejorative. Muslims see Islam as a corrective to Judaism and Christianity, and as a response to revelation rather than secondhand faith compiled piece-meal.[26]

Therefore, though it has greatly contributed to the growth of a body of research in the field of Islamic studies, there are several reasons why the question raised by Geiger is neither definitively nor helpfully answered. While this chapter gleans from much of the scholarship generated by Geiger's question, it will ask the opposite question: "What didn't Muhammad borrow from Judaism?" One glaring omission revealed by answering this question is the Qur'an does not include a doctrine of sacrificial atonement, despite its claim to continuity with—and perfection of—biblical Judaism and Christianity.

The subsequent question, and the question with which this project is centrally concerned, thus presents itself, "How does Islam explain the absence of Yom Kippur and sacrificial atonement that is so central to Judaism and Christianity?" As will be seen, traditionally Ramadan has been understood to take the place of Yom Kippur—the Jewish Day of Atonement—in Islam. As this project contends, however, the Qur'an suggests ʽid al-Aḍha as Islam's earliest explanation for Yom Kippur's absence. In Islam, the annual celebration of ʽid al-Aḍha is a celebration of Abraham's willingness to sacrifice his son as recorded in *Surat as-Saffat* 37:100–107, a story that has parallels in the Hebrew Bible (Gen 22). This sacrifice is not based upon the atoning power of sacrificial blood, but rather as a ritual of demarcation, setting apart the final and perfect dispensation of revealed religion. For the missiologist seeking to communicate the Christian perspective of atonement, however, it is vitally important to consider how Islam's treatment of the concept of atonement does not merely exchange one ritual for another, but rather, using shared vocabulary and history, tells a different story based upon a different worldview.

---

25. Wansborough, *Sectarian Milieu*. Referring to the variety of Jewish expression already at the time of Christ, see also Wright, *People of God*.

26. Regarding the Orientalist accusation of borrowing, see Reynolds, *Qur'an*, 35, who says, "Muhammad was usually assumed to have borrowed material from Jews and Christians. The Qur'an consequently was seen as something of a scrapbook of earlier religious ideas." Regarding the claim to be a response to revelation, see Brinner, "Islamic Decalogue," 67.

Linguistic Analysis: Kipper (כִּפֶּר) and Kaffara (كَفَّر)

In order to begin this investigation, then, it is helpful to consider the words used in the Bible and the Qur'an that are often translated in English as "atone." While one cannot hope to exhaustively compare two faith systems across two languages using only a lexical approach, such a starting point lays bare the distinct ways that each text uses shared lexemes.[27] Likewise, by focusing on a comparative word study, one begins in neutral territory, at least initially avoiding commitment to either the traditional or the intertextual approach to understanding the Qur'an's meaning. Finally, this word study investigates the component parts of atonement as exhibited in the Bible in order to consider whether or not the Qur'an also includes each element.

Recalling the conclusions of chapter 2, atonement in the Hebrew Bible involves a concept-cluster involving sacrifice, ransom/forgiveness, and cleansing that is centrally focused on blood.[28] Turning to the concept of atonement in the Qur'an, however, one discovers that the word translated "atone" functions in a different way. Furthermore, while most of the component parts of Old Testament atonement feature in the Qur'an, they also mean something different.

Arabic Atonement Language

When considering the difficulty of explaining Christian atonement to Muslims, one barrier to communication that presents itself derives from the fact that Arabic speaking Christians and Muslims use shared language to describe divergent concepts. As indicated above, the Arabic Bible uses

---

27. Smart, *Dimensions of Sacred*, 1–8. Smart argues that one must consider a cluster of related concepts to compare religions rather than assuming that words are used in the same way in different faiths.

28. Sklar, *Sin, Impurity*, 185. See also Wenham, *Book of Leviticus*, 62, who comments on the idea of an animal taking the worshipper's place vicariously, stating, "Both fit in well with sacrifices making atonement, i.e., the animal serving as a ransom for the life of man. One may regard the animal either as dying in the worshipper's place as his substitute, or as receiving the death penalty because of the sin transferred to it by the laying on of hands." Regarding the contentious issue of substitution in atonement theology, see Gathercole, *Defending Substitution*, 28, who defends the idea of substitutionary atonement, saying, "A response that one might make to any such challenges is that biblical exegesis simply demands substitution; therefore it cannot be avoided.... there is actually very good evidence for seeing substitutionary atonement as intrinsic to the biblical presentation of how God has reconciled the world to himself in Christ."

the word *kaffara* (كفّر) to translate the Hebrew word *kipper* (כִּפֶּר).²⁹ However, while *kaffara* functions similarly to *kipper* within its biblical context, it is freighted with different meaning in its qur'anic context. The following section will consider the different features of the word where it occurs within the Qur'an.

Atonement Language in the Arabic Bible and in the Qur'an

Scholars and translators have often claimed that the Hebrew word *kipper* (כִּפֶּר) and its derivatives serve as cognates with the Arabic word group from *kaffara* (كفّر).³⁰ On a superficial level, one might argue that both *kipper* and *kaffara* do exhibit similarity in that they refer to a way of dealing with sin. As seen above, part of the effect of making atonement in the HB is dealing with sin.³¹ Likewise, in the Qur'an atonement entails God dealing with sins. However, the Qur'an promises God's atonement in response to a worshipper's good deeds.³² However, despite similarity in these most general of terms, examination of the usage of the *kaffara* reveals that the Qur'an refers to a process that is significantly different than that of the Hebrew Bible when it speaks of "atoning."

The Subject of Kaffara

One of the clear distinctions between the qur'anic and biblical concepts is the agent involved in the process. In the Qur'an, the subject of the verb *kaffara*—translated variously as "atone," "expiate," and "efface"—is almost

---

29. Van Dyke, *Al Kitab*; Lev 16:30: "لانه في هذا اليوم يكفّر عنكم لتطهيركم. من جميع خطاياكم امام الرب تطهرون."

30. Wensinck et al., *First Encyclopaedia*, 1148. The encyclopedia takes the qur'anic use of *kaffara* as being equivalent to the Hebrew *kappara* and presupposes that it is an instance; Cuypers, *Banquet*, 360. Clarifying a point of vocabulary, Cuypers writes, "The term "expiation" *kaffara* . . . appears to be derived directly from the Hebrew *kappara*." Additionally, Sklar, *Sin, Impurity*, 2, 44–45, n2, notes the widespread tendency to conflate the Hebrew and Arabic words in nineteenth and twentieth century scholarship.

31. Sklar, *Sin, Impurity*, 2. Sklar concludes, "There is basic agreement that כִּפֶּר refers to sin being dealt with in such a way that the broken relationship between the LORD and the sinner is mended."

32. The result of God's act of *kaffara* (كفّر) seems to be connected with forgiveness of sins (Qur'an 3:193; 8:29) and entry into heaven (Qur'an 3:195; 4:31; 5:12, 65; 48:5; 66:8). See Appendix B for a list of qur'anic uses of *kaffara* (كفّر).

always God.³³ This differs from the priestly literature of the Hebrew Bible where the subject is another agent—often a priest—who effects atonement on behalf of the individual or group presenting the offering. An example of the formula used to indicate the priestly role in making atonement comes from Leviticus 4:31, which states, "And the priest shall make atonement for him for the sin that he has committed, and he shall be forgiven."³⁴ In the Hebrew Bible, then, God provides a means by which humans might make atonement, whereas in the Qur'an it is God himself who directly atones for the "bad/evil deeds" (سيئات) of humans.

Likewise, as has been shown above, the Hebrew word *kipper* is used in the Hebrew Bible in contexts of both ritual impurity and of sin. The verb *kipper*, then, effects both cleansing and ransom.³⁵ However, in the Qur'an, *kaffara* is used exclusively to expiate "bad/evil deeds" (سيئات).³⁶ God in the Qur'an, as the subject of *kaffara*, acts on behalf of the transgressor by covering over the bad deeds of the one who has committed them. In each instance this expiation is effected by God, though he does so in response to the faith-filled piety of the believer demonstrated variously by fasting, faith, repentance, charity, or martyrdom.³⁷ Thus God

---

33. There is one exception to this rule in Qur'an 2:271 where charity given in secret serves as the subject: "إِن تُبْدُوا الصَّدَقَاتِ فَنِعِمَّا هِيَ ۖ وَإِن تُخْفُوهَا وَتُؤْتُوهَا الْفُقَرَاءَ فَهُوَ خَيْرٌ لَّكُمْ ۚ وَيُكَفِّرُ عَنكُم مِّن سَيِّئَاتِكُمْ ۗ وَاللَّهُ بِمَا تَعْمَلُونَ خَبِيرٌ" Likewise, in the nominal form *kaffara* (كفّارة) acts of charity are considered to be themselves atonement. See Appendix A and B for charts of the qur'anic uses of the verb *kaffara* (كفّر) and the noun *kaffara* (كفّارة). English translations in the Appendix come from Asad, *Meaning of the Qur'an*. Asad prefers the verb "efface" as his translation of كفّر, though he uses "atone" for Qur'an 2:271. See also Ali, *Qur'an*. Ali uses the words "remove/blot out/expel/wipe out/turn off" in the place of كفّر throughout his translation; Droge, *Qur'an*. Droge uses "absolve" consistently throughout his translation in place of كفّر.

34. In Hebrew, וְכִפֶּר עָלָיו. This recurs throughout the priestly literature, notably repeated during the Day of Atonement prescription recorded in Lev 16:16 and 16:33.

35. Sklar, *Sin, Impurity*, 182, sums up his lengthy treatment of the idea of atonement in the priestly literature saying, "In either context, however, it was seen that the end point of sin and impurity is the same: both endanger (requiring ransom) and both pollute (requiring purgation). . . . In short, due to the similar ending points of sin and impurity, even when the emphasis is upon ransom (כֹּפֶר), it is a purifying ransom that is in view, and even when the emphasis is upon purgation, it is a ransoming-purgation that is in view. The verb that describes this dual event is כִּפֶּר, and the ability of the כִּפֶּר-rite to accomplish this dual event is due to the blood of the sacrifice which both ransoms and purifies."

36. See Appendix B for a chart of the qur'anic uses of the verb *kaffara* (كفّر).

37. See Appendix A and B for charts of the qur'anic uses of the noun and verb derived from the كفّر root to consider the causes of atonement.

will "atone for" one's evil deeds in response to one's faith-driven good deeds. Purification, however, is not a part of the Qur'an's *kaffara* process.

Purification in the Qur'an

Lest one conclude that the Qur'an is disinterested in purification due to its absence from the concept of *kaffara*, it is necessary to consider the role of purification separately. In so doing, one discovers that cleansing is actually discussed more than atonement throughout the Qur'an. This occurs through the use of a second word family: *tahhara* (طهّر).[38] Where *kaffara* is an act almost exclusively performed by God in the Qur'an, *tahhara* can be performed by an individual through washing (*Surat al-Mā'idah* [5]:6) or by charity (*Surat at-Tawbah* [9]:103).[39] God can also purify someone directly (*Surat al-Aḥzāb* [33]:33). As in the Hebrew Bible, impurity in the Qur'an can be an external element of contamination, stemming from menstruation or sexual activity, or it can be due to an impure heart that motivates lying or disgraceful behavior (*Surat al-Mā'idah* (5):41).[40]

Summary of Linguistic Analysis

This section has demonstrated that there is sufficient warrant to claim that, despite the appearance of *kaffara* in both the Qur'an and the Arabic Bible, each text exhibits significant differences in its use of the term. The context in which the Arabic Bible uses *kaffara* maintains the emphasis of the original Hebrew: *kaffara* means a ransom-purgation of sin and defilement. Yet the context in which the Qur'an employs *kaffara* reveals a process that is singularly focused on the covering or expiation of evil deeds.

---

38. According to "The Qur'anic Arabic Corpus," the trilateral root طهّر occurs thirty-one times throughout the Qur'an and always refers to purity and the process of purification and cleansing. In the context of the usage, one sees a relationship between sexual contact (5:6), menstruation (2:222), idolatry (74:4), and improper motives (58:12) in making one impure. The removal of idols and idolatry (2:125), ritual washing (5:6), and charity (9:103) are connected as means by which effecting purity might occur.

39. See Appendix B to illustrate the subjectival role of God in instances of *kaffara*. Regarding *tahhara* (طهّر), this is similar to the Hebrew cognate, טהר, used in the HB to effect purification through blood or water washing. See Sklar, *Sin, Impurity*, 125.

40. See particularly the section focused on impurity laws in Lev 11–15.

One might, at this point, contend that the Qur'an merely utilizes two words (كَفَّر and طَهَّر) to convey the same components of atonement as the Bible does with one. Therefore, one might claim that the Qur'an incorporates Jewish and Christian teaching on atonement by dividing the concepts of forgiveness and purification. While this answer may initially seem satisfactory, it provides only a very superficial answer to the deeper question that we are asking: "How does the Qur'an incorporate sacrificial atonement into its claim to continue previous revelation?" The biblical concept addressed above contained four components: sacrifice, ransom/forgiveness, purification, and blood. Two elements thus remain for consideration: sacrifice and blood.

These two elements, however, require a foray into contemporary literature on Islamic studies. While a lexical study of *kaffara* and *tahhara* suffices to identify the basic corresponding concepts within the Bible and the Qur'an, consideration of the meaning and symbolism of ritual, sacrifice, and blood requires more nuance. The following section elucidates the Qur'an's teaching on this topic by approaching the remaining concepts of sacrifice and blood from both the perspective of traditional Islamic studies and emerging intertextual proposals.

Approaching Islam: A Tale of Two Medinas

As indicated in the introduction to this chapter, there are at least two approaches to understanding and interpreting the Qur'an. The approach of most of the Islamic world, along with that of most Orientalist scholarship, takes for granted the historical reliability of the *sira* (The biography of Muhammad) and reads the Qur'an in its light.[41] As indicated above, however, there is little reason to trust the historical reliability of these traditional sources. Thus, while this approach may not actually provide much insight into the origins of Islam in history, it does serve as the basis upon which most standard Islamic theology is built and is suggestive of how contemporary Islam perceives itself.[42]

41. Reynolds, *Qur'an*, 8, offers a list of significant scholars of Islam who "all work from the basic premise, inherited from Islamic tradition and enshrined in the work of Nöldeke, that the Qur'an is to be understood in light of the biography of Muhammad."

42. Reynolds, *Emergence of Islam*, 206. Having traced important developments in qur'anic studies that lead away from the traditional material, Reynolds concedes, "Of course, from the perspective of most Muslims there is no reason to doubt the traditional biography of the Prophet. . . . Moreover, those traditions with precise reports on the words and deeds of the Prophet—that is, the *hadith*—are to most Muslims

For that reason, the answer to the question of continuity given by this perspective is yet valuable to the Christian missiologist in that it provides insight into the presuppositions and worldview of most of the Islamic world. Therefore, this section will first consult the traditional material and those who follow its lead in interpretation of the Qur'an, while also turning to the second, and perhaps more fruitful, approach of intertextual analysis and interpretation following emerging historical-critical scholars who prefer to approach the Qur'an in light of biblical literature.[43]

One of the central claims made by the traditional material is that Muhammad emigrated to a city named Yathrib/Medina in 622 CE. It was in Medina, then, that tradition depicts Muhammad's community growing and becoming established.[44] While this account is often taken for granted, many of the emerging scholars have begun to doubt even this geographical information.[45] With that in mind, the two approaches to understanding the Qur'an and Islam itself will be considered in turn under the headings "Medina 1.0: A Traditional Approach" and "Medina 2.0: An Intertextual Approach."

Medina 1.0: A Traditional Approach

According to traditions, as Islam in its infancy engaged other monotheistic faiths, it was both drawn to and repulsed by what it found, alternately claiming to be of the same heritage as the Jews and Christians and dismissing adherents of both other faiths as having gone astray and being in need of correction.[46] Because the traditional biography depends upon Muhammad's interactions with Judaism in Medina, it is instructive to begin with a summary of what Judaism taught at the time of the rise of Islam. Specifically, this section will focus on the role of temple, sacrifice,

---

more than an important source of historical information. They are also a source of revelation."

43. Reynolds, *Qur'an*, 22.

44. Guillaume, *Life of Muhammad*, 235, records Ibn Ishaq reporting, "When the apostle was firmly settled in Medina and his brethren the emigrants were gathered to him and the affairs of the helpers were arranged Islam became firmly established."

45. Ohlig, *Early Islam*, 12, summarizes the conclusions of the authors included in his edited work, saying, "The beginnings of a qur'anic movement originated from a specific form of Christianity and came from regions much farther east of Mesopotamia and not from the Arabian Peninsula."

46. Ali, Qur'an 2:52; 5:69, 82; 9:30–31, etc.

and priesthood in the Day of Atonement in the Judaism of the seventh century CE.

Post-Biblical Yom Kippur in Medina

As discussed above, for ancient Israel, Leviticus 16 served as the central record of the ritual requirements for the high priest's annual entrance into the holy place. This passage in Leviticus clearly shows that the ritual sacrifices pertaining to the Day of Atonement were to occur at the Tent of Meeting and later at the Jerusalem temple.[47] However, upon the destruction of the Jerusalem temple in 70 CE, all Jews were forced to reconfigure their practice in order to observe the Yom Kippur rituals in the absence of the prescribed place of sacrifice.[48] At this point, historian József Zsengellér indicates that the various divisions of the Jews "gave up all their sacrificial activities but developed a theoretical system on how to perform the non-existing rituals all the more [sic] better."[49] According to the prolific author of Middle Eastern history, Bernard Lewis, these theoretical systems developed over time, adding elaborate *halakha*—official rabbinic teaching—to the core teaching of the Torah in the absence of sacrifice.[50]

Tracing this line of theological development, Jewish scholar Jacob Neusner shows that *halakhic* teaching on the Day of Atonement between 200 CE and 600 CE shifts attention from the cultic actions of the high priest to an attitude of repentance as the "precondition of reconciliation with first humanity, then God."[51] Elsewhere, Neusner indicates that the Hebrew word for repentance, *teshuva*, is "built out of the root for 'return,' . . . [and] is generally understood to mean 'returning to God from a situation of estrangement.' The turning is not only from sin but toward God, for sin serves as an indicator of a deeper pathology, which is utter estrangement from God—man's will alienated from God's."[52] Thus rabbis

---

47. Zsengellér, "Day of Atonement," 141. Zsengellér highlights the permanence of the requirement that the holy place is to be the place of service, saying, "This holy place as the location of the high priest's service is presented to be a continuous tradition except during the time of the exile."

48. Zsengellér, "Day of Atonement," 143.

49. Zsengellér, "Day of Atonement," 143.

50. Lewis, *Faith and Power*, 47.

51. Neusner, *Performing Israel's Faith*, 123.

52. Chilton and Neusner, *Classical Christianity*, 195.

began to teach that, in lieu of the opportunity to sacrifice, the posture of repentance could restore relationship between God and man.

Corroborating this trend, the ten days leading up to Yom Kippur became known as "Ten Days of Repentance," during which Jews and Samaritans remember their sins while visualizing God's love and forgiveness as a way of cleansing the individual and corporate conscience prior to the celebration of the Day of Atonement.[53] These ten days of preparation, along with the reconceptualized observation of Yom Kippur noted above, were filled with prayer, reading of Scripture, fasting, and charity. By the time of Muhammad, then, this repentance-centered cleansing had become, for many post-biblical Jews, a satisfactory substitute for the actual sacrifices prescribed for Yom Kippur.

While it would be fascinating to know which specific sects of Judaism early Islam may have encountered, Steven Wasserstrom summarizes the historical obscurity of the period, saying, "The end of late antiquity is a period of Jewish history best known for being unknown."[54] Furthermore, commenting on the anonymity of Jewish tribes in the Qur'an and traditions, Wasserstrom writes, "Much if not most of recorded Muslim knowledge of Judaism and Jewish life concerns generic Jews (*Yahud*) [and] is denominationally non-specific."[55] It is thus difficult to know exactly which sects of Judaism may have been in contact with Muhammad and the early Muslim community, or what their specific practices and theologies looked like.

However, while myriad questions about the specific practices and beliefs of the Jews of the seventh century remain, what is obvious is that, post-70 CE, the lack of an officiating priesthood had caused all sects of Judaism to reimagine how they might fulfill the Torah sans temple. The Jewish populations with whom Muhammad and the early Islamic community would have had contact, then, were neither practicing physical expressions of animal sacrifice nor relying upon it for atonement, having theologically reconstructed their religious practice to accommodate their inability to literally carry out the prescribed rituals.

Thus, since traditional Islamic teaching holds that Muhammad was an "unlettered" man (traditionally taken to mean that he was illiterate or only partially literate), it is assumed that his understanding of Judaism

---

53. Zsengellér, "Day of Atonement," 150.
54. Wasserstrom, *Between Muslim and Jew*, 17–18.
55. Wasserstrom, *Between Muslim and Jew*, 162.

would have come directly from its practitioners rather than from personal interaction with Jewish Scriptures.[56] For that reason, and since animal sacrifice had long since been replaced in Judaism with metaphor and symbolism, it is easy to understand how a robust biblical understanding of blood-wrought atonement was never a necessity in his understanding of Jewish theology. From this traditional understanding, then, it is helpful to investigate some of the early Islamic sources to better understand their reaction to Judaism, sacrifice, and atonement.

Islamic Interactions with Judaism

In the tenth century, a Muslim writer named al-Maqdisi created a list of Jewish practices and beliefs. From this list of beliefs and practices, one is granted a glimpse into relatively early Islamic understanding of Judaism. For example, al-Maqdesi records an account regarding the pilgrimages required of Jews living in the diaspora, noting, "While the Temple still stood and the altar existed, they had to make the pilgrimage (*hajj*) three times each year."[57] Explaining the Yom Kippur pilgrimage, al-Maqdisi indicates his understanding of the significance of the day, writing, "Isaac was ransomed from the sacrifice . . . [and] on this day, God forgives them all their sins and offenses, except three: adultery with a married woman, injustice of a man towards his brother, and the denial of God's divinity."[58] By using terminology of the *hajj* (the word used for the compulsory Islamic pilgrimage to Mecca) and the story of Abraham's son being ransomed by God as the basis for forgiveness, al-Maqdisi closely connects Islamic thought with Jewish practice without referring to blood atonement or temple cult.

Likewise, the Qur'an itself gives evidence that the various expressions of Judaism traditionally understood to have inhabited Medina in the early seventh century had already reimagined themselves without the temple as the central feature of their religious practice. For example, despite the fact that the Jewish and Christian communities use the word *haykal* (هيكل) to specifically refer to the Jerusalem temple, this word does

---

56. Ali, Qur'an 7:158, n1132, notes the importance of Muhammad as being untainted by education, yet miraculously in possession of a "most wonderful knowledge of the previous Scriptures."

57. Adang, *Muslim Writers*, 260.

58. Adang, *Muslim Writers*, 260.

not appear in the Qur'an.⁵⁹ Instead the word *masjid* (المسجد) is used–the same word applied to mosques to refer to a place of prostration or prayer.⁶⁰ This linguistic conflation of the holy place of Judaism and the places of prayer in Islam indicates the sense of seamlessness that early Islam saw between its own proclamation and practice and that of Judaism.

With all of this in mind, tradition depicts Muhammad expecting that his message would be understood as an extension of original Jewish and Christian teaching. In an effort to secure a warm welcome with his would-be brethren of the Jewish community in Yathrib (later Medina), the *sira* and *hadith* record that Muhammad enjoined his followers to keep the Jewish fast of *'Ashura* (This fast is widely understood to be Yom Kippur) and to pray facing Jerusalem.⁶¹ Happily, upon his arrival, Muhammad indeed found many residents—chiefly the Jews of the Banu Nadir and Banu Quraiza—who welcomed his strong, authoritative hand in their politically volatile region.⁶² As a political figure, then, he was initially welcomed as he expected, which encouraged his optimism for a positive religious reception as well.

Contrary to his expectation, however, tradition records that the Jewish leaders rejected Muhammad's teaching and prophethood. Bernard Lewis summarizes the traditional understanding of Muhammad's reception, saying:

59. Reynolds, *Qur'an*, 138.

60. Ali, *Qur'an*, 695. Q. 17:7. The note on this section recognizes the destruction of the Jerusalem temple in 70 CE, and the English text records the translation "temple" though the Arabic word is المسجد. This indicates the lack of distinction between Islamic worship practices and their understanding of the ritual of Judaism.

61. Regarding the change of direction for the *qibla*, see Guillaume, *Life of Muhammad*, 258–59. Regarding the fast of *'Ashura* that was adopted by Muhammad, see Al-Bukhari, *Sahih Bukhari*, Book 31: Hadith 218–25. Regarding *'Ashura* as Yom Kippur, see Peters, *Origins of Islam*, 203–6, 215. Peters, having drawn from hadith narrated by Aisha, the favorite wife of Muhammad, concludes that *'Ashura* is, in fact, Yom Kippur, and that, alluding to Qkur'an 2:185, "Muhammad discontinued the *Ashura*, or at least made it purely voluntary, and on the apparent testimony of the Qur'an substituted for it the fast of the full month of Ramadan." It should be acknowledged that *'Ashura* as Yom Kippur is a debated issue. See the argument by Nadwi, "Fast of Ashura." However, in light of the Jewish development of ten days of fasting prior to Yom Kippur mentioned above, it is likely that *'Ashura* was understood the be the culminating day of what had become of the fast. Furthermore, the traditional material understands *'Ashura* to be a solemn period of fasting followed by a great celebration that would coincide with the manner in which Yom Kippur was celebrated at the time of Muhammad's traditional advent.

62. Lewis, *Arabs in History*, 40.

> Muhammad had hoped to find a friendly welcome among the Jews, whose faith and scriptures would, so he thought, cause them to receive the claims of the Arabian Prophet with greater sympathy and understanding. In order to appease them, he adopted a number of Jewish practices including the fast of Kippur and the prayer towards Jerusalem. The Jews, however, rejected with contempt the pretensions of the Gentile Prophet and opposed him on precisely the religious level where he was most sensitive.... Muhammad, realizing that no support was to be received from this quarter, later dropped the Jewish practices that he had adopted, substituted Mecca for Jerusalem as the direction of prayer, and generally gave a more strictly Arabian and national character to his faith.[63]

In fact, J. J. Saunders notes that Muhammad's acceptance of some Jewish rituals "failed to secure recognition from the Jews, whose rabbis taunted him with ignorance of their faith, and the Prophet's attitude changed to bitter hostility."[64] Likewise, Clare Alena Wilde shows that tradition records a universal rejection of Muhammad, among the variegated Jewish tribes in the region, saying, "The three notable Jewish tribes of Medina... were rather uniform in their rejection of Muhammad and his followers.... [thus] encounters with individual Jews in Muhammad's own lifetime are generally portrayed as unsatisfactory."[65] These interactions serve as the traditional explanation for the Qur'an's largely negative attitude towards Jews.

Muhammad, the Day of Atonement, and Ramadan

Having distanced himself from the Jews early in his ministry, then, it would be understandable that Muhammad would not display a nuanced understanding of Jewish theology. Yet despite this, central elements of Jewish and Christian history, theology, and practice—as he is said to have understood them—remained an integral part of Muhammad's teaching and self-understanding.[66] Of central concern to the current study is Mu-

63. Lewis, *Arabs in History*, 39.
64. Saunders, *History of Medieval Islam*, 27.
65. Wilde, *Approaches*, 180–81.
66. Schofield, *Emerging Scriptures*, 165, cites the Qur'an in several places, eliciting this conclusion, including Qur'an 46:9, which states, "Say, 'I am nothing new among God's messengers." Also, Qur'an 13:39, states, "There was a Scripture for every age: God erases or confirms whatever He will, and the source of the Scriptures is with

hammad's assimilation of post-temple Jewish observance of the Day of Atonement into Islamic theology. Abraham Katsh details the process, saying,

> At first Muhammad accepted the Day of Atonement as a day of fast. It was known as '*Ashura*,' meaning the tenth day and corresponding to the Jewish Day of Atonement, which occurs on the tenth of *Tishri*. Muhammad later substituted for it the month of Ramaḍan, and required every Moslem to fast a whole month.... It is probable that Muhammad took for his pattern the Jewish month of '*Elul* which precedes *Rosh Hashanah* and *Yom Kippur*, a month devoted to repentance and asking for forgiveness.[67]

Having already seen that post-70 CE Judaism had substituted repentance, prayer, fasting, and Torah reading for the temple-sacrifices, it is easy to see how seamlessly Muhammad was able to incorporate the Islamic holiday of Ramaḍan as a natural extension of Jewish practice. The resonances between the post-temple Day of Atonement rituals and the Islamic practices during Ramaḍan are unmistakable: Fasting, prayer, gifts of charity, and seeking forgiveness are all marks of this month, paralleling and extending the Jewish practices.[68] Without the need for animal sacrifice, the connection between the biblically prescribed presentation of blood-as-life and atonement might easily have gone unnoticed.

Taking this traditional development of history, Muhammad could claim to fulfill and extend Judaism without having to incorporate sacrificial blood. It is understandable, then, that contemporary Muslim writers, such as Ulfat Aziz-us-Samad, confidently assert, "We see no connection at all between sin and blood. What is necessary to wash away sin is not blood but repentance, remorse, persistent struggle against evil inclinations, development of greater sympathy for mankind and determination to carry out the will of God as revealed to us through the prophets."[69] Indeed, if Yom Kippur can be fulfilled by Ramadan without reference to sacrifice, the Christian doctrine of atonement through Christ's blood seems absurd at best.

Aziz-us-Samad summarizes contemporary Islamic disapproval of the Christian idea of the atoning blood of Christ, writing,

---

Him."

67. Katsh, *Judaism in Islam*, 128.
68. Al-Bukharī, *Sahih Al-Bukhari*, 438 §919; 435 §958, §959; 458 §972.
69. Aziz-us-Samad, *Islam and Christianity*, 54.

> The Christian scheme of salvation is not only morally and rationally unsound, but also has no support of the words of Jesus. Jesus may be said to have suffered for the sins of men in the sense that, in order to take them out of darkness into light, he incurred the wrath of the evildoers and was tortured by them; but that does not mean that his death was an atonement for the sins of others and that only those who believe in his blood would be forgiven. Jesus had come to rescue men from sin by his teaching and the example of his godly life, and not by deliberately dying for them on the cross and offering his blood as a propitiation for their sins.[70]

Likewise, Aziz-us-Samad cites the Qur'an in saying that God does not receive flesh and blood sacrifices; rather, he wants individuals to act in righteousness.[71] This attitude pervades contemporary Islamic teaching, despite the fact that it seems to neglect the precedent of blood-wrought atonement in the teaching of the Torah.

Summary: Fulfillment of Post-Biblical Judaism

In summary of the findings above and in following the traditional understanding of Muhammad's ministry, one traces modern denial of blood atonement and representative sacrifice back to the early misunderstanding of biblical Judaism. A myriad of Islamic approaches to the Bible and its teaching regarding atonement have arisen since the early days of Islam.[72] However, this survey of traditional material indicates that Islamic practice developed without apparent consultation of the prior revelations. Since nothing from post-temple Judaism's reconfiguration of the sacrificial system was left unfulfilled through the practices of Ramadan, early Islam could claim to stand in Judaism's stead without having to address

---

70. Aziz-us-Samad, *Islam and Christianity*, 55.

71. Aziz-us-Samad, *Islam and Christianity*, 54. See Qur'an 22:37.

72. Wasserstrom, *Between Muslim and Jew*, 149–52, discusses several Islamic approaches to the Bible, citing Muhammad Abu Bakr al-Razi's rejection of biblical sacrificial commands as being satanic in contrast to multiple others who approach biblical sacrifices and rituals allegorically. Further, Adang, *Muslim Writers*, 219, cites Ibn Hazm as an example of an Islamic scholar who seeks precedent in the Hebrew Scriptures for the Islamic concept of abrogation, or cancellation of previous divine revelation. Also, Accad, "Final Criterion," 231, highlights yet more examples of Islamic approach to the Bible in his citation of Ibn Taymiyya and Ibn Qayyam who search the biblical material for predictions of Muhammad's advent and support of Islamic practice.

its teachings regarding blood atonement. From an Orientalist perspective of the material, then, it might be said that Muhammad, ignorant of the true teaching of the HB, claimed that Ramadan supersedes Yom Kippur. One answer to the question "How does Islam explain the absence of Yom Kippur and sacrificial atonement?" then, is that it was a historically and biblically deficient understanding of Israelite religion that thus allowed Islam to make its claims of fulfillment of the Torah.

This conclusion, though derived from an understanding of history as narrated by the traditional Islamic perspective, results in a rather simplistic and pejorative view of the Qur'an. Not unlike some standard Orientalist opinions, it appears from this perspective that the Qur'an was mistaken or negligent in its treatment of previous revelation, and, as such, it left out teaching on blood atonement. While a more mature intertextual approach to the question may yield a similar conclusion— that the Qur'an is not interested in the symbolism of blood-as-life in the same way as the Hebrew Bible—it may be that dialogue between Jews, Christians, and Muslims might move forward on more congenial and respectful terms after inspection from a different angle. It may be that the Qur'an is actually self-consciously engaged with the biblical material that precedes it, and that its position on sacrifice and atonement is more nuanced than what would be indicated by the traditionally-informed understanding of its message given above.

Medina 2.0: An Intertextual Approach

While all of the information above follows the traditional telling of Islamic history, a historical-critical perspective reveals that major issues remain with interpretive methodologies that are based upon reading the Qur'an in light of the *sunnah* and *sira*. One major issue confronting the line of thought from the previous section is the complete lack of archeological or extra-Islamic evidence that there ever was a Jewish presence in Yathrib/Medina at the traditional time of Muhammad's emigration.[73] If the presence of a Jewish community practicing Yom Kippur as detailed above cannot be proven, the claim to patterning Ramadan after an expanded version of the *'ashura* fast is unverified and misguided.

---

73. Shoemaker, *Death of Prophet*, 248, notes, "Although the Islamic tradition describes a sizable Jewish community in Yathrib (Medina), its existence is not confirmed by any non-Islamic sources."

In order to provide a more nuanced and respectful approach, this chapter turns now to consider the qur'anic material as an intertextual conversation with the biblical and extra-biblical material that precedes it. In particular, this section will approach the Qur'an from the perspective suggested by Gabriel Said Reynolds in his book, *The Qur'an and Its Biblical Subtext*. In this work, Reynolds rejects the traditional Islamic and Orientalist presupposition that the *sira* gives an accurate account of Islamic origins.[74]

Instead, Reynolds proposes that the Qur'an appears to be much more of a dialogue with the Bible, utilizing biblical material and allusions in order to impact the reader in a certain manner and according to its own purposes.[75] In fact, it appears that the Qur'an is much more familiar with the biblical material than one following the traditional histories might be led to believe. The following section, then, will investigate shared vocabulary, concepts, and narrative as it pertains to atonement, sacrifice, and blood to illumine the manner in which the Qur'an claims to take up and transcend previous biblical material.

Qur'anic Teaching Regarding Sacrifice and Atonement

Throughout the Qur'an, one finds references to nearly all of the concepts discussed above regarding the HB teaching on atonement. At least four different words are used to refer to sacrifice, *qurban*, *nahar*, *dhabih*, *nusuk*.[76] Likewise, one finds the word group treated above that is trans-

---

74. Reynolds, *Qur'an*, 12–13, leaning on Wansborough, writes, "The stories which exegetes tell to explain the Qur'an are not historical records, but rather the literary product of a community developing a salvation history in an environment charged with sectarian rivalry.... I will argue that the Qur'an—from a critical perspective at least—should not be read in conversation with what came after it (*tafsīr*) but with what came before it (Biblical literature)." Here, the point has already been made that the *tafsīr* are dependent upon the *sira* for its historical orientation of the qur'anic material. This is suggested to be a false basis, and thus disorients subsequent explanation by way of a faulty origin.

75. Reynolds, *Qur'an*, 239, argues, "The Qur'an does not seek to correct, let alone replace, Biblical literature, but instead to use that literature for its homiletic exhortation.... For the Qur'an all that matters is the impact on the reader, the degree to which its discourse on these characters and places might lead the reader to repentance and obedience."

76. See Appendix C for a list of the qur'anic use of words for sacrifice: نُسُك، ذبح، نحر، قربان. It should also be noted that the word "*hadī*" هدي is used to refer to animals that are set apart for sacrifice, or sent on behalf of one who cannot complete the pilgrimage.

lated "atone" or "expiate." Additionally, the Qur'an includes discussion of ransom and the provision of purification. Perhaps the most obvious conceptual similarity between the sacrificial practice of Islam and Judaism comes from the annual Hajj sacrifice offered on the Feast of the Sacrifice, or 'id al-Aḍha. This feast commemorates the near-sacrifice of Abraham's son along with God's provision of a substitutionary sacrifice on behalf of the son of Abraham.[77]

While Judaism, Christianity, and Islam all tell this story in some form, Christians have understood it as a symbol of the advance of salvation history. Much extra-biblical literature has been produced by Christians offering embellishments upon this story and explaining it as an allegorical picture of God's willingness to save the lives of his people by providing a suitable substitute.[78] This is indeed a powerful image that does serve the Christian church with an important understanding of the theological claim to Christ's crucifixion and the atonement he achieved according to the Bible.

In light of this Christian understanding of the story, and perhaps overly anxious to find common ground, some Christian missionaries have seized upon the similarities between the Islamic story of Abraham's sacrifice and the biblical story as a way to explain Christ as the ultimate substitute.[79] For example, one of the most well-known Protestant mis-

See Qur'an 2:196 and 5:2, 97.

77. Most of the early commentators relate the story of Abraham's sacrifice to the biblical story and suggest that the substitutionary sacrifice was a ram. See Al-Ṭabari, "Tafsīr As-Saffaat." Al-Ṭabari's comments on Qur'an 37:107 begin stating that the sacrifice or ransom payment for Abraham's son was a great ram (جزيناه بأن جعلنا مكان ذبحه ذبح كبش عظيم،) before continuing on to give accounts of the various proponents of Isaac or Ishmael as the son Abraham almost sacrificed. Interestingly, one sees that, though later commentators conclude that the son is Ismaʻil, among the earliest jurists there were many who taught that Ishaq was the son who was offered. There does not appear to be any discussion of the ransom idea as being out of place, however the phrasing of Qur'an 37:107 seems to fit more with Christian theology than with Islamic understanding.

78. Geiger, *Monk's Topical Bible*, 234, records what St. Ephrem, the prolific Syrian author of the fourth century CE, wrote regarding Abraham's sacrifice, saying, "The ram hanging on the Sabek plant mystically redeemed Isaac alone. While the Lamb of God hanged on the cross delivered the world from Death and Hell." The conceptual proximity between ransom and redeem suggests that the qur'anic expression of this story might parallel already-existing Christian writings.

79. Indeed, though none of the early Muslim exegetes consulted in the research for this paper seem concerned with the use of "ransom," the language used in the Qur'an is evocative of Christian theology. (See Appendix D for qur'anic use of the word group

sionaries to engage the Muslim world, Samuel Zwemer, compares Yom Kippur to 'id al-Aḍha, insinuating that both Jews and Muslims cling to animal blood for atonement, while Christians rely on the eternal blood of Jesus for a better salvation.[80] Though this comparison merely serves as a background for Zwemer's intent to show Christ's sacrifice as better, 'id al-Aḍha is not intended to provide Muslims with the atonement promised by Yom Kippur. Instead, the rhetoric of the Qur'an suggests that 'id al-Aḍha serves as an ebenezer of remembrance that God has ushered in the final dispensation of revelation. As such, 'id al-Aḍha, not Ramadan, may be the Qur'an's answer to why Yom Kippur and sacrificial atonement do not feature in Islam. A study of the Qur'an's teaching related to sacrifice will help to bear this claim out.

Sacrificial Rites in the Qur'an

While sacrifice in the Qur'an does not result in the same kind of atonement as in the Hebrew Bible, it does in several places refer to animal

from "fadī" [فدي] meaning "ransom.") The majority of the conversation among the early jurists focuses on the question of which son is in view—Isma'īl or Ishaq. See Ibn Kathīr, "Tafsīr As-Saffaat"; and Tabari, "Tafsīr As-Saffaat." Perhaps one might find a fruitful path for further research in attempting to find precedent in Christian literature previous to the sixth century as a clue to reception history. Regardless, the context of the Qur'an makes it clear that Abraham and his son's faith were being tested in this act (Qur'an 37:106). Likewise, the following verse (37:108) indicates that this sacrifice is to be repeated throughout time until the day of resurrection. See Ali, Qur'an 37:103 footnote 4100. "Note that the sacrifice was demanded of *both* Abraham and Ismail. It was a trial of the will of the father and the son. . . . The whole thing is symbolical. God does not require the flesh and blood of animals (22:37), much less of human beings. But he does require the giving of our whole being to God, the symbol of which is that we should give up something very dear to us, if Duty requires that sacrifice." While this explanation focuses on the Qur'an's test of Abraham and his son's wills, the question yet lingers, "Why, when Abraham and his son had proven their intent to go through with the sacrifice, was there yet a need to sacrifice an animal?" This again indicates the possibility that the story has been handed down from Christian sources, though further research would be required to verify this.

80. Zwemer, "Atonement," 192, concludes, "The great day of Atonement, *Yom Kippur,* and the annual sacrifice at Mecca seem to have much in common. . . . The Jewish high-priest offered sacrifice for himself and for all the people annually, as not at Mecca there is the annual sacrifices. In both cases we have 'ordinances of divine service and a worldly sanctuary.'" Zwemer goes on to show that Christ is seen in the NT as a better sacrifice than bulls or goats, thus Islam and Judaism's sacrifices are not as good as Christ's.' While this is a helpful missiological direction, it presumes that Muslims are looking to their sacrifice for atonement. As will be shown below, this is not the case.

sacrifice. In fact, there are at least four words that appear throughout the Qur'an that refer to the process of slaughtering an animal ritually.[81] Perhaps the clearest example of qur'anic injunction to sacrifice is found in *Surat al-Kawthar* (108):2: "Hence, pray unto thy Sustainer [alone], and sacrifice [unto Him alone] (فَصَلِّ لِرَبِّكَ وَانْحَرْ)." Apart from this command, all other references found in the Qur'an are narrative accounts of slaughter or descriptions of sacrifices.[82]

Furthermore, examples of biblical stories of sacrifice are evoked throughout the Qur'an through references to Cain and Abel (*Surat al-Mā'idah* [5]:27), Abraham (*Surat as-Ṣaffāt* [37]:100–13), and Moses (*Surat al-Buqarah* [2]:67–71), though without the corresponding detail found in the biblical accounts. Thus, while the details or implications of animal sacrifice are not discussed at length in the Qur'an, it seems taken for granted that sacrifice is a legitimate means of worshipping God.[83] The references to previous instances of sacrifices also serve to instantiate the Qur'an's claim that God appoints particular sacrifices as a way of demonstrating and authenticating revelation.

Sacrifice as Distinction

The clearest explanation of the purpose of sacrifices in the Qur'an appears in *Surat al-Ḥajj* (22):34 and (22):67. In *Surat al-Ḥajj* (22):34, one reads, "To every people did we appoint rites (of sacrifice), that they might celebrate the name of God over the sustenance he gave them from animals (fit for food). But your God is one God: Submit your wills to Him (in Islam): and give thou the good news to those who humble themselves." Verse 67 includes the same recognition of the claim that certain forms of worship or sacrifice have been appointed to different groups of believers throughout time. One finds, then, that the Qur'an understands sacrifice to serve as a symbolic ritual or an outward expression of inward piety

---

81. See Appendix C for a list of sacrificial vocabulary present in the Qur'an.

82. As evidenced in Appendix C, occasionally words related to sacrifice are used in reference to non-sacrificial slaughter of living things (such as Qur'an 14:6, which refers to Pharaoh's killing of the sons of Israel) or as references to methods of worship in which sacrifice is included, but not always clear (as in the various uses of *nusuk* (نسك).

83. See, for example, the reference to sacrificial cattle and camels (البدن) as signs from God to be sacrificed in Qur'an 22:36–37. There is here no command to sacrifice, but rather instruction for saying the name of God over the animals in the process of sacrifice, which is assumed.

that is given to a people for a time to distinguish them as God's people. Thus, various sacrifices symbolize the provision of identity and legitimate worship to each dispensation of divine revelation.

This identifying function of sacrifice is further verified by the fact that the Hajj sacrifice is referred to as being among the "signs or symbols of God" (شعائر الله), which are understood to mark off particular groups of people for God.[84] Sacrificing an animal is seen in the Qur'an as an outward symbol of gratitude, trust, and worship of God. Further, it is a symbol that is given to each people in order that they might both worship and demonstrate their faithful allegiance to God.

Therefore, since the Qur'an claims that sacrifice serves as one of many acceptable forms of worship and as a way to distinguish the followers of a particular dispensation of revelation, it need not view sacrifice as substitutionary in any way. Thus, *Surat al-Ḥajj* (22):37 can assert, "It is not their meat not their blood that reaches God: it is your piety that reaches Him."[85] The blood of sacrifices in the Qur'an is not presented before God, nor does its manipulation feature anywhere in the text.

Animal sacrifice in the Qur'an, then, is not the provision of a ransoming and purifying substitute, but rather sacrifice is an act of piety by which a worshipper identifies as a member of a faith community marked by divine revelation and subsequent ritual. The piety exhibited by faithful keeping of sacrificial rituals, then, functions similarly to the acts, such as charity and fasting mentioned above, which result in atonement. Blood is explicitly incidental to the process of observing piety, yet a closer look to the Qur'an's teaching on blood provides a vista from which to see how the Qur'an claims continuity.

---

84. Ali, Qur'an 22:32, n2807. Ali says, "*Sha'air*, symbols, signs, marks by which something is known to belong to some particular body of men.... Here it seems to be applied to the rites of sacrifice. Such sacrifice is symbolical: it should betoken dedication of piety and heart." Likewise, verses 36–37 make this connection between sacrificial animals and signs of God (شعائر الله) more explicitly, saying, "The sacrificial camels We have made for you as among the Symbols from God." Again, referring to this section, Ali notes in footnote 2810 that, "This is the true end of sacrifice, not propitiation of higher powers, for God is One, and He does not delight in flesh or blood (22:37), but a symbol of thanksgiving to God by sharing meat with fellow men." See also the reference in Qur'an 5:2 to the symbols of God in connection with sacrifices and rituals of the Hajj.

85. Ali, Qur'an 22:37a. "لَن يَنَالَ اللَّهَ لُحُومُهَا وَلَا دِمَاؤُهَا وَلَٰكِن يَنَالُهُ التَّقْوَىٰ مِنكُمْ"

Blood in the Qur'an

The linchpin of the Hebrew concept of sacrificial atonement, as discussed above, is the role of blood as a substitutionary representation of life. This teaching of substitution and representation is vehemently denied in much Islamic scholarship.[86] However, in one area the Qur'an does echo the biblical material regarding blood. References to biblical teaching can be found in *Surat al-Ma'idah* (5):3, which, among other dietary laws, prohibits the consumption of meat with blood remaining in it.[87] In fact, the context in which this prohibition is found is strikingly similar to the prohibitions given to gentile Christians in Acts 15:29.[88]

This reference in Acts, however, hearkens back to the dietary laws given to the Israelite community at the foot of Mount Sinai, and specifically to Leviticus 17:10–16.[89] It is in this section of Leviticus that God

---

86. Along with the references above to scholarly rejection of the connection between blood and forgiveness, see Ali, Qur'an 22:34, footnote 2810, who writes, "This is the true end of sacrifice, not propitiation of higher powers, for God is One and He does not delight in flesh or blood (22:37), but a symbol of thanksgiving to God by sharing met with fellow-men. The solemn pronouncement of God's name over the sacrifice is an essential part of the rite." Likewise, Wasserstrom, *Between Muslim and Jew*, 149. Wasserstrom cites Islamic philosopher, Muhammad Abu Bakr Al-Razi, who rejects Leviticus' sacrificial scheme stating, "it is absurd to believe that God *needs* burnt sacrifices.... [so] these detailed biblical descriptions could only be satanic work."

87. Ali, Qur'an 5:3a, writes, "Forbidden to you (for food) are: dead meat, blood, the flesh of swine, and that on which hath been invoked the name of other than God; that which hath been killed by strangling or by a violent blow, or by a headlong fall, or by being gored to death; than which hath been (partly) eaten by a wild animal; that which is sacrificed on stone (altars)."

88. The one qur'anic distinction is that pork is included among the prohibitions, though this further points the reader back to the HB dietary code. Acts 15:29 states, "That you abstain from what has been sacrificed to idols, and from blood, and from what has been strangled, and from sexual immorality. If you keep yourselves from these, you will do well. Farewell." I am indebted to Dr. Gabriel Said Reynolds for making this connection. Similarly, Cuypers, *Banquet*, 84 points out that there are similarities between the qur'anic list and the prohibitions extended to the gentile believers in Acts 15.

89. Lev 17:10–16 includes prohibition against eating blood, eating meat from an animal that has died of natural causes, or by being killed by other animals. However, as shown above, Lev 17:11–12 reveals the logic of sacrifice in the eyes of God, connected to which is the explanation of the prohibition from consuming blood: "For the life of the flesh is in the blood, and I have given it for you on the altar to make atonement for your souls, for it is the blood that makes atonement by the life. Therefore, I have said to the people of Israel, no person among you shall eat blood, neither shall any stranger who sojourns among you eat blood." See also Cuypers, *Banquet*, 83, who,

gives the rationale for the prohibition against the consumption of blood: it is representative of the life of the animal that is given by God for making atonement. As such it is unfit for casual human consumption.

The Qur'an incorporates the biblical prohibitions, though it rejects the blood-as-life rationale given in Leviticus 17, insisting above that neither the blood nor the meat of sacrifices reaches God, providing only a symbol of the worshipper's piety.[90] That being so, one wonders why the Qur'an would maintain such seemingly arbitrary dietary laws? Why might the Qur'an focus on this particular issue when it elsewhere seems to intend to distance itself from the Levitical conception of sacrificial blood?

Blood and Rhetorical Analysis of Surat al-Mā'idah (5)

In fact, it may very well be that, on a rhetorical level, the Qur'an is here invoking central moments in biblical history in order to lay claim to a new and final stage of redemption history. In Acts, the gentiles who had come to faith in Jesus and received the Holy Spirit were received into the community of Jewish-background Christians with the dietary stipulations mentioned above. This served as a major development for the community of Jesus-followers as it officially broke the nationalist claim to being the covenant people of God. The book of Acts itself highlights the importance of this decision by recording it in duplicate.[91]

The community of Jesus-followers, then, has at this point in Acts transcended ethnic boundaries and become inclusive of all those who believe in Jesus. Many of the Jewish traditions and identifiers, such as

---

though recognizing the connection with the "Apostolic Decree" found in Acts, prefers to directly link the dietary laws to Deuteronomy due to the presence of the pork prohibition. While this is a correct impulse, it appears that the Qur'an is also intent upon reasserting the epoch-shifting scene in which the Christian community maintains an aspect of the previous law, while also advancing into a new stage in revealed history wherein the gentiles are included.

90. As has already been noted, Qur'an 22:37 distinguishes between the sacrificial meat/blood and the piety involved in the act of sacrificing and animal.

91. Acts 15:19–21 and Acts 15:28–29. The context of this ruling is a gathering of the Jerusalem council of apostles and leaders wherein they are deliberating about what customs are to be followed by the gentile believers. Specifically, this council was concerned with the necessity of circumcising gentile converts. The two tellings of this event noted here are first the council's declaration, and then the reading of the declaration to the churches and the gentile believers.

circumcision, then, are seen to be non-binding upon these gentile believers except for the prohibition against consuming blood, the meat of strangled animals or that which was offered to idols, and sexual immorality. Perhaps, then, this is the very intent of the passage in the Qur'an—to harken back to the time when heavenly religion took a leap forward—in order to capture the epoch-shifting power of gentile inclusion and leverage it similarly to indicate the advent of Islam.

This suggestion is further evidenced by the context of the prohibition against consuming blood in *Surat al-Mā'idah* (5):3, in the midst of which is the bold claim, "This day I have perfected your religion for you, completed my favor upon you, and have chosen for you Islam as your religion."[92] Michel Cuypers, whose book, *The Banquet*, analyzes *Surat al-Mā'idah* (5) rhetorically, indicates that this reference at the beginning of the *sura* connects to its conclusion where Jesus speaks of a banquet table that will come down from heaven and that will be for all generations.[93] Throughout the work, Cuypers shows that the reference in *Surat al-Mā'idah* (5):3 to "this day" upon which human religion is perfected, in the context of discussion regarding the Islamic pilgrimage, has become the reason for the celebration of *'id al-Aḍha*, which is viewed as "the celebration of Islam's day of completion for all, not just the Muslims, but also the Jews and Christians."[94] Thus, *Surat al-Mā'idah* (5) appears to be a foundational document for Islam and a summons to those under previous dispensations to convert to Islam as the divine perfection of religion.

Furthermore, throughout Deuteronomy the author employs the formulaic "this day/today" to indicate the people of God crossing a religious threshold by receiving YHWH's law and preparing to enter the promised land (Deut 4:20, 38–39; 6:6, 24; 7:11; 8:1; 9:1; 11:2). Thus, as the Qur'an employs this formula in *Surat al-Mā'idah* (5):3, the author intends to make the same epoch-shifting claim for its own revelation that was found for Israel in Deuteronomy and for Christians in Acts. In fact, Cuypers argues that the entire fifth *Sura* of the Qur'an is to be read

---

92. Ali, Quran 5:3b; See also Cuypers, *Banquet*, 81, who points to the central location of this claim to perfection in the midst of the dietary laws as a Semitic way of highlighting the claim. He goes on to show, through the rest of his work, that the reference to "Today" (اليوم, which is translated as "This day" by Ali as quoted in the text above) occurs three times in Qur'an 5, in reference to the day upon which God has completed and perfected religion.

93. Ali, Qur'an 5:114.

94. Cuypers, *Banquet*, 87.

through the lens of the claim that Islam is the perfection of religion in verse three, and subsequently as a summons to Christians and Jews.

Regarding the Jews, Cuypers demonstrates that the qur'anic employ of the formulaic use of "today" language intends to recall the great moments in Israel's history. The word "today" is used sixty-nine times throughout the book of Deuteronomy, usually to indicate a moment of salvation or adoption of the Jewish people through the direct act of God. Thus, along with the direct references to the Deuteronomic and Levitical codes of conduct and dietary laws, this passage invokes great moments of identification and divine "setting apart" in Israel's history.

Likewise discussing key moments in Christianity, then, *Surat al-Mā'idah* (5):114 has Jesus asking for a sacred table to be sent down from God as a sign for his people. While commentators have assigned this reference various meanings, Cuypers convincingly reveals a mature use of intertextuality, whereby the Qur'an depends upon John 6 and Jesus's claim to be the new manna that has come down from heaven.[95] The John 6 passage is left somewhat open-ended with a promise of provision, though Christian interpreters have regularly taken this to be a reference to the Eucharist.[96] The Qur'an, however, utilizes the open-ended promise of John 6 to offer itself as the bread from heaven that Jesus requested, claiming Islam as the perfection of all revealed religion and the hajj along with *'id al-Adha* as the ritual given to establish a pattern of worship suitable to the final dispensation of revelation.

Finally, Jesus refers to the coming feast as a feast for all generations that will serve as a sign for all humanity. Taking advantage of the fact that the account in John 6 of Jesus's discussion on bread coming from heaven does not immediately result in its fulfillment, the Qur'an is able to suggest that, though the Eucharist belonged to the Christians and the Passover belonged to the Jews, there is yet a more universal and perfect feast that has come to Islam. Thus, Islam's advent claims to be the perfection of

---

95. Cuypers, *Banquet*, 422, concludes, "Jesus' discourse in John 6 is a rereading of several Old Testament texts—the account of the manna in Exodus 16; Psalm 78 (itself a rereading of Exodus, v. 24 of which is quoted textually in John 6:31). This psalm sees the manna as the food of the messianic people, which for Christians has become an image of the Eucharistic feast, the main celebration of Christianity, a memorial of Jesus' Passover, prefigured by the Jewish Passover."

96. Cuypers, *Banquet*, 440. Cuypers connects John 6 as a prediction of the bread coming down from heaven with the Farewell Discourse, or high priestly prayer, of John 17 that takes place during the Last Supper, which is the setting for Jesus's establishment of the Eucharist in the Synoptic Gospels.

religion, and this is demonstrated to be from heaven through the institution of *'id al-Aḍha*, the means of worship given to the final form of people of God.

The Day of Atonement and *'id al-Aḍha*

The rhetorical connection between the dietary laws found in *Surat al-Mā'idah* (5):3 and the introduction of a feast for all generations, promised by Jesus himself in *Surat al-Mā'idah* (5):114 allows Cuypers to posit, "The feast *par* excellence [*'id al-Aḍha*] will be the celebration of Islam's day of completion for all, not just the Muslims, but also the Jews and Christians. The everlasting feast announced by Jesus at the end of the *Sura* will then be supplanted by the celebration of the pilgrimage mentioned at the beginning."[97] Thus, the Feast of the Sacrifice or *'id al-Aḍha* serves as a reminder of both the return to a pre-Jewish and pre-Christian practice of the faith of Abraham, while also providing the emerging religion of Islam with a sacrifice by which it might distinguish itself.[98]

More than merely distinguishing itself, however, the fifth *Sura* of the Qur'an claims Islam and its sacrifice supersede and complete previous revelation and sacrifice, as has already been seen. To this point, Cuypers summarizes his treatment of the *Sura*, saying, "Thus the final monotheistic religion to arrive revives the common past of the three, and in this way is able to both claim temporal primacy and completion for itself, making other, intermediary worship obsolete."[99] Thus, the reference to blood in the Qur'an that most closely resembles the teaching of the Bible is used to evoke and transcend common history.

If this is the case, then, the prohibition of blood in the Qur'an is not tied to its sacred ability to represent life before God as in the Hebrew Bible or the New Testament's teaching regarding Jesus's blood. Instead, this prohibition is a rhetorical move as much as an instance of dietary

---

97. Cuypers, *Banquet*, 87.

98. See Ali, Qur'an 22:34a: "To every people did We appoint rites (of sacrifice), that they might celebrate the name of God over the sustenance that He gave them from animals (fit for food)." Also Ali, Qur'an 22:67a: "To every People have We appointed rites and ceremonies [منسكًا] which [*sic*] they must follow." Further, see Cuypers, *Banquet*, 463, who writes, "The Mecca festival existed before Islam, but the Prophet maintained it, giving it a new meaning, joining it to the recollection of Abraham's sacrifice (Which Christian tradition prefigures as Christ's)."

99. Cuypers, *Banquet*, 463.

law. Here one finds the summation of the Qur'an's sustained claim to be the final religion that confirms and completes all that has come before it. This also makes sense of the otherwise strange implementation of the *hajj* sacrifice. If, following the Qur'an's own idea that God grants a sacrifice or means of worship to each dispensation, it may very well be that the *hajj* sacrifice is the annual reminder of Islam's claim to being the final revelation, the final paradigm shift in revealed religion. As such, it is as much a reminder of the final religious threshold that has been crossed by the emergence of Islam as a commemoration of Abraham's faith.

By reading the Qur'an with the expectation that it is intentionally engaging in an intertextual dialogue with previous Scripture, then, one sees that it is self-consciously unconcerned with the rationale given for the sacrifices as practiced in Israel. Rather than viewing itself as being necessarily tied to that which has come prior to it, it appears to treat Judaism and Christianity as distinct dispensations, demarcated by their own sacrificial celebrations. For Islam, then, the necessity to fulfill Yom Kippur is not in mind as much as the necessity to establish that there is a specific Islamic sacrifice that is indicative of a new dispensation in revealed religion. Where the traditional material leads one to conclude that a biblically uninformed Muhammad instituted Ramadan as an Islamic counterpart to Yom Kippur, an intertextual approach sees the Qur'an as being very intentionally in dialogue with biblical concepts of sacrifice.

The claim that is made by the Qur'an, then, is not that the *'id al-Aḍha* sacrifice provides the atonement promised to the Israelites through Yom Kippur. Instead, this sacrifice, as seen through the rhetoric of the Qur'an, is the definitive symbol of the perfect and final dispensation of revelation that has been given to Islam. Rather than a ritual that effects atonement, then, *'id al-Aḍha* serves Islam as an ebenezer of its Abrahamic origins, prior to Judaism and Christianity, and perfect in its finality.

Summary

It appears, then, that whether one takes the view of Islamic origins provided by the *Sira* (the authorized biography of Muhammad's life) or whether one sees the Qur'an as a sort of homiletical treatment of biblical material, the Levitical perspective on blood has not been incorporated into Islam *per se*. The *Sira*-driven Orientalist perspective tends to rely on the presence of Jews who had already given a theological definition to their sacrificial system. Therefore, Ramadan can replace Yom Kippur without having to deal with blood. However, if one investigates the Qur'an as a conversation with biblical literature, one sees that perhaps the Qur'an is not interested in taking up Yom Kippur or atoning sacrifice into its own context as much as it is with establishing that, having crossed the final religious threshold, a new pattern of acceptable worship has descended from God to those who would follow Islam.

On either approach, this paper's question, "What didn't Muhammad borrow from Judaism?" is answered, at least in part, with a recognition that Islam does not incorporate substitutionary blood into the logic of its sacrificial ritual or theology. While the Qur'an offers ways to forgiveness and purification, it does not do so by following the same logic as espoused in the Hebrew Bible regarding the ransom-purging effected by blood. Likewise, while animal sacrifice is practiced, it is viewed to be a religious ritual that identifies a faith-community and that is accepted by God, though, again, not on the basis of substitutionary and atoning blood.

Ultimately, the qur'anic treatment of the biblical teaching regarding the importance of blood will likely remain unsatisfactory within the Jewish or Christian understanding of redemption history. However, this chapter has sought to understand the Qur'an's own logic of sacrifice in order to advance interreligious dialogue and mutual understanding. While all three of the Abrahamic faiths treat the idea of sacrifice differently, the concept of sacrificial ritual remains a part of all three teachings. Perhaps, as evidenced by Zwemer's superficial comparison of Yom Kippur and 'id al-Aḍha, the similarities between the faiths and their respective rituals have at times obscured the distinctive teachings or meaning behind them.[100]

As this chapter has labored to show, despite the presence of sacrifice in Islam, the understanding of the ritual is vastly different than that of ancient Israel's Yom Kippur. Where Judaism and subsequently Christianity have held together the concepts of sacrifice and atonement based upon the logic of blood-as-life, the Qur'an has rejected blood-as-life while maintaining the concepts of sacrifice and atonement separately. Because blood-as-life serves as a linchpin for Jewish and Christian theology of atonement and sacrifice, Islam's removal of this teaching radically redefines the concepts of sacrifice and atonement.

100. Zwemer, "Atonement," 192.

While Christian theology maintains the importance of blood-as-life in its conception of Christ's eternal atoning blood offered in the heavenly tabernacle as the fulfillment of Yom Kippur (Heb 10), the Qur'an employs sacrifice as a means of establishing its own uniqueness and veracity as a heavenly religion. In this way, the Qur'an appears to treat history episodically, while the Bible presents a continuous narrative. For the Christian missiologist explaining atonement, it is crucial to understand that the distinction between the Bible and the Qur'an or Christianity and Islam is not merely one of competing rituals, but of the competing stories that stand behind the rituals.

Conclusion

This chapter began by asking, "What *didn't* Muhammad borrow from Judaism?" While one finds difficulty confirming instances of Islamic borrowing from previous religions, it is relatively easier to demonstrate the absence of Jewish or Christian elements in qur'anic teaching. In order to provide the broadest treatment, this chapter consulted both traditional historical accounts and emerging historical-critical approaches to the Qur'an. Having focused on both linguistic and thematic elements of both the Hebrew Bible and the Qur'an, it became evident that significant differences exist between the two traditions regarding the process and logic of atonement. The locus of these differences is the divergent understanding of the role of blood.

The Hebrew Bible depicts blood as a substitutionary representation of life that, when offered to God through the sacrificial ritual of Yom Kippur, serves as a ransom for sin (a mitigated penalty accepted by God instead of the forfeited life of the impure or the sinner) and also an agent of cleansing (in that it represents life that exerts power over the pollution of death). The Qur'an, however, utilizes sacrifice to symbolize a distinct approach to worship given specifically by God to Islam, as the final dispensation of revealed religion. Blood does not play a special role in Islamic tradition nor in the Qur'an because sacrifice is merely one of several expressions of one's piety.

For the Christian missiologist, seeking to clearly articulate the Christian perspective of atonement, then, it is crucial to hear the stories being told by one's audience prior to assuming that communication has occurred. Though similar words might feature in the theology of each faith, one must be aware that those words are freighted with different meaning according to the narrative of each faith. Comprehension of the Christian concept of atonement requires more than shared vocabulary. It requires telling and retelling the stories through which meaning is apprehended.

It is this recognition of the importance of narrative-driven conceptual understanding that drives the following chapter to consider the worldview level effects of the Qur'an's teaching on sacrifice, atonement, and blood. Having discussed two potential qur'anic answers to the question of continuity with the *tawrah* and *injil*, chapter 5 will follow the same procedure as the previous two chapters, seeking to dig out the assumed worldview foundations of the Qur'an to consider whether or not they are compatible with the biblical narrative and subsequent worldview. Ultimately, the following chapter will demonstrate that the Qur'an's claim to continue biblical revelation is, at best, radically different than the continuity exhibited by the book of Hebrews.

5

Hebrews and the Qur'an
Conflicting Worldviews and the Narratives That Form Them

As INDICATED IN THE introduction, the purpose of this project is to argue that the book of Hebrews can be used to explain atonement in Christ to an audience influenced by the Qur'an. To argue this, it has been necessary to investigate the concept of atonement and its component parts as they appear in Leviticus, in Hebrews, and in the Qur'an. Thus chapter 2 extrapolated Leviticus' teaching on atonement through the lens of Yom Kippur and chapter 3 concluded that the book of Hebrews portrays the Christ event as the perpetual fulfilment of Yom Kippur. Along with attention to the doctrine of atonement in Leviticus and Hebrews, chapters 2 and 3 also considered atonement's role in shaping the narrative and subsequent worldview of the reader of each respective text.

Turning to the concept of atonement in the Qur'an, however, chapter 4 demonstrated that one encounters several difficulties equating atonement in the Bible to the concept of atonement as it appears in the Qur'an. The fact that the Qur'an and Bible use the same word (*kaffara*) differently causes problems of understanding at a lexical level. Furthermore, when one considers the component parts of the Day of Atonement discovered in Leviticus and Hebrews—sacrifice, forgiveness/ransom, purification, and blood—one finds each aspect in the Qur'an performing a different function. Most centrally, chapter 4 highlighted the fact that for the Qur'an, blood does not function as the conceptual linchpin holding together the logic of sacrifice, forgiveness/ransom, and purification.

Chapter 4 labored to show how the Qur'an separates sacrifice, forgiveness, and purification into different rituals. In so doing, the Qur'an tells and participates in an alternative metanarrative, implicitly producing an alternative worldview.

Furthermore, due to the Qur'an's claim to continue and complete the revelation found in the *Tawrah* and *Injil*, this project has sought answers to how the Qur'an can sustain such a claim while maintaining an understanding of sacrifice that is much different than that which one finds in Leviticus and Hebrews. This book intends to avoid the pejorative conclusions that might be reached by the Orientalist approach outlined in chapter 4 as Medina 1.0: that the Qur'an is merely ignorant of the robust array of biblical concepts related to atonement, and has thus overlooked Yom Kippur and the role of blood in Leviticus as it claims to continue and complete the *Tawrah*.

Instead, this chapter builds upon the previous chapter's conclusion showing that the qur'anic claim to completion works from a different understanding of the world that can be unearthed by investigation at the point of the qur'anic narration of Abraham's sacrifice and the subsequent prescription of the *'id al-Adha* sacrifice. Furthermore, building the larger argument of this project, this chapter argues that the overarching biblical narrative (OBN) presented through Hebrews can be used to overcome the communication barriers that exist at the lexical, ritual, and worldview level, while demonstrating the Christ event's continuity with a biblical understanding of sacrificial atonement, thus challenging the Qur'an's claim to continuity with prior revelation.

Therefore, following the conclusions of Medina 2.0 and attempting to maintain continuity with chapters 2 and 3, the present chapter will draw upon theologian N. T. Wright's six "worldview" questions in order to discern the implicit worldview foundations that undergird the Qur'an's claim that sacrificial rites function differently than they do in the biblical material. Rather than serving an atoning function in the biblical sense, sacrifice in the Qur'an is a ritual of demarcation, separating dispensations of divine revelation from one another and giving divine approval to the religion proceeding from the sacrifice. In light of the divergence between the biblical and Quranic conceptions, therefore, it behooves the Christian communicator to consider the way the Qur'an tells and uses the story of Abraham's sacrifice in its doctrinal, ritual, and narrative forms prior to speaking of Christ's crucifixion as a fitting continuity thereof.

The Akedah and Atonement

Focusing on Abraham's sacrifice in the Qur'an, or what is known as the Akedah (Akedah translated from the Hebrew means "binding," as in Abraham "bound" his son Isaac and placed him on the altar for sacrifice; see Gen 22:9) in Jewish tradition, serves the purposes of this book on multiple levels.[1] First of all, this story features in the Torah, in Hebrews, and in the Qur'an.[2] Thus, this common story affords a helpful starting point from which to trace the divergent trajectories of Hebrews and the Qur'an as they incorporate this micronarrative in their respective metanarratives.

For example, Hebrews 11 utilizes the Akedah micronarrative as a vignette concerning one who exhibited radical faith in the promises of God that culminate in Christ.[3] While in the context of Hebrews 11 the Akedah is not overtly connected to Jesus's death, it serves the author as an example of a moment within God's progressive revelation of his plans to one day fulfill his promises in Christ as Hebrews 12:2 makes explicit.[4] For the Qur'an, however, the Akedah provides the prototypical response of submission (*islam*) to God and provides a summons to the reader to submit to the perfected and final version of Abraham's faith in Islam.[5] Such a divergence in the subsequent interpretation and metanarrative trajectories of Hebrews and the Qur'an provides a point at which to assess each text's claim to continuity with prior revelation.

Second, many of Christianity's leading historical theologians—including a number of early church fathers—have viewed the Akedah as foreshadowing Christ's substitutionary death.[6] In a book entitled *Inheriting Abraham*, Jon Levenson highlights this tendency, writing, "The Sacrifice of Isaac served as a key resource by which the early church developed its understanding of the role of Jesus, and especially his death, in the

---

1. Levenson, *Inheriting Abraham*, 66.
2. See Gen 22:1–19; Heb 11:17–19; Qur'an 37:100–13.
3. Lane, *Hebrews 9–13*, 361–63.
4. Lane, *Hebrews 9–13*, 363.
5. Qur'an 5:3.
6. Lane, *Hebrews 9–13*, 363, recognizes this history of interpretation while also acknowledging that the context of Heb 11 does not make such an explicit connection to Christ's sacrificial death. Making the same point regarding the history of interpretation, see also Attridge, *Hebrews*, 334.

history of salvation."[7] Commenting on Genesis 22, Kenneth Mathews likewise acknowledges that some NT scholars assume the Akedah story to foreshadow atonement in Christ, writing, "The relationship between the Jewish Akedah interpreted as expiatory and Paul's doctrine of forgiveness of sin by faith in the atoning blood of Christ has been an important topic among scholars."[8] Thus, there is a history of interpretation within Christian theology that sees the Akedah as being related to atonement in Christ.

What is important for the current project, however, is to recognize that without the intervening narrative, particularly the prescription for the Day of Atonement recorded in Leviticus 16–17, one does not find warrant to consider the biblical story of the Akedah in Genesis 22 an account of atonement. Mathews highlights this insight strongly, writing, "There is a fundamental theological difference between the substitutionary doctrine of Christ's atonement and the developed Jewish Akedah, so that a simple exchange of Abraham for God and Isaac for Christ is not a satisfactory explanation for Paul's soteriology."[9] This is not to say that the Akedah cannot serve a preparatory role for the subsequent stages of the history of redemption, but rather that one must be cautious about jumping from Abraham and Isaac to Christ without intervening explanation. Such a jump is not without precedent in Christian missions among Muslim populations.[10]

Additionally, since sacrifice is a component part of the Christian concept of atonement, it will prove important to consider the ritual function of sacrifice in the Qur'an prior to assuming conceptual similarity. As the previous chapter demonstrated, the Qur'an seizes upon the story of Abraham's sacrifice and the subsequent ritual of *'id al-Adha* as an opportunity to receive its own distinguishing ritual as a sign from God that Islam is the perfection of religion (*Surat al Mā'ida* [5]:3). The Qur'an

---

7. Levenson, *Inheriting Abraham*, 66.

8. Mathews, *Genesis 11:27*, 304.

9. Mathews, *Genesis 11:27*, 305.

10. This tendency to jump from Abraham and Isaac to Jesus is exhibited clearly in the work of Masri in his book, *Adha and Injeel*, 14. Signaling this jump, Masri writes, "Since Christians believe in both the Passover and the Adha events, why don't they celebrate them? Is there a Christian Passover too? To answer these questions, we need to look in the 'Injeel' (the New Testament) and examine its teachings on the character of God and His plan for mankind." See also from a more polemic angle, Shamoun, "Where is the Blood?"

does not commend this sacrifice as a means of atonement that can be paralleled to the biblical concept and ritual. Rather, in commending such an annual sacrifice, the Qur'an intends to separate observers of 'id al-Adha from the adherents of prior revelations.

Ultimately, the Qur'an intends to point through Abraham to Muhammad. Thus, reference to Abraham in prescribing 'id al-Adha as a commemoration of the Qur'an's account of the Akedah is incidental except for the convenience of referencing a sacrifice that precedes the revealed religions the Qur'an is attempting to supersede. In using the story of the Akedah to tell a different story than the Bible tells, the Qur'an affords the reader ritual (symbols and praxis), doctrine (answers to questions), and narrative material (story) required by N. T. Wright by which to access its worldview.[11]

Sacrifice, Metanarrative, Worldview, and Continuity

In extrapolating the underlying worldview of Leviticus and Hebrews, the previous chapters have utilized N. T. Wright's analogy of the foundation of a house to illustrate the concept of worldview. For Wright, a worldview functions as the formative but often unnoticed substructure that supports the more visible components of a system of faith, such as rituals, stories, and doctrines.[12] Chapters 2 and 3 argued that the book of Hebrews extends and expands upon the worldview foundations laid by Leviticus and the Yom Kippur ritual while yet incorporating all the component parts in its exposition of the Christ event. Thus, the book of Hebrews claims and demonstrates continuity with the Hebrew Bible by projecting Leviticus' prescriptions for Yom Kippur on Jesus as the great high priest and the perfect sacrifice (Heb 9–10).

The purpose of the present chapter, then, is to revisit what the preceding chapters have concluded about the Qur'an's claim to continuity by

---

11. Wright, *People of God*, 123–24; see also Smart, *Worldviews*, 8, who distinguishes six categories by which to assess worldview: doctrinal, narrative, ethical, ritual, experiential, and social. While these categories are helpful for further distinction, one might easily consider the social and experiential elements as coming under the ritual dimension. Likewise, the ethical dimension can be treated under the doctrinal dimension. Therefore, this project leans on Wright's more streamlined approach including Smart's dimensions as components of Wright's broader categories.

12. Wright, *People of God*, 117.

uncovering its implicit worldview through its incorporation of sacrifice into its metanarrative. In the process of uncovering the Qur'an's worldview, then, multiple barriers to communication emerge. Such barriers emerge from the Qur'an's alternative understanding of the Akedah and are exacerbated by its prescription of *'id al-Adha* as a symbol of distinction. Thus, the Qur'an's use of the Akedah narrative offers a glimpse into its underlying worldview and its metanarrative that is in conflict with the worldview and metanarrative of Hebrews.

Sacrifice in the Qur'an and Wright's Worldview Questions

In order to understand the extent of the divergence exhibited in the metanarratives of the Qur'an and the book of Hebrews, it remains for this project to make the worldview of the Qur'an explicit. Since chapter 4 showed that the Qur'an imports different meaning into the shared story of the Akedah, the following section will inspect the effect that such a narrative alteration has on the Qur'an's worldview through the lens of *'id al-Adha*.

To maintain a consistent approach, this section will pose N. T. Wright's worldview questions to the Qur'an, focused particularly on its narration of Abraham's sacrifice (*Surat as-Saffat* [37]) and the annual commemoration thereof that takes place during the Islamic ritual of *'id al-Adha* (*Surat al-Mā'ida* [5] and *Surat al-Hajj* [22]). Though many similarities might emerge as each text answers the worldview questions, this section focuses primarily on the distinctive answers that the Qur'an and Hebrews offer in order to highlight the communication barriers that the Christian must overcome in order to explain the role of the Christ event as an eternal, atoning sacrifice.

Who Are We?

The first of Wright's questions is a question of identity: Who are we? Perhaps the most basic answer that the Qur'an gives to this question is not far removed from a biblical answer: a human is created by God to be a servant (عبد) and steward/vicegerent (خليفة).[13] One finds the voca-

---

13. These two roles provide a summary of humanity's responsibility on earth for

tion of vicegerent in the creation account recorded in *Surat al-Baqarah* (2):30a, which states, "Behold, thy Lord said to the angels, "I will create a vicegerent on earth.""[14] Furthermore, in *Surat al-Dhariyat* (51):56, the Qur'an makes the human role of servant clear, stating, "I have only created Jinns and men, that they may serve me."[15]

While a full treatment of qur'anic anthropology is beyond the scope of this project, these two functions of vicegerent and servant emerge from the Qur'an's version of the Akedah narrative. The most complete narration of the Akedah story, *Surat as-Saffat* [37]:99–113, involves Abraham being commended as a model representative of belief in God as is recorded throughout the account.[16] Therefore, in telling the Akedah story as a story of Abraham's faithfulness to submit to God, the Qur'an employs Abraham as one in whom both vocations are satisfied.

Divergence: Qur'an Followers

While neither of the vocations mentioned above are foreign to the teaching of the Bible, the Qur'an diverges from Hebrews in an important identity-giving way through its prescription to keep the '*id al-Adha* sacrifice as an annual ritual. As such an exemplar, however, the Qur'an capitalizes on Abraham's pre-Jewish and pre-Christian faithfulness in claiming supersession of both. The conclusion reached in chapter 4 is that the sacrifice of Abraham in the Qur'an, repeated annually as '*id al-Adha*, is part of the rehearsal of the summons to submit to Islam as the perfect religion (See *Surat al-Mā'ida* [5]:3). In fact, Gabriel Said Reynolds concludes that the Qur'an's purpose in linking contemporary believers to Abraham is to highlight Abraham's role as a prototype for the Qur'an's own prophet.[17]

Hanapi, "Conceptual Elements," 50. As a scholar of Islamic worldview, and in addressing humanity's purpose through the lens of the Qur'an, Hanapi writes, "Man is to function as a servant ([*Surat*] *al-Dhariyat* [51]:56) and *khalifa* of Allah SWT on this earth ([*Surat*] *al-Buqqarah* [2]:30)."

14. Qur'an 2:30a: وَإِذْ قَالَ رَبُّكَ لِلْمَلَائِكَةِ إِنِّي جَاعِلٌ فِي الأَرْضِ خَلِيفَةً

15. Qur'an 51:56: وَمَا خَلَقْتُ الْجِنَّ وَالْإِنسَ إِلَّا لِيَعْبُدُونِ

16. Qur'an 37:85, Abraham confronts his idolatrous father about his polytheism; Qur'an 37:94–96, Abraham confronts his community about their idolatry; Qur'an 37:102–103, Abraham and his son both submit their wills to God. In narrating this story, then, Abraham both represents God as a vicegerent (خليفة) who calls others to worship rightly and who himself serves God as a slave (عبد).

17. Reynolds, *Qur'an*, 86–87.

By connecting themselves to Abraham, then, *Surat al-Mā'ida* encourages observers of *'id al-Adha* to connect themselves further to the Qur'an and its prophet. The question "Who are we?" provokes the Qur'an to answer, "We are the people of Abraham's religion, though through the final revelation of the Qur'an and its prophet."

Hebrews, on the other hand, links its audience through Abraham to Jesus. In Hebrews 11:17–19, Abraham's story is told as an example of one who believes God to be faithful to unfold his promises. For Hebrews 11, the account of the Akedah is one episode in the progressive revelation of God's faithfulness to fulfill his promises. As Harold Attridge notes, Hebrews 11 recounts faithful recipients of the progressive revelation of God's promises that culminates in Hebrews 12:1–3 where Jesus stands as the end to which God's promises point.[18] Therefore, with the Akedah included in the long list of exemplars of the faith, Hebrews 11 answers the question "Who are we?" by claiming that the faithful to whom the letter is addressed are the people of God in Christ.

Where Are We?

Wright's second worldview question focuses on the nature and history of the world. Again, the Qur'an's answer to this second question exhibits both consonance and dissonance with biblical teaching. While there are questions as to what exactly the Qur'an teaches regarding the intent of earth (was earth to be humanity's domain, or was it the place of post-fall punishment?), the basic fact that the earth and the heavens are created by God are tenets held in common between both texts.[19] However, the more

---

18. Attridge, *Hebrews*, 354–55, connects the faithful witnesses of chapter 11 with the cloud of witnesses who both received God's testimony and promises in their lives, and now who bear witness to God's faithfulness. Their faith was ultimately founded in and perfected by Jesus, despite being chronologically prior. As Heb 11:13–16 indicates, these forefathers and foremothers looked into the future without seeing the details, but believing in God's faithfulness to his promises.

19. In reading the account of the fall found in Qur'an 2:30–39 one sees that humanity is created in a garden from which they are cast down to earth. However, in the same section, God declares his intention to create vicegerents on earth. It is difficult to say whether man was intended to dwell on earth, or whether earth is a punishment for the fall. See Reynolds, *Qur'an*. Elsewhere, in *Surat al-Dhariyat* [51]:47–48, God claims, "With power and skill did we construct the firmament: for it is we who create the vastness of space. And we have spread out the (spacious) earth; how excellently do we spread it out!" Qur'an 51:47–48: وَالسَّمَاءَ بَنَيْنَاهَا بِأَيْدٍ وَإِنَّا لَمُوسِعُونَ وَالْأَرْضَ فَرَشْنَاهَا فَنِعْمَ الْمَاهِدُونَ

specific answer that the Qur'an gives through the command to observe *'id al-Adha* proves to be another point of divergence from the worldview assumptions of Hebrews.

Divergence: Mount Moriah Versus Mount Zion

As seen above, the Qur'an praises Abraham as a *muslim* before the coming of either Judaism or Christianity. Explicitly in *Surat al-'Imran* [3]:67, the Qur'an states, "Abraham was not a Jew nor yet a Christian; but he was true in Faith, and bowed his will to God's (which is Islam), and he joined not gods with God."[20] As followers of the Qur'an perform the *hajj* ritual and the reenactment of Abraham's sacrifice, then, they metaphorically stand on Mount Moriah with Abraham, imitating his commendable submission to God and practicing the fullness of his primordial religion. Thus, when one looks backwards in time and metaphorically stands with Abraham on Mount Moriah, the result is to stand with the predecessor of Islam before the coming of the Qur'an.

In contrast, the book of Hebrews calls its readers to envision themselves approaching a different mountain: Mount Zion (Heb 12:22). This summons to Mount Zion serves to push the reader forward to the time to when the heavenly dwelling of God will descend to also be the dwelling place of man.[21] Thus, as chapter 3 argued, in considering the atoning sacrifice of the Christ event, the book of Hebrews calls its audience to approach Mount Zion as a way of anticipating to God's dwelling with man in the future.[22] The Qur'an, on the other hand, answers the question, "Where are we?" by calling its readers to look backward in time and to stand on the biblical Mount Moriah.

---

20. Qur'an 3:67: ما كانَ إِبْراهيمُ يَهودِيًّا وَلا نَصْرانِيًّا وَلٰكِنْ كانَ حَنيفًا مُسْلِمًا وَما كانَ مِنَ الْمُشْرِكينَ One of the words used to describe Abraham in this verse is *muslima* (مُسْلِمًا) which means "submitted one" as an adjective. This is the source of the word commonly used to identify followers of the Qur'an as Muslims.

21. Attridge, *Hebrews*, 374, comments on Hebrews 12:22 saying, "The first of the series of eight items to which they draw nigh is 'Mount Zion' (Σιὼν ὄρει). Zion, of course, was, since the establishment of the Davidic monarchy, the traditional locus of God's presence on earth, ether by itself or in close association with Jerusalem as a whole."

22. Attridge, *Hebrews*, 374, highlights the apocalyptic function of Hebrews' reference to Zion, saying, "Hebrews similarly relies on traditional apocalyptic imagery and uses it to contrast the old and the new."

What Is Wrong?

While Hebrews and the Qur'an exhibit some similarity in answering the previous two questions, they offer radically divergent answers to the next two questions. For the Qur'an, the source of humanity's problem is human ignorance and inability to remember God's ways. The Qur'an combats ignorance and forgetfulness throughout, from its narration of the fall,[23] to its claims about itself as a book of reminders.[24] Highlighting ignorance and forgetfulness as the source of human problems within the Qur'an, Shia theologian Seyyed Hossein Nasr states, "Islam addresses the human being not primarily as will, but as intelligence. If the great sin in Christianity is disobedience, which has warped the will, the great sin

---

23. Perhaps the clearest point at which one sees the problem of sin in the Qur'an comes from the account of Adam and Hawa's sin recorded both in *Surat al-Baqarah* (2):35-36 and in greater detail in *Surat aṭ Ṭaḥa* (20):115-124. According to *Surat al-Buqarah* (2):36 Adam and his wife were deceived by the *shaytan* (الشيطن), and the result is that God forced them to depart from "the state (of felicity) in which they had been. Immediately after God forces Adam to depart from the garden, *Surat al-Baqarah* (2):37 states, "Then learnt Adam from his lord words of inspiration, and his Lord turned towards him; for He is Oft-Returning, Most Merciful." The account in *Surat aṭ Ṭaḥa* (20):123 is rendered more explicitly as, "He said: 'Get ye down, both of you—all together, from the Garden, with enmity One to another: but if, as is sure, there comes to you Guidance from me, whosoever Follows my guidance will not lose his way, nor fall into misery.'" Therefore, if what Adam required after the fall from felicity was knowledge, the Qur'an indicates that humanity's problem is rooted in a lack of knowledge or forgetfulness.

24. In *Surat as-Sad* (38):1, the Qur'an refers to itself as a book for reminding people of God's ways: "And the Qur'an, this is the reminder." The English recorded here is the author's translation of Qur'an 38:1: وَالْقُرْآنِ ذِي الذِّكْرِ. Yusef Ali translates this verse as, "By the Qur'an, full of Admonition (this is the Truth)." However, Reynolds also follows the author translating الذكر as "the reminder." See Reynolds, *Qur'an*, 235. Likewise, and further confirming the fickleness of human memory as the source of humanity's problem throughout the corpus of the Qur'an, one might appeal to the ubiquity of the Arabic root *dhkr* (ذكر), by which the Qur'an calls its audience to "remember" God's law and the words of former prophets. This verb appears nearly one hundred times throughout the Qur'an as an appeal to remember what God has said in order to please him, to avoid punishment, and to live rightly. See the Qur'an study tool, the Qur'an Corpus: the root ذكر occurs 108 times in the Qur'an. Of those occurrences, 96 are references to the verb "remember" and its derivatives; On this point, see Reynolds, *Qur'an*, 236, who writes, "Thereby the Qur'an, 'the reminder,' fulfills the role of the homilist. The homilist brings to mind that which his audience once knew, but due to the human tendency to forget (Q. 2.44; 6.68; 7.53; 9.67, passim), no longer heeds."

in Islam is forgetfulness and the resulting inability of the intelligence to function in the way that God created it as the means to know the One."[25]

Reinforcing this point, Islamic scholar Annemarie Schimmel summarizes the Qur'an's position on the human problem, setting it against the Christian doctrine of original sin, writing, "Man, despite his ignorance and weakness, accepted the *amana* [a "trust" from God] (Sura 33/72).... This means to observe history and nature; one's own heart and soul can lead the way to a deeper religious understanding. Warnings and lessons from history and from nature may help reveal the right path; such insights can be applied to one's own life."[26] Thus, the problem facing mankind from the perspective of the Qur'an is ignorance and forgetfulness. Yet again, this perspective finds reinforcement in the Qur'an through the attention given to the Akedah.

'id al-Adha and Human Forgetfulness[27]

While Hebrews celebrates the once-for-all nature of Christ's sacrifice as the culmination to which all other sacrifices pointed, the Qur'an unabashedly commends the institution of the annual *hajj* ritual and its attendant sacrifice, *'id al-Adha*. In so doing, the Qur'an exposes its view that humanity's problem is a matter of forgetfulness by proposing an annual reminder of the faithful submission of Abraham. Not only does the event cause the participant recall and rehearse Abraham's submission to God's will, but, as chapter 4 demonstrated, the believer also participates in the distinguishing ritual given through the Qur'an to those receiving the final revelation of divine knowledge and guidance.

---

25. Nasr, *Heart of Islam*, 7.
26. Schimmel, *Islam*, 32–33.
27. In preparing to make a comparison between the Qur'an and Bible, it is helpful to note that forgetfulness of the Lord and his ways is a key theme throughout both texts. (Attestation of the exhortation to remember Allah in the Qur'an is included in the treatment above; examples of such exhortation in the Bible abound, particularly in Deut 4:9–14;6:12; 7:18; 8:2; etc.) For the Qur'an, however, the emphasis on remembering the straight path and the ways of Allah and also exerting effort in attempting to obey and follow such guidance are the means of salvation. For the Bible, however, and for the book of Hebrews in particular, sins cannot be forgiven nor purged without the shedding of blood (Heb 9:22), thus requiring the substitutionary sacrificial system and a priestly intermediary.

The Qur'an explicitly links the *'id al-Adha* ritual with divine guidance in *Surat al-Hajj* (22):36–37, by commanding the *'id al-Adha* sacrifice and then clarifying, "It is not their meat nor their blood that reaches God: it is your piety that reaches him: He has thus made them subject to you, that ye may glorify God for His guidance to you and proclaim the Good News to all who do right." Thus, the Qur'an itself claims to exist as a reminder to its audience to recall the ways of God, and its prescription for the *id al-Adha* is an example of such guidance.

Ultimately, then, for the Qur'an, the problem facing humanity is a lack of knowledge, a tendency toward forgetfulness, and ignorance of divine guidance. Therefore, while the book of Hebrews celebrates the end of sacrifice due to Christ's completion thereof (Heb 10:11–14), the Qur'an celebrates the perpetuity of observing Abraham's sacrifice as another reminder to keep the ways of God, thereby addressing the human tendency toward forgetfulness. Therein is the Qur'an's answer to the next question: What is the solution?

What Is the Solution?

Considering that the Qur'an's teaching regarding humanity's problem is distinct from the problem proposed by Hebrews, it follows that the Qur'an also offers a solution that is distinct from Hebrews' solution. Hebrews highlights the sin-caused division that exists between humanity and God along with Christ's atonement as the key to reconciliation (Heb 9:8; 10:19–22). Contradicting this from an Islamic viewpoint, however, Al-Furuqui writes, "In the Islamic view, human beings are no more 'fallen' than they are 'saved.' Because they are not 'fallen,' they have no need of a savior. But because they are not 'saved' either, they need to do good works—and do them ethically—which alone will earn them the desired salvation."[28] Therefore, the Qur'an can contend that man's problem is resolved by guidance without needing to incorporate a savior or intercessor (*Surat al-Taha* [20]:123).[29]

Islamic scholar Seyyed Houssein Nasr concurs with this claim in his book, *Ideals and Realities of Islam*. Therein, Nasr claims that God's mercy

---

28. Al-Faruqi, *Islam*, 9.
29. Qur'an 20:123: قَالَ اهْبِطَا مِنْهَا جَمِيعًا ۖ بَعْضُكُمْ لِبَعْضٍ عَدُوٌّ ۖ فَإِمَّا يَأْتِيَنَّكُم مِّنِّي هُدًى فَمَنِ اتَّبَعَ هُدَايَ فَلَا يَضِلُّ وَلَا يَشْقَىٰ

and grace extends to humanity through the law (*Sharīʿah*) that is given to guide humanity to felicity in the present and in the eschaton, saying, "In the Islamic perspective God has revealed the *Sharīʿah* to man so that through it he can reform himself and his society.... The presence of *Sharīʿah* in the world is due to the compassion of God for his creatures so that he has sent an all encompassing Law for them to follow and thereby to gain felicity in both this world and the next."[30] While Nasr here refers to an extra-qurʾanic body of Islamic jurisprudence as law sent from God, the Qurʾan repeatedly claims to be a book of guidance sent to lead believers to felicity.[31] Of particular concern to this project, the *ʿid al-Adha* ritual reinforces the claim that the solution to humanity's problem is guidance.

Divergence: Guidance Versus Atonement

Chapters 2 and 3 argued that the biblical concept of atonement provides a way of dealing with sin and impurity based on the power of blood to represent life before God's presence. Thus, the book of Hebrews demonstrates that Jesus's blood offered in the heavenly places allows for an eternal ransom-purgation of sin (Heb 1:3; 2:17; 5:9–10; 7:27; 10:12–14, 19–22).[32] If the Qurʾan offers guidance to show the believer how to remove sin and impurity, then guidance functions more like the concept of atonement than any other aspect of qurʾanic teaching. In fact, as the Qurʾan prescribes the *ʿid al-Adha* sacrifice in *Surat al-Māʾida* (5) and *Surat al-Hajj* (22), one finds evidence to support such an assertion.

The clearest example of this dual function of guidance comes from *Surat al-Māʾida* (5):1–11. The previous chapter revealed the role of the *hajj* and *ʿid al-Adha* in the logic of *Surat al-Māʾida* (5):3 whereby the reader is instructed about unlawful foods that defile. Following the defiling effects of such foods, verses 6–11 offer guidance regarding the solution to such defilement: washing or bathing (*Surat al-Māʾida* [5]:6).[33] The

30. Nasr, *Ideals and Realities*, 117.

31. According to the Qurʾan Study tool, the Qurʾan Corpus, of the 118 occurrences of the root *hda* (112 ,هدى) refer to guidance. The six remaining references are to sacrificial animals (Qurʾan 2:196 [three occurrences]; 5:2 [one occurrence]; 5:97 [one occurrence]; 48:25 [one occurrence]).

32. Moffitt, *Atonement*, 265.

33. Ali, *Qurʾan: Text, Translation, and Commentary*, 242n702, links such

remainder of the section, *Surat al-Mā'ida* (5):7–11, guides believers to remember the ways of God and to do works of righteousness and receive forgiveness.[34] In this short section, then, the Qur'an confronts the problems of impurity and guilt with guidance.

Likewise, immediately preceding the prescription for the *'id al-Adha* sacrifice, *Surat al-Hajj* (22) reinforces the connection between the recitation of Abraham's sacrifice and divine guidance. In *Surat al-Hajj* 22:23–24, the author of the Qur'an promises, "God will admit those who believe and work righteous deeds to Gardens beneath which rivers flow: they shall be adorned therein with bracelets of gold and pearls; and their garments there will be of silk. For they have been guided (in this life) to the purest of speeches; they have been guided to the Path of Him Who is worthy of (all) praise."[35] This promise that those who follow God's guidance will receive admittance into gardens introduces the prescription for keeping the *hajj* pilgrimage and *'id al-Adha* as a sacred rite given to Abraham (*Surat al-Hajj* [22]:26–33). Thus, the performance of the *hajj* ritual is intimately connected to the promise that God will reward those who follow his guidance.

Following this section and reinforcing the connection between *'id al-Adha* and the guidance of God, *Surat al-Hajj* (22):34–38 goes on to include explicit reference to the sacrifice to be performed during the *hajj*, writing in verse 34, "To every people did We appoint rites (of sacrifice) that they might celebrate the name of God over the sustenance He gave them from animals (fit for food). But then your God is One God: Submit then your wills to Him (in Islam): and give thou the good news to those who humble themselves."[36] As seen in the section above, just three verses later, this sacrifice is directly linked to God's guidance.[37] Summing up the section on the sacrifice that attends the *hajj* ritual, then, the Qur'an

---

rituals for cleansing to man's duty to follow God's law and guidance, commenting, "As always, food, cleanliness, social intercourse, marriage and other interests in life, are linked with our duty to God and faith in him. Duty and faith are for our own benefit, here and in the Hereafter."

34. Qur'an 5:9: وَعَدَ اللَّهُ الَّذِينَ آمَنُوا وَعَمِلُوا الصَّالِحَاتِ ۙ لَهُم مَّغْفِرَةٌ وَأَجْرٌ عَظِيمٌ

35. Qur'an 22:23–24: إِنَّ اللَّهَ يُدْخِلُ الَّذِينَ آمَنُوا وَعَمِلُوا الصَّالِحَاتِ جَنَّاتٍ تَجْرِي مِن تَحْتِهَا الْأَنْهَارُ يُحَلَّوْنَ فِيهَا مِنْ أَسَاوِرَ مِن ذَهَبٍ وَلُؤْلُؤًا ۖ وَلِبَاسُهُمْ فِيهَا حَرِيرٌ وَهُدُوا إِلَى الطَّيِّبِ مِنَ الْقَوْلِ وَهُدُوا إِلَىٰ صِرَاطِ الْحَمِيدِ

36. Qur'an 22:34: وَلِكُلِّ أُمَّةٍ جَعَلْنَا مَنسَكًا لِيَذْكُرُوا اسْمَ اللَّهِ عَلَىٰ مَا رَزَقَهُم مِّن بَهِيمَةِ الْأَنْعَامِ ۗ فَإِلَٰهُكُمْ إِلَٰهٌ وَاحِدٌ فَلَهُ أَسْلِمُوا ۗ وَبَشِّرِ الْمُخْبِتِينَ

37. Qur'an 22:37: لَن يَنَالَ اللَّهَ لُحُومُهَا وَلَا دِمَاؤُهَا وَلَٰكِن يَنَالُهُ التَّقْوَىٰ مِنكُمْ ۚ كَذَٰلِكَ سَخَّرَهَا لَكُمْ لِتُكَبِّرُوا اللَّهَ عَلَىٰ مَا هَدَاكُمْ ۗ وَبَشِّرِ الْمُحْسِنِينَ

explicitly refers to the sacrifice given to the people of the Qur'an as a part of the divine guidance given to them.

Therefore, the Qur'an proposes guidance as the solution to humanity's problem of ignorance and forgetfulness. Further, chapter 4 argued that the rhetorical structure of *Surat al-Mā'ida* (5):3 allows the Qur'an to prescribe *'id al-Adha* as a way to distinguish the followers of the Qur'an from the followers of previous dispensations of heavenly revelation. Further, what the present section recognizes is that, in the context of *Surat al-Hajj*, the flow of thought from verse 23 through to 38 reveals that God's intention in prescribing the *hajj* and *'id al-Adha* is also to provide the final dispensation of guidance, which leads naturally into the answer to Wright's fifth question: What time is it?

What Time Is It?

As with the Bible, the Qur'an is a document that discusses the past, the present situation in which humanity finds itself, and the future towards which history is heading. When one asks the question, "What time is it?" of the Qur'an, the concept of sacrifice as delineated in the previous chapter provides an answer that is both similar to and divergent from the answer provided by Hebrews. Both texts intend their readers to understand themselves to be in the final epoch of history, awaiting eternity (Heb 13:14 and *Surat al-Mā'ida* [5]:3). For Hebrews, that entails waiting to enter God's rest, to draw near to God in Christ, and to anticipate a city that is to come (Heb 4:8–12; 10:19–25; 13:14). But for the Qur'an, particularly as seen through the command to observe *'id al-Adha*, the current epoch finds the believer practicing the fidelity to the final and perfect form of religion in anticipation of the coming pleasures of God.

Divergence: Following the Qur'an as the Final Revelation

As chapter 4 argued, the rhetorical structure of *Surat al-Mā'ida* (5) intends the reader to see the *hajj* ritual and particularly the *'id al-Adha* sacrifice as the rite given to authenticate the divine origins of the Qur'an and its message. In so doing, the Qur'an calls the reader back to the days of Abraham to stand on Mount Moriah alongside of one who received commendation for being faithful and submissive to God's will.

At the same time, as chapter 4 revealed, reference to Abraham's submission allows the Qur'an to propose Abraham as a prototypical *muslim*, thus pointing forward to the revelation of the Qur'an and its prophet. Therefore, answering the question "What time is it?" through the lens of the *'id al-Adha* sacrifice, the Qur'an intends to establish itself as the indication that humanity has entered the final age prior to the eschaton.

Furthermore, as already mentioned, the Qur'an prescribes observance of *'id al-Adha* as a way of recalling the distant past, rehearsing the faith exhibited by Abraham, and submitting to the fullness of Abraham's religion that is now revealed through the Qur'an (*Surat al-Mā'ida* [5]:3). Those who have received the Qur'an as the final dispensation of guidance are those most fully equipped with the means to worship, do righteous deeds, avoid impurity, and receive the rewards of God. It remains to ask Wright's final question in order to understand the purpose of such guidance: "Why?"

Why?

This final question provides the reader access to the crux of the distinction between the worldviews of the Qur'an and Hebrews. By asking each text "Why?" one evokes a response that includes God's original purposes in creation, ongoing purposes in addressing humanity's problems, and the ultimate purposes to which everything is heading. In other words, the "Why?" question allows one to summarize the overarching narrative holding together the answers provided by the previous five questions.[38]

In brief, the Qur'an contends that life is a test. Such a conclusion comes from *Surat al-Mulk* (67):2, which states, "He who created Death and Life, that He may try which of you is best in deed: and He is the Exalted in Might, Oft-Forgiving."[39] Again, *Surat al-Mā'ida* (5):48b states, "To each among you have We prescribed a Law and an Open Way. If God had so willed He would have made you a single People, but (His plan is) to test you in what he hath given you: so strive as in a race in all virtues."[40] These two verses provide insight into the purposes of the Qur'an as a

---

38. Wright, *Paul and Faithfulness*, 27.

39. Qur'an 67:2: الَّذِي خَلَقَ الْمَوْتَ وَالْحَيَاةَ لِيَبْلُوَكُمْ أَيُّكُمْ أَحْسَنُ عَمَلًا ۚ وَهُوَ الْعَزِيزُ الْغَفُورُ. See also Qur'an 2:214; 29:2–3.

40. Qur'an 5:48b: لِكُلٍّ جَعَلْنَا مِنكُمْ شِرْعَةً وَمِنْهَاجًا ۚ وَلَوْ شَاءَ اللَّهُ لَجَعَلَكُمْ أُمَّةً وَاحِدَةً وَلَٰكِن لِيَبْلُوَكُمْ فِي مَا آتَاكُمْ ۖ فَاسْتَبِقُوا الْخَيْرَاتِ

means by which the people of the Qur'an might be tested for faithfulness and fidelity to their dispensation of divine law.

Reinforcing the Islamic understanding of life as an ethical and moral test, well known Islamic scholar, Fazlur Rahman offers a summary of the Qur'an's answer to the question of "Why?" in his acclaimed book, *Major Themes of the Qur'an*, concluding,

> While the purpose of man is to "serve" God, i.e., to develop his higher potentialities in accordance with the "command" (*amr*) of God, through choice, and to use nature (which is automatically *muslim*, "obedient to God"), he must be provided with adequate means of sustenance and of "finding the right way." Hence God, Who in His outgoing mercy brought nature and man into being, in His unbroken and sustained mercy has endowed man with the necessary cognition and volition to create knowledge and use it to realize his just and fair ends. It is at this point that man's crucial test comes: will he use his knowledge and power for good or for evil, for "success or loss," or for "reforming the earth or corrupting it" (as the Qur'an constantly puts it).... For this reason, God's mercy reaches its logical zenith in "sending Messengers," "revealing Books," and showing man "the Way." This "guidance" (*hidaya*) is also kneaded into man's primordial nature insofar as the distinction between good and evil is "ingrained in his heart."[41]

Rahman's lengthy quote deserves to be recorded in full due to its ability to weave together the conclusions already purported above. God's purpose in creating was to test humanity in order to see who would believe in him and obey him.

In so doing, humanity is tasked with the responsibility to use God-given cognition and volition to do rightly on earth. Man's forgetfulness causes God in his mercy to send guidance as a reminder of how to please God so that humanity will be prepared for the test and receive God's rewards both here and in the afterlife.[42]

41. Rahman, *Major Themes*, 8–9.

42. To this point, from a Muslim point of view, see Sachedina, "End-of-Life," 774, who writes, "Muslims believe they were created to discover God's work in the universe and to appreciate and serve God's ends for His creation. Although shouldering the great responsibility of serving God, the Merciful and the Compassionate, human beings often forget their purpose. To overcome this tendency, God from time to time appoints prophets as reminders and guides to lead people to the right path of success in this world and the next."

Turning again to the sacrifice of *'id al-Adha* and its role in the Qur'an, one finds an example of two humans receiving divine rewards for their obedience and submission. The Qur'an commends both Abraham and his son as it recounts the Akedah story in *Surat al-Saffat* (37):103–6: "So when they had both submitted their wills (to God) and he had laid him prostrate on his forehead (for sacrifice), We called out to him, 'Oh Abraham! thou hast already fulfilled the vision!'—Thus indeed do we reward those who do right. For this was obviously a trial."[43]

In this account, both Abraham and his son exemplify the obedience of those who have received guidance, and God promises to reward both for their obedience in doing that which is right (*Surat as-Saffat* [37]: 105, 110). Such commendation fits into the repeated theme of the Qur'an that belief and obedience serve the faithful as means to both temporal and eternal rewards. Likewise, as believers annually rehearse Abraham's story during the *'id al-Adha* sacrifice, they recall Abraham's faithfulness and seek to imitate his belief and submission in order to receive similar rewards. For the Qur'an, then, life is a test of how one will respond to divine guidance and one's rewards hang in the balance.

---

43. Qur'an 37:103–106: فَلَمَّا أَسْلَمَا وَتَلَّهُ لِلْجَبِينِ وَنَادَيْنَاهُ أَن يَا إِبْرَاهِيمُ قَدْ صَدَّقْتَ الرُّؤْيَا ۚ إِنَّا كَذَٰلِكَ نَجْزِي الْمُحْسِنِينَ. إِنَّ هَٰذَا لَهُوَ الْبَلَاءُ الْمُبِينُ

TABLE 5.1
Worldview Questions and Answers Comparison: Hebrews and the Qur'an

QUESTION	HEBREWS	QUR'AN
Who are we?	THE PEOPLE OF YHWH IN CHRIST The descendants of the people whom YHWH rescued from slavery in Egypt. The people with whom YHWH has made a new covenant in Christ. The people who are still waiting for a lasting city that is to come. The people whose uniqueness is demonstrated by Jesus leading them into YHWH's presence.	ABRAHAM'S CHILDREN SUBMITTED TO THE PERFECT HEAVENLY REVELATION By observing ʿid al-Aḍha, Muslims acknowledge continuity with Abraham without having to account for later details revealed to Moses and Jesus. Thus, as God has given Muslims this sacrifice, he affirms them as Abraham's children, submitted to perfect religion.
Where are we?	MOUNT ZION At the foot of Mount Zion, waiting for the lasting city that is to come. Outside the camp, following Jesus and offering a sacrifice of praise to God. Having passed through the true curtain of Jesus' flesh, believers stand in the holy place, the intersection of heaven and earth.	MOUNT MORIAH On Mount Moriah with Abraham, exhibiting the faithful obedience of Abraham and his son. Waiting for the last day to give account before God and to hopefully enter the heavenly garden by the mercy of God.
What is wrong?	OLD-COVENANT IMPERMANENCE Sin and impurity endanger humanity in the presence of the holiness of YHWH. The old covenant way of managing sin and impurity was impermanent.	FORGETFULNESS Humanity has forgotten the ways of God and needs to be reminded of what to obey and how to worship correctly.
What is the solution?	PERPETUAL ATONEMENT IN CHRIST The Christ event provides the image of which the Day of Atonement was but a shadow. Jesus' eternal blood and sacrifice perpetually forgive, cleanse, and redeem.	GUIDANCE Those who follow divine guidance should obey the commands to "atone" for their bad deeds and purify themselves. Ultimately, the judgment of the last day is dependent upon the mercy of God.
What time is it?	BETWEEN ATONEMENT AND HEAVENLY JERUSALEM A time of sojourning without a city, awaiting the heavenly Jerusalem's descent. The time to draw near to God by drawing near to Jesus.	THE FINAL DISPENSATION God has sent Muhammad as the seal of the prophets and has given Islam as the perfection of religion. This is the final dispensation of heavenly religion. It is time to submit to God by following Islam.
Why?	YHWH'S PERMANENT PRESENCE YHWH has provided in Jesus a means by which he might create a people for himself, and that he might dwell among them through the Holy Spirit (see Heb 6:4). The Christ event provides the image of which the Day of Atonement was a preparatory shadow, thus Jesus's priesthood and sacrifice offer a once-for-all solution to the problem of sin and impurity.	ACHIEVE THE PLEASURES OF GOD Humanity exists because of the secret purposes of God. However, throughout a human's life, they are tested as to how well they will submit to the commands of God. Those who follow God's commands provide "covering" for their sins and purification for their defilement and so exhibit their obedience. It is likely that these will be admitted to heaven's pleasant gardens, but ultimately admittance depends upon God's mercy.

Summary

Finally this project has arrived at a point where the fundamental distinctions between the Qur'an and Hebrews emerge most clearly. Up to this point, it may appear that rather than providing tools to aid in communication, this book has actually multiplied the barriers to Christian communication of biblical atonement. The purpose of investigating the extent of the problem, however, is to provide greater clarity in assessing how one might move forward in overcoming such barriers. Thus, this project has labored to demonstrate that there are problems for the communicator at the lexical, narrative, ritual, and worldview levels.

What remains is to consider whether or not the book of Hebrews provides the means to overcome the extensive communication barriers that the preceding study has exposed. The following section will thus demonstrate that Hebrews' argument includes the contours of the OBN by claiming Christ provides the eternal atonement that the annual Yom Kippur celebration pointed toward but could not provide. In so doing, Hebrews overcomes the communication barriers listed above while challenging the Qur'an by demonstrating a different kind of continuity.

Hebrews and the OBN

The preceding discussion has utilized the role of the Akedah and the subsequent 'id al-Adha ritual as employed by the Qur'an as an entry point for exploring the worldview effects such a narrative has upon the reader. In Hebrews 11:17–19, Abraham and his sacrifice provide a single episode in the unfolding of redemptive history culminating in Christ. The Qur'an, however, prescribes rehearsal of the Abrahamic sacrifice as a validation of the Qur'an and a ritual of demarcation for Islam as the final dispensation of religion. Therefore, while the Bible and Qur'an both recognize Abraham and tell the story of the Akedah, the larger controlling narratives in which Abraham and his sacrifice are situated in each text set the reader on divergent trajectories of interpretation, thus producing divergent answers to the worldview questions posed above.

Due to the divergent function of such concepts and stories in the Qur'an, missiologist Theodore Curry contends, "Any presentation of the Gospel message to Muslims must begin by laying out a framework for the proper interpretation of the Bible's comprehensive narrative:

creation-fall-redemption-restoration."[44] Curry's insight pushes the reader to recognize that individual micro-narratives, extracted from their purpose within the biblical metanarrative, take divergent trajectories in the Qur'an. The preceding treatment of the telling of the Akedah story in the Qur'an demonstrates the veracity of Curry's claim, as he writes, "The stories of Adam and Eve, Noah, Abraham, Moses, and Jesus do not make sense when abstracted from their narrative context.... Ultimately, the Bible must be allowed to exert its narrative control over how the story of the prophets is told."[45] Scope limits Curry's article from prescribing a specific means and method by which one might incorporate the whole OBN into one's ministry, but his contention that the biblical narrative should be allowed to control meaning and encourage understanding finds affirmation in variety of disciplines.[46]

The burden of the current section, then, is to demonstrate that Curry's concern for the OBN-driven communication of Christian concepts such as atonement is satisfied by the book of Hebrews. Therefore, the remainder of this chapter will focus on how the book of Hebrews demonstrates continuity between the HB and the NT by viewing the Christ-event as the fulfillment of Yom Kippur. In so doing, Hebrews incorporates Curry's four plot moves that summarize the OBN: creation, fall, redemption, and restoration. As Hebrews includes each of these elements into its treatment of Yom Kippur in the light of the Christ event, it becomes apparent that what the Bible means by atonement, sacrifice, blood, and continuity is based upon a different way of telling the story of the world.

As argued by missiologist Lesslie Newbigin, such a competing metanarrative challenges other alternatives to offer a better story, and it "compels one to challenge every understanding of the human story that looks to an end other than that which is disclosed in Jesus."[47] The author issues exactly this kind of narrative-driven call to look to Jesus in

44. Curry, "Mission to Muslims," 234–35.

45. Curry, "Mission to Muslims," 235.

46. This argument for a narrative-driven articulation of doctrine not only finds advocates such as Curry within the narrow field of mission to Muslims, but biblical scholars such as Wright, *People of God*, 139–43; theologians such as Bartholomew and Goheen, "Story and Biblical Theology," and Vanhoozer, *Drama of Doctrine*; and missiologists such as Newbigin, *Open Secret* and Hiebert, *Transforming Worldviews* also contend that the metanarrative of Scripture should determine the meaning of any given motif, concept, or doctrine.

47. Newbigin, *Open Secret*, 89.

Hebrews 12:2, having established the context of the larger story in which the Christ-event as the once-for-all Yom Kippur makes sense.

Creation in Hebrews

As Curry rightly claims, "If one is to properly comprehend the Bible's teaching on the triune nature of God, the incarnation, the atonement, the church, eschatology, or ethics, these must be understood within the context of their organic relationship to the story narrated in the Bible and its redemptive theme."[48] Starting at the beginning of the story with the idea of creation, then, the book of Hebrews provides the reader with not only the idea that God is the Creator, but the author also provides a hint toward understanding God's purposes in creation.

Hebrews 1:1–4 records the opening verses of the book with the author writing,

> Long ago, at many times and in many ways, God spoke to our fathers by the prophets, but in these last days he has spoken to us by his Son, whom he appointed the heir of all things, through whom also he created the world. He is the radiance of the glory of God and the exact imprint of his nature and he upholds the universe by the word of his power. After making purification for sins, he sat down at the right hand of the Majesty on high, having become as much superior to angels as the name he has inherited is more excellent than theirs.

This magisterial introduction to the book is what Harold Attridge refers to as, "A single, elaborately constructed periodic sentence that encapsulates many of the key themes that will develop in the following chapters."[49] Bearing this claim out, William Lane notes that in this sentence both the royal Son of Psalm 2 and the high priest of Psalm 110 appear as a single active agent through whom God created the world and the one who will be the heir of all things (Heb 1:3).[50] Since the high priest and the royal son coalesce into an individual who attains a superior status

---

48. Curry, "Mission to Muslims," 222.
49. Attridge, *Hebrews*, 36.
50. Lane, *Hebrews 1–8*, 6, identifies in these opening verses references to both Ps 2:8 (Heb 2:2, "whom he appointed heir of all things.") and Ps 110:1 (Heb 1:4, "he sat down at the right hand of God.").

even to the angels, one is warranted to claim that the author is frontloading the major themes of the book in these opening statements.

However, not only does one see that the opening section prepares the reader to encounter these themes in the following argument, but it also provides the reader with a glimpse of the Son's involvement in all four plot movements required by Curry for communicating the Bible's message to Muslims. First, Hebrews 1:3a states, "He is the radiance of the glory of God and the exact imprint of his nature, and he upholds the universe by the word of his power." This reveals that the Son was the active agent through whom God created all things.

Second, Hebrews 1:3b continues, saying, "After making purification for sins, he sat down at the right hand of the Majesty on high." As this part of the verse references the Son making purification for sin, the author hints at the separation between God and humanity whereby a priest is a necessary intermediary.[51] Third, when Hebrews 1:3 mentions the Son's position as being seated, having made purification for sins, the reader calls to mind the role of atonement in the process of redemption.[52] Finally, restoration is included through the allusion to Psalm 110:1, wherein the Son is called to await the time when his enemies will be made a footstool.

Most pertinent to challenging the metanarrative and subsequent worldview of the Qur'an, however, is that the reference to creation in these opening verses comes in the context of an indication of the purpose of creation. While both the Qur'an and Hebrews identify God as the Creator, Hebrews shows that God creates so that he might communicate himself to man. Exhibiting this self-communication, Hebrews 1:1–2 posits that God has been speaking to his creation consistently throughout history, though "in these last days he has spoken to us by his Son."[53]

Commenting on the impact of this verse for the ensuing argument of Hebrews, Attridge writes, "God . . . speaks through this Son not only in word, but in deed, in the entirety of the Christ-event, providing for

---

51. Attridge, *Hebrews*, 45–46, comments on Heb 1:3, saying, "Although the terminology of high priest and explicit reference to the cross are absent here, an essential feature of Christ's priestly work is adumbrated in this phrase."

52. This theme of atonement provides the author with his most sustained and concentrated argument, particularly as Heb 7:1–10:18 articulate the Christ-event in terms of the *telos* to which Yom Kippur was always pointing. See Lane, *Hebrews 1–8*, 9; see also Attridge, *Hebrews*, 36.

53. The Son as communication links to Heb 2:14–18, which references the Son's incarnation.

humanity atonement for sin and an enduring covenant relationship."[54] By linking the Son's activity in creation with his exalted status as the ultimate means of God's self-communication, God's self-revelatory purpose weaves its way throughout the rest of the narrative. While the effects of the fall threaten God's abiding presence, humanity is invited to approach God once again, restored by the high priestly work of the Son, and to be ultimately consummated in the age to come. While the author assumes most of the narrative of creation, referencing creation only in Hebrews 1:3, the purpose of creation is a thread woven through the entire OBN as presented in Hebrews.

Fall in Hebrews

The second of Curry's plot moves involves attention to the fall and its effects. While the author of Hebrews nowhere directly addresses the story of the fall, and Adam and Eve are conspicuously absent from the account, the sin of the first couple is present within Hebrews' narrative through the author's consistent reference to its effects.[55] Within the first two chapters the author identifies sin as the cause of impurity requiring purification (Heb 1:3) and of guilt requiring propitiation (Heb 2:17). Such recognition parallels the findings of chapter 2 that determined the underlying logic of the Day of Atonement to depend upon blood as a remedy for sin and impurity.[56] Thus in the first two chapters of Hebrews, one finds that sin has caused both defilement and guilt, and the only means of escaping the just retribution such sin earns is by the eternal atonement that the Christ as the great high priest achieves.

The reference to Christ as a high priest who might make atonement, however, prepares the reader for Hebrews 7:1—10:18, where the author

54. Attridge, *Hebrews*, 39.

55. Moffitt, *Atonement*, 129–44. Despite the lack of direct reference, Moffitt argues that Adam appears in Heb 2 through allusion to a second temple and rabbinic tradition wherein Adam is exalted above the angels.

56. The Arabic Bible translates this verse using the verb *kaffara* for ἱλάσκεσθαι. Hebrews 2:17: من ثم كان ينبغي ان يشبه اخوته في كل شيء، لكي يكون رحما، و رئيس كهنة امينا في الله حتى يكفّر خطايا الشعب. This word choice allows a Christian communicator to make the direct relationship to the action of Christ as the high priest and atonement than what comes through in the English version. At the same time, the English-speaking communicator will recognize the expanded idea of atonement endorsed by the author of Hebrews and demonstrated in chapter 3. Regarding the role of blood in ransom-purification, see Sklar, *Sin, Impurity*, 187.

explicitly demonstrates that Christ's atonement removes the separation between humanity and God. The author highlights this separation most vividly in chapter 9:6–14 by focusing on what the Spirit communicates through the curtain that divides the holy place of divine dwelling from the people of God. As Attridge comments, "What the spirit reveals is the lack of access to the true presence of God."[57]

As demonstrated in chapter 2, because of sin and its attendant guilt and defilement, a curtain divided the people of Israel from the presence of their God, reminding the people that sin threatened the purposes of their God who had promised to dwell in their midst.[58] While the curtain of division represents the effects of the fall, the annual entry of the high priest into the holy place provides the reader with assurance that atonement and redemption remain possible. In Hebrews 9–10, the author seizes upon the annual ritual of Yom Kippur, demonstrating that the Christ event eternally fulfills and expands the restorative hope to which Yom Kippur pointed.

Redemption and Restoration in Hebrews

For the author of Hebrews, the remedy for the separation between God and humanity continues along the arc of ancient Israel's history by completing once and for all the ritual of Yom Kippur. Following William Lane's commentary on Hebrews, and as chapter 3 demonstrated, the author of Hebrews draws on Leviticus 16–17 to demonstrate that the component parts of the Day of Atonement ritual are satisfied by the eternally atoning blood provided by the Christ event.[59] Thus, the idea that the Day of Atonement was a shadow of the Christ event is central to the author's argument that the former times prepared the people of God to receive his solution.[60]

---

57. Attridge, *Hebrews*, 240.

58. Bartholomew and Goheen, *Drama of Scripture*, 71, claim that the purpose of God through creation, covenant, tabernacle, and sacrifice is to dwell among his people as their God. Their assertion fits well with the burden of the author of Hebrews to demonstrate that the purpose of God to dwell among his people is the undergirding feature of all four plot moves.

59. Lane, *Hebrews 9–13*, 235, comments, "The manner in which the argument is set forth presupposes the cultic orientation of 9:1–10 and its leading motif, that access to God is possible only through the medium of blood (9:7)."

60. Attridge, *Hebrews*, 241. See also Lane, *Hebrews 9–13*, 259. The theme of

In fact, looking back on the claims made throughout Hebrews 7–10, the author summarizes the Christ event's atoning effects in Hebrews 12:22–24, declaring,

> You have come to Mount Zion and to the city of the living God, the heavenly Jerusalem, and to innumerable angels in festal gathering, and to the assembly of the firstborn who are enrolled in heaven, and to God, the judge of all, and to the spirits of the righteous made perfect, and to Jesus, the mediator of a new covenant, and to the sprinkled blood that speaks a better word than the blood of Abel.

The climax of Hebrews' argument recapitulates the purpose of the Day of Atonement by claiming that those who receive the atonement offered in Christ by faith are invited to approach God in a way that was previously impossible. Where the barrier of the curtain to the holy place formerly served as a reminder that the people could only go before the presence of God once a year, and even then, only by way of the high priest as a vicarious representative, the Christ event has achieved the purposes of the Day of Atonement once and for all (Heb 9:6–14).

Commenting on the declaration of Hebrews 12:22–24, Attridge concisely sums up the teaching of Hebrews regarding the ultimate purpose of atonement, writing,

> What Christians ultimately have approached is not some distant or ethereal eschatological reality, but "blood" (αἵματι). Like that of the *Yom Kippur*, red heifer, and covenant sacrifices this blood is "sprinkled" (ῥαντισμοῦ) and the epithet recalls the interpretation of Christ's death in terms of those various sacrificial acts of the Old Testament. It was through the "sprinkling" of Christ's blood that true atonement was effected and thereby a true and lasting covenant relationship with God established.[61]

---

foreshadowing is central to the manner in which the author of Hebrews conceives of the Christ event's proper continuation of prior revelation. Commenting on the shadow-image motif in Hebrews, Lane points out, "Now the law is described as a 'foreshadowing (σκιά) of the good things which are to come.' The term σκιά does not signify unreal or deceptive, as in Platonism, but rather imperfect or incomplete." For the author of Hebrews, then, Christ has perfected and completed the annual atonement offered by Yom Kippur by fulfilling the role of the high priest and by offering atoning blood before God. In other words, discontinuity between Leviticus and Hebrews regarding atonement pertains more to scope than to kind.

61. Attridge, *Hebrews*, 376–77.

Attridge's summary succinctly defines the author of Hebrews' teaching regarding the purpose of creation: to approach God. As chapter 2 and 3 both contended, the Day of Atonement ritual was a reminder of God's repeated promise throughout the Hebrew Bible that he would come to dwell among his people as their God.[62]

Likewise, the warning passages throughout Hebrews exhibit the author's intent to connect the three previous movements of the OBN with its final *telos* found in the restoration of the age to come. Such warning passages urge the reader not to neglect the revealed salvation (Heb 2:3), to enter God's rest (Heb 3:7, 15; 4:3, 5, 9–13), and to await the coming of the heavenly Jerusalem (Heb 11:16; 12:18–24, 28; 13:14). All of these passages involve a way of living in the present that anticipates a coming future in God's presence. Throughout Hebrews, the author contends that the single purpose of atonement is to restore human capacity to approach God in worship, and that fulfillment of this purpose is the *telos* of history, ensured through Christ's eternal atonement.[63]

Summary

The book of Hebrews contains much more content that might be drawn into its retelling of the story of the people of God than discussed above. However, what has been covered suffices for the purposes of satisfying Curry's requirement that a presentation of Christian doctrine be defined and carried by the OBN. Furthermore, such a construction of the OBN focuses on what this project has established as a point of divergent narrative trajectories between the Qur'an and Hebrews: atonement and sacrifice. For the missiologist intent on explaining Christian atonement to an audience versed in the Qur'an, then, the way the author of Hebrews incorporates the Day of Atonement ritual into the explanation of the Christ event is crucial: the author utilizes the OBN to define atonement and explain the purpose of sacrifice, while implicitly developing a biblical worldview and challenging alternative renderings of history.

This project has referenced multiple scholars from various disciplines who claim that worldviews are formed by metanarratives, that principles and doctrines only make sense within overarching stories of how the world really is, and those who argue that Muslim ministry

---

62. Exod 25:8; 33:14–17; Lev 26:11–12; Zech 2:10–11; Isa 12:6; passim.

63. Attridge, *Hebrews*, 371–77.

requires presentation of the OBN.[64] It remains, then, to consider how the OBN presentation contained in Hebrews might justify such claims. In other words, does the metanarrative of Hebrews, presented with a focus on how the Christ event continues and completes the Day of Atonement, help the Christian communicator to overcome the lexical, ritual, and worldview barriers to communication listed above?

Narrative as Communication

It is true that many of the same prophets and stories exist in the Qur'an and the Bible, and it is true that many of the basic ethical commands by which Muslims live are similar to those taught within Christianity. In fact, Hebrews specifically contains multiple elements that might be considered commonalities. For example, Hebrews 11 provides a list of the faithful throughout history who have counterparts in the Qur'an.[65] Hebrews 2:2 indicates that angels are mediators of divine revelation and the Qur'an concurs.[66] Hebrews also warns the reader that judgment is coming and decisions made in the present will affect one's eternity, an idea exhibited routinely throughout the Qur'an.[67]

Yet, as this chapter has demonstrated, the story of the Akedah provides an excellent example of how such apparent similarity, upon scrutiny, often proves superficial, revealing more fundamentally divergent narrative trajectories. As is true of the conflicting uses of the Akedah story, such claims of basic similarity obscure the undergirding distinctions rooted in divergent worldviews, metanarratives, and doctrines related to atonement in both faith systems.

Therefore, when attempting to communicate a complex concept such as biblical atonement, one must first orient the audience to the

64. Regarding the narrative-driven formation of worldviews, see Wright, *People of God*, 135; see also Hiebert, *Transforming Worldviews*, 266. Regarding propositions in narrative context, see Newbigin, *Open Secret*, 81; see also Bartholomew and Goheen, "Story and Biblical Theology," 151. Regarding Muslim ministry, see Curry, "Mission to Muslims," 224.

65. Cf. Heb 11 with Qur'an 37: both texts list characters from the past as models of faithfulness.

66. Qur'an 2:97 claims that Gabriel was the messenger who recited the Qur'an to its prophet.

67. Ex. Heb 4:7 11 calls for believers not to harden their hearts as they hear the Spirit speaking. Likewise, Qur'an 5:13–19 calls on the people of the book (اهل الكتب) to remember how covenant disobedience leads to hardened hearts and punishment.

larger narrative in which doctrines of atonement, sacrificial rituals, blood, and ultimately Christ's cross and resurrection exist in order to avoid importing qur'anic, and thereby divergent, understanding of the component parts. The following section will highlight the points at which the OBN as told by Hebrews will challenge the worldview and metanarrative proposed by the Qur'an. At the same time, it will demonstrate that, by allowing the biblical metanarrative to control the meaning of such concepts, one is able to overcome the communication barriers discussed previously.

Lexical Conflict: Defined by Narrative

The preceding chapters have demonstrated that the Christian communicating in Arabic will encounter difficulties in explaining a Christian understanding of atonement to a Muslim because both the Bible and the Qur'an use the word *kaffara* to convey different ideas. By providing the missiologist with a summary of the OBN structured around the Day of Atonement, however, the book of Hebrews defines atonement in the context of the OBN, explaining atonement in a way that can overcome the divergent understanding of shared lexemes.

Exhibiting this in the very first verses, Hebrews 1:3 draws attention to the Son's work and its accomplishment of purification for sins. Additionally, Hebrews 9:22 states that sin requires forgiveness. In between these references, Hebrews 2:17 presents Jesus as a high priest who is able "to make propitiation for the sins of the people." The word translated in English as "propitiation" is rendered in Arabic by the root *kaffara*.[68] Therefore as Jesus purifies sins (Heb 1:3) and sheds his blood to achieve forgiveness of sins (Heb 9:22) the author provides definition for what it means when Jesus provides *kaffara* for sin.

As chapter 2 demonstrated, the dual accomplishments of this atoning work are intimately connected to the story of ancient Israel as the means by which YHWH's presence might remain in her midst. This connection reinforces Hebrews' claim that atonement in Christ is directly connected to the atonement elicited from the Day of Atonement as recorded in Leviticus 16–17.

---

68. Heb 2:17: من ثم كان ينبغي ان يشبه اخوته في كل شيء، لكي يكون رحيما، و رئيس كهنة امين في ما الله حتى يكفّر خطايا الشعب.

Furthermore, through explaining Christ's eternal atonement, the author of Hebrews draws together all the components of the concept cluster related to atonement seen in chapter 2's treatment of Leviticus 16–17. For the author of Hebrews, Jesus serves as the fulfillment of the role of high priest (Heb 8:1–2) who offers eternal blood (Heb 9:13–14) of his own sacrifice (Heb 10:12–14) that opens the way to the holy place of God's presence (Heb 10:19–22).

By recounting the Christ event in light of the OBN, Hebrews allows the Christian communicator to highlight the continuity of Christian use of *kaffara* with the OT concept of atonement. As such, Christian atonement emerges from the book of Hebrews being shaped by the Day of Atonement ritual of Leviticus 16–17 and reenvisioned through Christ. Therefore, it also reinforces the central purpose of atonement: approaching the presence of God.

Ultimately, then, while *kaffara* appears in the Qur'an in a more limited sense referring only to expiation of sins, the book of Hebrews defines *kaffara* in an alternative and more robust manner, drawing directly upon the understanding of atonement that Leviticus records. Furthermore, since Hebrews' presentation of atonement in Christ depends upon the story of ancient Israel and the promises of Yom Kippur, it also presents an alternative understanding of the second barrier to communication: sacrificial rituals.

Ritual Conflict: Explained by Narrative

Ultimately, atonement in the Bible is tied into the story of God's faithfulness to his promise to dwell among his people.[69] Hebrews 2:17 introduces the claim that Christ accomplished atonement as a merciful and faithful high priest. Later, Hebrews 10:11–25 explains how this accomplishment fits in the larger biblical understanding of atonement as sacrifice, forgiveness, purification, and blood manipulation. In the context of this explanation, particularly as found in Hebrews 9–10, the reader recalls the purpose of the original Day of Atonement: the opportunity to draw near to the presence of God.

---

69. Sklar, *Leviticus*, 206, comments, "The Lord, however, was Israel's redeeming King, who always desired to continue in covenant fellowship with his people. He therefore provided this day—the Day of Atonement (23:27)—to make full atonement for their sin and impurity, thus removing the threat of his judgment and assuring the Israelites that they could continue in covenant fellowship with him."

As the author begins to expand upon the claim that the Christ event is the *telos* to which previous sacrifice pointed, Hebrews 9:11–22 recalls the instructions for blood manipulation that effect purification for the flesh (Heb 9:13) and forgiveness of sin (Heb 9:22). The author argues that, since Christ's offering has "perfected for all time those who are being sanctified (Heb 10:14)," the reader can now "draw near with a true heart in full assurance of faith, with our hearts sprinkled clean from an evil conscience and our bodies washed with pure water (Heb 10:22–23)." Christ's sacrifice is mentioned (Heb 10:14), forgiveness of sins is accomplished (Heb 10:18), purification from defilement is achieved (Heb 10:22), and Christ's sprinkled blood provides the linchpin to the idea, allowing the reader to draw near (Heb 10:22–23). Therefore, one sees that atonement is both defined and completed in this section in terms of sacrificial ritual.

Such an understanding of sacrifice conflicts with the role of sacrifice as a marker of distinction in the Qur'an. Yet, since the author connects the accomplishments of the Christ event with the purposes of the Day of Atonement ritual, one can demonstrate consistency with the purpose of sacrifice revealed in Leviticus and thereby explain the purpose of sacrifice in terms determined by the OBN rather than by prior qur'anic understanding. In addition to that, by demonstrating such consistency of purpose, one comes into contact with one of the controlling elements of worldview formation: the answer to the question, "Why?"

Worldview Conflict: Formed by Narrative

Having investigated the divergent answers to Wright's worldview questions, it appears that the point of distinction looming largest between the worldviews of the Qur'an and the Bible is each text's answer to the question, "Why?" For the Qur'an, the preceding research has demonstrated the pervasiveness of the concept of life as a test. If life is a test, then information is the solution, and success is determined by one's capacity to recall and apply information. The Qur'an is unblushing in contending that God might reveal different laws by which to test different dispensations of people, as in *Surat al-Mā'ida* (5):48b, which states, "To each among you have We prescribed a Law and an Open Way. If God has so willed He would have made you a single People, but (His plan is) to test you in what he hath given you: so strive as in a race in all virtues."

Likewise, since the Qur'an portrays God as wholly transcendent as Seyyed Hossein Nasr contends, then fellowship with him will not factor into the ultimate purpose of life.[70] Furthermore, Nasr concludes, "[Man] has in himself the possibility of being God-like but he is always in the state of neglecting that possibility. That is why the cardinal sin of Islam is forgetfulnessreenvisionedRevelation is there to awaken man from this dream and remind him what it really means to be man."[71] Thus, knowledge of God and of his straight path is key to navigating one's way to salvation.

Further reinforcing the Qur'an's revelatory purposes, Islamic scholar Kenneth Cragg claims that, for Islam, "Revelation is conceived of, not as a communication of the divine Being, but only of the divine will. It is a revelation, that is, of law, not of personality. God the revealer remains unrevealed."[72] More succinctly, Cragg summarizes the concept of qur'anic revelation, writing, "God sends rather than comes."[73] For the Qur'an, then, if the purpose of life is to endure a divine test, the controlling metanarrative takes a different trajectory than the Bible takes, thereby producing a divergent worldview.

Thus, where *'id al Aḍha* summons the reader of the Qur'an to submit to the distinct and final dispensation of guidance, the unified story related by the book of Hebrews sees the Christ event as the long-awaited opportunity to draw near to God by joining Jesus outside of the camp. Utilizing the four movements of the OBN, Hebrews reveals that creation, the fall, redemption, and restoration are all unified by the overarching purpose that God might dwell with his people. Therefore, despite the existence of significant conflict between the Qur'an and Hebrews at a worldview level, communication of a Christian perspective of atonement is yet possible because of the OBN structure of Hebrews that recounts the unified story from which its worldview develops. Furthermore, by rehearsing the OBN in light of Christ, Hebrews challenges the Qur'an's claim to continuity by demonstrating the unity of progressive divine self-disclosure, culminating in God speaking through the Son.

---

70. Nasr, *Ideals and Realities*, 18, writes, "The divine essence (*al-dhat*) remains absolutely transcendent and no religion has emphasized the transcendent aspect of God more than Islam."

71. Nasr, *Ideals and Realities*, 23.

72. Cragg, *Call of Minaret*, 41.

73. Cragg, *Call of Minaret*, 42.

Continuity Conflict: Demonstrated by Narrative

All of the preceding research and comparison has provided the backdrop against which to see that the Qur'an and Hebrews maintain claims to continuity with prior revelation distinctively and irreconcilably. As the Qur'an describes life as a test, with different laws assigned to different dispensations of divine revelation, it becomes apparent that it does not concern itself with connecting the details of previous revelation with its own law. The Qur'an claims continuity with previous revelation without being compelled to demonstrate how the component parts of prior dispensations are incorporated into its teaching because it understands history as the arena of humanity's great test. Each people has received its own law for serving the one transcendent God. Thus continuity of revelation is found not in the details included in subsequent stages of progressive revelation, but in the fact that the same God is responsible for providing various people with guidance as to how they should worship and obey him as servants and vicegerents.

For Hebrews, however, the Christ event is both intimately connected to and continuous with the story begun in the Hebrew Bible. Particularly important for the purposes of this project, the argument that the Day of Atonement ritual serves as a precursor to the final and complete sacrifice of Christ is a point at which the author demonstrates such continuity and completion. Atonement has provided a window to the implicit worldview of Hebrews, and the attention Hebrews gives to explaining ancient Israel's concept of atonement as being completed in Christ allows the reader to see that the author intends to incorporate the details of prior revelation into the final revelation in Christ due to the unifying purpose of the biblical God to dwell among his people.

Since Hebrews demonstrates significant continuity with the atonement prescribed for Israel, now completed in Christ, it reveals the divergent claim to continuity made by the Qur'an that does not concern itself with the fulfillment of the Day of Atonement or the details of worship given to prior dispensations. Ultimately, such a presentation does not undermine or defeat the Qur'an as some debates focused on atonement in Islam attempt to do. Seen in the light of the previous research, the Qur'an lays its claim to continuity in a way that is different from the Bible, though not illogically. However, utilizing the OBN of Hebrews allows the Christian missiologist an opportunity to uphold the beauty of the one God whose singular purpose throughout redemptive history has prepared the people through the ritual and sacrifice of the law to grasp the grandeur of the completed the way through Christ to the presence of God himself.

TABLE 5.2
Communication Barriers and OBN Resolution

Barrier	Hebrews	Qur'an	OBN Resolution
Lexical Barriers Atonement and *kaffara* (كفّر)	*Kaffara* extends and expands the effects of the Day of Atonement as prescribed in Leviticus 16–17. Jesus is the actor as high priest.	*Kaffara* functions as expiation of sins and is achieved by doing good deeds. God is the actor. (See Appendix A and Appendix B.)	The OBN in Hebrews defines *kaffara*: Hebrews 2:17 – Jesus as high priest secures atonement (*kaffara*). Hebrews 1:3; 9:22–28; 10:22 – Jesus's blood purifies and forgives sin.
Ritual Barriers Sacrifice	Sacrifice is the ritual by which atoning blood is procured. The sacrifice of Jesus precedes the resurrection and ascension.	Sacrifice is part of the *hajj* that distinguishes Islam. Sacrifice connects believers to Abraham who precedes Judaism and Christianity.	The OBN in Hebrews explains sacrifice: Hebrews 9–10 draws ancient Israel's sacrificial cult into the light of the Christ event showing Christ to fulfill it perpetually.
Worldview Barriers Why?	Humanity was created to dwell in God's presence. Atonement makes that possible again.	Life is a test during which believers must heed guidance, believe, worship, and obey in order to gain the pleasures of God.	The OBN in Hebrews forms a biblical worldview: Hebrews 3:7–18; 4:14–16; 7:18–19; 10:19–25; 12:18–28; 13:13–14 all speak of drawing near to God, reinforcing human purpose.
Continuity Barriers Completion Claims	The story begun in the HB continues naturally into and through the Christ event, taking into account the details that came before and satisfying them in Christ; progressive revelation.	Continuity is maintained not in looking back to how other religions have been guided and satisfying their laws, but by recognizing the common source of revelation and guidance.	The OBN in Hebrews demonstrates continuity: Hebrews 1:1–2 claims that God has been speaking through the prophets and now through the Son. Hebrews 7:1—10:18 shows Jesus fulfilling the details of the priesthood, sacrifice, and Day of Atonement perpetually.

For this reason, Curry is correct to contend that the Christian missiologist must make the OBN explicit to demonstrate that the Christ event is fitting. What this book has argued, then, is that the book of Hebrews demonstrates such fittingness, showing that the Christ event includes and extends the narrative, ritual, and doctrine that precedes it. In so doing, Hebrews challenges the Qur'an's claim to continuity directly at the point of Christ's atonement. The barriers to communication are significant, but the book of Hebrews can be leveraged to overcome such barriers by telling history distinctly.

Conclusion

This book has attempted to allow the Qur'an to speak about atonement, sacrifice, and the overarching story of the world in order to better understand what it means by and does with stories with at least superficial biblical counterparts. In so doing, this project intends to recognize the truth in Patrick Cate's statement, "To begin outside of the Muslim mind, driving home points which [sic] Muslims categorically reject, is similar to banging our heads against the wall."[74] Therefore, great effort has gone into preparing the Christian missiologist to hear the book that is influencing the Muslim audience in front of them because hearing the Qur'an on its own terms allows the Christian communicator to avoid imposing extra-qur'anic meaning on shared words and concepts. Likewise, such attention helps the communicator understand how the words that one uses will be received by the audience.

While this chapter has demonstrated that Hebrews, through its presentation of the OBN, contains content important for overcoming the significant barriers to communication investigated herein, it remains to consider how one might utilize this content to explain Christian atonement to an audience influenced by the worldview and teaching of the Qur'an.

Returning to the introduction, one might recall the three categories of contextualization models with which this project concerns itself: combative models, conversational models, and OBN models. While each model exhibits certain strengths and weaknesses, the burden of the next chapter will be to offer a contextualization model driven by the content provided by Hebrews that capitalizes on each one's strengths while mitigating some of the weaknesses. It should be stated clearly from the outset that no model should ever claim to provide the means for convincing people of the truth of the Christian message. Instead, this model proposes

---

74. Cate, "Gospel Communication," 281.

to overcome the communication barriers listed above while also providing freedom for cultural appropriation of the message.

The final chapter argues that using the content of Hebrews to drive a conversation with an audience that is in the process of encountering, understanding, and applying a different worldview than their own requires contextual sensitivity and conscientiousness. Therefore, rather than leaving the reader with content but no model for contextual application, chapter 6 will propose a trialogical and critical contextualization model to be employed as the Christian sits under Scripture with those raised under the Qur'an.

6

Hebrews and Contextual Communication

The Cross-Cultural Communicative Power of the OBN

It has been the burden of this project to argue that the book of Hebrews can be used to challenge the Qur'an's claim to completing prior revelation while also helping to communicate a biblical perspective on atonement in Christ. The preceding chapters have demonstrated that the content of Hebrews and its teaching on atonement in Christ conflicts with the Qur'an on multiple levels. However, the narrative structure of Hebrews' argument helps to overcome the communication barriers that arise from such points of conflict by defining its terms in context, by demonstrating continuity with previous ritual and revelation, and by establishing and reinforcing a biblical worldview along the way. Therefore, the content of Hebrews naturally aids the Christian communicator by demonstrating the Christ event's fittingness within the OBN in which it functions.

However, communication and understanding are but the first steps in contextual appropriation of a concept such as atonement. As the introduction demonstrated, there are at least three broad models of contextual approach that Christians dedicated to a high view of Scripture utilize in ministry to Muslims. Addressing the strengths and weaknesses of each, then, this final chapter proposes a contextualization model that employs Hebrews as its initial content and that allows for cultural expression of application and theology. Prior to doing so, however, it is important to consider the two factors in faithfully executing the mandate to contextualize.

Biblically Faithful and Culturally Meaningful Contextualization

Despite the prevalence of contemporary literature promoting contextualization, it is not merely recent scholarly journals or monographs that encourage such efforts. Rather, Matthew 28:18–20 provides a biblical basis for the church's work of contextualization. In this passage, after Jesus's resurrection and in his final earthly address to his disciples prior to his ascension, Jesus sends out his followers as witnesses called to make disciples of all nations. Since Matthew 28:19–20 records that the disciples are explicitly called to "go and make disciples of all nations . . . teaching them to obey all that [Jesus has] commanded them," Jesus commits them to the task of faithfully communicating across national, linguistic, and cultural barriers the testimony of his kingship, the instructions of his rule, and the atonement it makes possible.[1] Such a task has been the work of the church throughout time; however, only in recent history have missiologists described this process with the term "contextualization."

As a term, contextualization entered into missiological vocabulary by way of the Theological Education Fund and its address to the World Counsel of Churches in 1972.[2] Two years later, Byang Kato employed the term as a conservative evangelical in his address to the Lausanne conference.[3] Since then it has been widely used by those identifying as evangelicals and by those who take the label liberal. As a term employed by those of widely different theological commitments, particularly regarding the authority of the Bible, contextualization manifests in a wide variety of ways.[4] For one who does not hold to a high view of Scripture, cultural concerns often outweigh biblical teaching when it comes to contextualizing faith. For one who does maintain a high view of Scripture, the understanding of biblical truth can at times lead to neglecting the cultural concerns that arise for the audience.

While this project takes a high view of biblical authority, inerrancy, and infallibility—and accordingly, affirms the universal nature of biblical truth, it also recognizes with Stephen Bevans that that human theologizing should not be equated with the universal truths of Scripture. The

---

1. Matt 28:18–20; Acts 1:7. See also Moreau, *Contextualization*, 63, who defines contextualization as communication of the unchanging word within a changing world.

2. Hesselgrave and Rommen, *Contextualization*, 28.

3 Moreau, *Contextualization*, 34.

4. Moreau, *Contextualization*, 34; see also, Hesselgrave and Rommen, *Contextualization*, 28.

work of expressing theology is a derivative process in which the human author extracts meaning from Scripture, systematizes it into categories, arranges it, and expresses it. As such, it is an inherently cultural process.[5] Thus, the question remains, "Is there a contextualization model for work among Muslims that is both biblically faithful and culturally meaningful?" In other words, is it possible for a Christian missiologist to read the Bible with a conversation partner influenced by the Qur'an so as to work out theology together in such a way that the Bible remains authoritative and application is expressed in culturally appropriate ways?

This final chapter argues that by combining the missiological insights of Paul Hiebert with the hermeneutical posture of N. T. Wright, a biblically faithful and culturally sensitive contextualization model emerges, allowing the Christian communicator to use the book of Hebrews as initial content and to propose a robust model for contextualization work among Muslims.

Finally, as the introduction argued, there are three broad categories of contextualization models into which Christians with a high view of Scripture fall: combative models, conversational models, and OBN models. Drawing together Hebrews, Hiebert, and Wright, then, this chapter will produce a trialogical critical contextualization (TCC) model that capitalizes on the strengths of each of the three models while mitigating their weaknesses.

Biblical Content, Narrative Theology, and Missiological Insight

The brief treatment above of the points of tension surrounding the process of contextualization suffices to reveal the poles of the debate. If those with a high view of Scripture define contextualization as the communication of the unchanging Word of God in changing contexts, then the camps are divided between those who allow the Word to exhibit more formative control and those who expect the culture to have more say in subsequent

---

5. So Bevans, *Models of Contextual Theology*, 3, whose book is a helpful assessment of various approaches to contextual theology that recognizes two *loci theologicus*: the Bible and human experience. Bevans does well throughout his work to militate against a slide into relativism, and instead argues that, since all reality is mediated by a meaning located within a culture, one cannot merely extract derivative teachings from Scripture without expressing them in some cultural garb.

expressions of theology.⁶ What this project argues, however, is that one might retain the Bible's ultimate place in the work of contextualization by reading Scripture together with someone from a different culture. At the same time, by encouraging the reader from the receptor culture to engage in the work of cultural appropriation of biblical teaching, one avoids at least some of the foreign influence and gains much insight by seeing the text through the eyes of the receiver culture.

It is appropriate, then, that a contextualization model draw from at least three streams of influence: a biblical starting point, a hermeneutical posture for doing biblical theology, and a rigorous commitment to cultural application. Therefore, as the preceding chapters have argued, the proposed model will argue that Hebrews is a helpful starting point as a biblical foundation while the following section will draw on insights from two leading scholars to complete this three-part model. From the perspective of a missiologist, Paul Hiebert's framework for critical contextualization will provide the skeleton for the proposed model. In addition, the contribution of biblical theology and hermeneutical posture will come from N. T. Wright's five-act-play approach to Scripture.

Critical Realist Epistemology

Of the many contributions made by both N. T. Wright and Paul Hiebert, their work in popularizing and applying a critical realist epistemology proves the most helpful in laying the methodological groundwork for a sophisticated critical contextualization model.⁷ With the collapse of modernity, its self-confident positivism has been rejected as no longer tenable. Therefore, one can no longer maintain the naïve claim to be apprehending reality directly without being historically and culturally located. Instrumentalism and its attendant relativism thus threaten to fill the epistemic void, rendering all truth claims subjective and impotent in the post-modern paradigm.⁸ Evangelicalism, maintaining commitments to divine revelation and biblical authority, can neither succumb to a

---

6. See Moreau, *Contextualization*. In this book, Moreau provides one of the most recent treatments of the spectrum of evangelical approaches to contextualization on the market. His findings reveal this binary tendency between those who prioritize the Word and those who prioritize the culture.

7. For Wright's treatment of critical realism, see Wright, *People of God*, 61–64. For Hiebert's presentation of critical realism, see Hiebert, *Missiological Implications*, 68.

8. Hiebert, *Missiological Implications*, 68.

non-realist epistemology, nor can it remain naively positivistic assuming its perspective to be entirely neutral and objective. Critical realism, then, is widely hailed as the appropriate way forward.[9]

As a realist, one can claim that there is truth to which our language and knowledge approximates itself. Yet as a critic, one is forced to maintain a humble approach, recognizing human limitations in the endeavor toward complete knowledge. As Hiebert claims, "Critical realist epistemology strikes a middle ground between positivism, with its emphasis on objective truth, and instrumentalism, with its stress on the subjective nature of human knowledge."[10] Taking this stance, then, one expects that God himself can speak truly to fallible mankind while ever drawing them nearer to truth. Critical realism lays a foundation of trust in biblical authority while expecting to be challenged, deepened, and expanded in one's theology through contact with both the Word and the world. This perspective makes the work of theological contextualization necessary, possible, and dialogical, and it provides the epistemological footing upon which Hiebert builds his critical contextualization model.[11]

Paul Hiebert's Critical Contextualization

One early attempt to provide a contextualization spectrum to chart the various approaches to contextualization comes from David Hesselgrave and Edward Rommen's book, *Contextualization: Meaning, Methods, and Models*.[12] Labeling the poles of the spectrum orthodox and liberal, one sees that both extremes exhibit shortcomings. As Hesselgrave and Rommen indicate, "orthodox" methodology takes a didactic posture, encouraging monologue in which the communicator takes the biblical message and gives it to a new culture.[13] On the other extreme, the "liberal" methods that Hesselgrave considers tend toward dialogue between two contexts with relatively little influence from the biblical text.[14] As an early attempt to define and describe various Christian approaches to contextualization, Hesselgrave's work was helpful; however, it lacks the nuance

---

9. Along with Wright and Hiebert, see also Clark, *To Know*, 199.
10. Hiebert, *Missiological Implications*, 69.
11. Hiebert, *Missiological Implications*, 75.
12. Hesselgrave and Rommen, *Contextualization*, 157.
13. Hesselgrave, *Communicating Christ*, 109.
14. Hesselgrave, *Communicating Christ*, 136.

required to include contextualization models that maintain a high view of Scripture while expecting the culture to wield shaping influence on contextual expressions of theology.

Along with other evangelicals espousing a critical realist epistemology, Hiebert's proposal of a critical contextualization model walks a middle road by way of four guiding principles: 1) the Bible is authoritative as the rule of faith and life; 2) the Holy's Spirit's work and leading in individuals is recognized; 3) the hermeneutical community is influential (though not determinative) in producing theology; 4) multiple cultures are involved in developing shared understanding on key theological issues.[15] His four criteria provide a basic foundation; however, they lack a sense of direction and momentum for approaching a new context with the gospel. In order to provide some traction, Hiebert's model requires more specificity in the area of posture, structure, and content. As the rest of this chapter will argue, N. T. Wright's contribution provides a helpful hermeneutical posture and structure while the book of Hebrews provides helpful initial content to that which is lacking in Hiebert's scheme.

N. T. Wright's Five-Act Play

In the first volume of Wright's *magnum opus*, *Christian Origins and the Question of God*, the image of a five-act play is used as a conceptual framework for the biblical metanarrative by which the Bible exhibits its authority. Wright imagines finding a previously unpublished copy of a Shakespearian play in which the first four acts are complete and intact. However, the fifth act includes only the first and last scenes with a conspicuous gap between them. Wright organizes the first four acts of the biblical story under the headings of "Creation," "Fall," "Israel," and "Jesus" before turning his attention to the fifth act in which Christians currently find themselves.[16] In his estimation, the task left to the church in the fifth act is to immerse itself in the story of acts 1–4 and the conclusion to

---

15. Hiebert, *Anthropological Reflections*, 91–92. Another evangelical theologian who advocates for critical realism is Clark, *To Know*, 386. See also Wright, *People of God*, 32–37.

16. Wright, *People of* God, 140–43. It is worth noting that Michael Goheen and Craig Bartholomew (*Drama of Scripture*) add a sixth act to their framework: new creation. Their emphasis on eschatology and teleology as part and parcel of the metanarrative is laudable and important, but for the purposes of this project, Wright's model illuminates the call to grounded-yet-dynamic contextualization.

which the final act is pointing. In light of this, the people of the church must act out their parts in fitting with what has come before, where the story culminates, and by submitting to the instructions given in the fifth act's first scene.[17]

The ramifications of Wright's suggestion for Christian theologizing, then, are manifold. As one approaches the biblical text from the posture of earnest desire to understand one's role in the fifth act of history, it also invites the global community into a common storyline. While his five-act structure intends to illustrate the outworking of biblical authority, Wright's hermeneutical posture to the biblical story develops Hiebert's criteria for critical contextualization into a more robust model as demonstrated below.

Biblical Basis

First, Wright's hermeneutical posture summons theologians back to the Old Testament in order to understand the present by way of the storyline. Likewise, and as suggested throughout the previous chapters, the author of Hebrews' understanding of atonement emphasizes the story of Israel and her interactions with YHWH. This is particularly helpful for cultures of non-Judeo-Christian backgrounds, though Wright argues that *all* proper early-Christian theology was self-consciously rooted in the soil of Judaism and subsequent expressions of theology should be likewise.[18]

Beyond worldview formation, the story of YHWH and Israel gives narrative-driven definition to the Bible's terminology. When one speaks in shorthand of "sin" or "atonement," it is not self-evident what these terms mean. Being able to demonstrate the effects of sin and the fall by way of Israel's interactions with YHWH and her religious practices gives a more robust and "lived" definition to subsequent propositions. When one reads the intricate and gory details surrounding the Day of Atonement, the words "sin" and "atonement" carry much more meaning than they do in what Scot McKnight refers to as "destoried propositions."[19]

Ultimately, attention to the story that the Bible tells and the way the Bible tells it demonstrates healthy hermeneutical practice and embodies a high view of Scripture. This opens a window into reality and extends an

---

17. Wright, *People of God*, 142.
18. Wright, *People of God*, 457–58.
19. McKnight, *King Jesus Gospel*, 50.

invitation to play one's part in God's world. By beginning with the book of Hebrews, then, a Christian communicator provides a biblically determined survey of the entire OBN as the author presents it to locate and explain the atonement that Hebrews presents as accomplished through the Christ event.

Work of the Spirit

Second, Wright's fourth and fifth acts are connected by Jesus' promise to send his Spirit, the dramatic arrival portrayed in act 2, and beyond.[20] God has attended to the storyline through creation and covenant in acts 1–3, has fulfilled and extended covenant in act 4 and has given his Spirit as the guarantee of the fifth act's fitting conclusion: a conclusion that establishes a new beginning. The opening scene to act 5 includes the Spirit being given to the church along with the Spirit-inspired writings upon which the actors will base their improvisation.[21]

While it seems risky to act out what Wright refers to as "missing parts" of the play, he notes, "The ultimate result is guaranteed, within the story itself, by the playwright's gift of his own spirit to the actors," though he goes on to say, "but this cannot be taken to validate in advance all that they do or say."[22] Therefore, as the Christian communicator opens the book of Hebrews with an audience influenced by the Qur'an, one does so expecting that the Holy Spirit will both challenge the audience through the points of divergence in worldview discussed in chapter 5, and also that the Holy Spirit will reveal aspects of Hebrews' teaching to the Christian communicator that were previously unnoticed due to the blind spots of the Christian's own contextual lens.

Community Hermeneutics

Third, the actors involved, having been immersed in the story, following the Spirit and Spirit-given instructions, are not left alone. The story so far has involved individuals, while never being individualistic. To that end, Wright notes, "We are looking, as the material is looking, for and at a

---

20. See Luke 24:49.
21. Wright, *People of God*, 143.
22. Wright, *People of God*, 143.

vocation to be the people of God in the fifth act of the drama of creation."[23] As the people of God, then, the church has the responsibility to extend the story corporately and to work together to examine the Scriptures, seek the Spirit, and forge ahead on the world's stage, telling and incarnating a story that makes sense of life as a whole. As Hebrews extends the story of Israel through the Christ event, it naturally also encourages each successive generation of readers to extend and apply its message as they join Christ outside of the camp, approaching Mount Zion and the heavenly city (Heb 12–13). This task requires the community of actors to immerse themselves in the script thus far, studying its warp and woof so as to appropriately improvise on an ever-changing stage, and encouraging other actors to likewise play their roles as they join Jesus outside the camp of their context (Heb 13:13).

Particularly for those far-removed geographically, chronologically, and culturally from the original texts, such proper improvisation will likely be a difficult task. The cultural world of the Bible, particularly the ancient communities of the Old Testament, will rub against the cultural trappings of many modern contexts. However, in order to act appropriately, the actors must subject themselves to the directives in the script so as to participate with the people of God. Again, Hebrews allows the Christian to encounter a canonical example of an OBN summary with an audience of a different culture so as to prompt this kind of reflection on the story thus far.

The Christian community has been called onto the stage in act five as a communally prophetic voice, embodying and communicating the gospel and its implications to the world. Wright's model capitalizes on Hiebert's desire to practice hermeneutics in community, but it also requires such communal exegesis to be enacted and embodied together in real life. Investigating the OBN through Hebrews with an audience of a different culture broadens the hermeneutical process by including the insight that emerges from reading the Bible through different cultural lenses. It also provides an opportunity to mutually chasten each other's theological conclusions.

---

23. Wright, *People of God*, 142.

Global Perspective

Finally, while there is to be a local component of the communal task of improvisation, there is great merit in recognizing the global scope of the narrative and of the stage. Wright's model does not envision a local troupe working on a small-time community theatre production. The model presupposes that the play in which the actors are immersing themselves in order to appropriately improvise a final act is in fact the story of everything. Of the "extant script" for act 5, one particularly beautiful piece is the closing scene that includes actors of every tribe, tongue and nation worshipping God (Rev 7:9–12). If that is the goal and the end to which the global story points, it is fitting that the global community would have a say in advancing the plot throughout the final act. Thus, when one reads Hebrews with a Muslim or formerly Muslim audience, one invites the opportunity for new insights as to how it is most appropriately performed.

Having established an epistemological posture and a basic, biblical definition of the gospel, one is able to engage the task with humble confidence. In light of this, then, Wright's five-act-play illustration enhances Hiebert's critical contextualization model by providing content, boundaries, and momentum. Prior to proposing a contextualization model, however, the issue of communication theory must first be addressed.

Trialogical Critical Contextualization

As noted above, David Hesselgrave has put forth a spectrum that attempts to chart the various models of contextualization and their correlative perspectives on biblical authority.[24] While helpful in providing generalities, recent theologians have challenged Hesselgrave's spectrum, showing that conservative views of Scripture do not necessarily exclude dialogical or synthetic models of contextualization. In fact, postured as a critical realist with a high view of Scripture, one is positioned to enter cross-cultural dialogue expectantly, removing cultural blinders and seeing the biblical message more fully.

A prime exemplar of this perspective is David Clark, who rejects simplistic didactic models of communication and theology on his way to proposing a robust dialogical model that will involve "actually doing

---

24. Hesselgrave, *Contextualization*, 157.

theology in the new context."²⁵ While Scripture remains preeminent, the gospel encountered by the fresh eyes and hearts of a different culture could shed light on long-held blind spots of traditional theology. In dialogical conversation under Scripture, then, "particular readings or traditional interpretations of the Bible—not to be equated with Scripture—may come under the searchlight of new insights that emerge from cultural perspectives of the Other."²⁶

Clark goes on to warn that this is not a search for new and novel readings, but rather it is the genuine pursuit of biblical illumination in the company of believers from different cultural settings. He writes, "*Evangelical* dialogical theology gives priority to Scripture due to its authority. Since the values embedded in cultures are not theologically neutral, the flow of influence must move dominantly from the Bible to culture. Yet theology includes feedback loops."²⁷ As Clark articulates, this model treats Scripture as the final authority while treating humans and culture with dignity, inviting conversation to better understand the Bible.

Given this understanding of cross-cultural theologizing, the process of missionary communication as a trialogue includes three ongoing dialogues: the Bible speaking to the missionary; the Bible speaking to the new culture; the missionary and the new culture speaking to each other under the authority of Scripture.²⁸ Through ongoing dialogues between the three planes mentioned above, each culture expands its own biblical understanding, while simultaneously sharpening, challenging, and encouraging the other culture.²⁹

The insights of Hiebert, Wright, and others referenced herein have shed a great deal of light on the process of faithful evangelical contextualization. Hiebert's critical contextualization has been given some structure and content by applying Wright's five-act-play approach to the biblical narrative, and Clark has been helpful in crafting a trialogical

25. Clark, *To Know*, 80.
26. Clark, *To Know*, 86.
27. Clark, *To Know*, 87. Emphasis original.
28. Hiebert uses "trialogue" to indicate his approach to Scripture, viewing systematic, biblical, and anthropological theology in conversation (Hiebert, *Anthropological Reflections*, 12). While this is a helpful hermeneutical position, this chapter will utilize the word "trialogue" to indicate the conversations between the Bible and the sender's culture, the Bible and the recipient culture, and the two cultures in dialogue under Scripture's authority.
29. Packer, "Infallible Scripture," 348, envisions a lifelong journey along the "hermeneutical spiral" described by Osborne, *Hermeneutical Spiral*.

communication model for how to theologize alongside of another culture under the authority of Scripture. Finally, the book of Hebrews has provided the content with which one might begin the process of the trialogical critical contextualization (TCC) model. What remains is to synthesize it all, sketch out a proposal for a TCC model, and to test it, which comprises the rest of the present chapter.

The Bible and Critical Realism

The proposed TCC model operates on two presuppositions. First, the Bible is the revealed, sufficient, inspired and authoritative word of God.[30] All theology is derivative and must ultimately be tried against the Bible. Second, however, critical realism recognizes the fact that, while knowledge gained in the interpretive process is genuine and coherent, it remains partial and localized. Thus, humbly with Paul, a critical realist admits, "Now we see in a mirror dimly, but then face to face. Now I know in part; then I shall know fully, even as I have been fully known."[31] Thus one can claim that biblically based theology touches that which is truly real, but that which is truly real is always greater than the partial and culturally biased understandings of it represented in various theologies.[32] These commitments ground theologians in the surety of the Scriptures while embracing a global hermeneutical community in order to better understand them together. Driven by these commitments, practice ensues.

Atonement and Israel

Proclamation of the message of atonement in Christ as seen through the OBN-driven argument of Hebrews is an ideal place to start because it relies upon the story of Israel to explain why Christ's death, resurrection, and ascension are meaningful. This requires investment of time, however, and the missionary committed to this model must not be concerned primarily with the quickest, most concise way to verbalize Christ's atonement.

---

30. 2 Pet 1:21; 2 Tim 3:16; Hiebert, *Anthropological Reflections*, 29.

31. 1 Cor 13:12.

32. Hiebert, *Anthropological Reflections*, 30.

Such a model views explanation of Hebrews' presentation of atonement in Christ as an invitation leading to deepening conversation and robust discipleship, including and building on the story of Israel that prepares the way for the Christ event.

Concepts of sin and salvation remain shallow if not rooted in the fall, the persistence of human sin, the temple and sacrificial system, and the story of Israel and her God. Wright's five-act-play approach encourages a narrative hermeneutic that will produce biblical understanding of biblical terminology and will reproduce communities of exegetes capable of understanding and applying the Word to their world.[33] As the previous chapters have demonstrated, the book of Hebrews defines and explains its use of atonement (*kaffara*) language by using it in the context of the OBN.

Ongoing Trialogue

Finally, this model is inherently open-ended and ongoing. As a worldwide troupe of players on God's stage, the global community is needed in order to make sense of this fifth act. Through intentional, cross-cultural conversation in light of what has gone before and where we will be when the curtain falls on this age, the worldwide church will benefit from—not despite—the wide variety of cultural lenses through which we all see the world. To that end, this model encourages persistent pursuit of mutually refined understanding through all three dialogues under Scripture's authority and supervision. Part of proclaiming the biblical message is embodying it in culturally diverse expressions of the biblically unified worship of God.

---

33. Bauckham, *Bible and Mission*, 12.

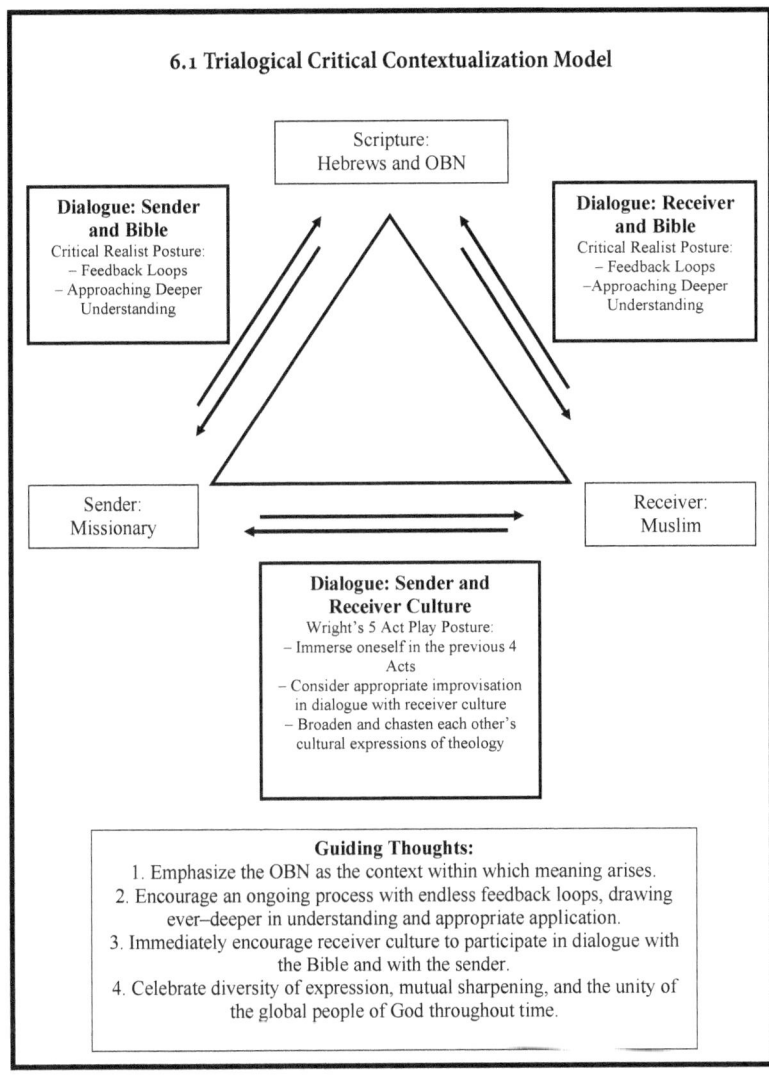

Addressing Contextualization Concerns

Along with Hiebert's concern to propose the critical contextualization guidelines considered above, he also includes seven concerns for those practicing contextualization. These concerns are valid, and prior to supposing the preceding argument to have satisfied Hiebert's four criteria for critical contextualization, it is advantageous to the reader to attend to

Hiebert's concerns in order to ensure that the TCC adaptation of Hiebert's work remains free of the dangers his concerns highlight.

Following Hiebert's general concerns, then, this section will also assess the TCC model against the three broad categories of approach to Mission among Muslims considered in the introduction. It will show that, though this model may not be without flaws of its own, it builds on the strengths of each of the three models while shoring up the weaknesses.

Hiebert's Concerns[34]

While Hiebert's four criteria for his critical contextualization model provide a helpful, positive set of guidelines for the work of contextually appropriate theologizing, his seven cautions prove equally helpful in providing guardrails that protect the missiologist from going too far in either allowing culture to play too formative a role or not giving it enough room to express itself at all.

Western Clothes

The first of Hiebert's concerns is that the message presented to the host culture might come dressed in Western clothes. In other words, the propositions and conclusions that have made their way into Western theology are robed in cultural garb and could potentially discourage the audience from accepting the underlying truth these propositions attempt to present.

By using the book of Hebrews as the content for explaining a Christian perspective of atonement in Christ, however, the missionary is able to begin with the supracultural biblical message. What the preceding chapters have shown is that, in seeking to further define the terms and propositions utilized, the OBN in Hebrews provides the context for understanding the robust concept of atonement as it appears in Leviticus 16–17 and culminates in Hebrews' presentation of the Christ event.

Thus, rather than presenting the derivative forms of atonement theory such as penal substitution, *Christus victor*, and the like, the narrative allows for the development of these concepts without requiring the host culture to import the Western contextualizations of these biblical truths

---

34. The following seven concerns are a part of Hiebert's chapter on critical contextualization in *Anthropological Reflections*, 75–92.

that emerge in Western compilations of systematic theology.[35] As chapter 3 demonstrated, the doctrines of penal substitution, *Christus victor*, and liberation motifs of the atonement arise from within Hebrews. However, such motifs emerge from within the OBN presentation of Hebrews, and by encountering such concepts in their narrative context, the audience is free to label and express such concepts for themselves.

Rather than presenting the atonement in Western cultural garb, a Christian may present the Bible's teaching about sin and atonement in a way that not only confronts a new culture but also depicts the meaning of shorthand terminology. While a Western missionary will likely yet view the narrative through Western eyes, the invitation to the new culture to read the story allows for fresh, organic insight. This encourages the message of atonement to be understood from within a variety of cultural settings, while also allowing its message to challenge and correct competing worldviews.

Forms and Meaning

Hiebert's second caution to the Western contextualizer calls for attention at the point of translation of the message along with what vehicles are used to convey the message. As a cultural outsider, the missionary may not understand the associations that attend various potential vehicles of communication, nor the nuances carried by specific vocabulary. Here again, while the vocabulary associated with atonement may be problematic when used in isolation, the story as it stands in Hebrews naturally informs the meaning of individual words and invites reflection. While some of the forms may be more rigidly fixed by the text than others, this method would encourage the new culture to recognize appropriate and inappropriate cultural forms for conveying Scripture's message and embodying it in practice and on stage.

This caution is particularly important for missionaries working among Muslim people who are forced to make decisions regarding vocabulary to use in telling biblical stories: should one use the Christian Arabic name for Jesus, *yasua'* (يسوع), or the qur'anic name for Jesus, *'aisa* (عيسى)? The TCC model encourages and provides space for the receptor culture to play a decisive role in such situations as the missionary will be

---

35. See the types of discussion that are part and parcel of Western styles of theology in Beilby and Eddy, *Four Views*.

less able to identify the unspoken connotations of a given form. In the process of trialogue, the new context and the missionary can more wisely select the mediums by which theology is transmitted.

Communication and Embodiment

The third of Hiebert's concerns is to ensure that any contextualized form of theology contains both a pedagogical and incarnational element. In other words, the theology produced by the TCC model must be both comprehended and lived out. Responding to this third concern, the image of the five-act play provides a helpful orientation to ensure embodiment.

While the missionary may initiate consideration of the biblical message, that message is clothed in a story into which the new context is invited. As a fellow actor, the missionary in trialogue with Scripture and the new culture will convey a desire to play the role correctly through embodiment and incarnation. The corporate nature of the trialogue naturally conveys an invitation into the fifth act, drawing on the story thus far as well as the responsibility of the audience to participate in its unfolding through the directives of the gospels and the ultimate destination to which it is all headed.

Likewise, as the book of Hebrews discusses atonement in Christ, the text summons the reader to draw near to God and to live as one surrounded by a great cloud of witnesses (Heb 12). Therefore, within the context of Hebrews, the teaching regarding atonement in Christ is inextricably related to a new way of living. Furthermore, as chapter 3 demonstrated, this new way of living continues the story that includes ancient Israel as a community of people identified by their God in their midst. As the audience engages Hebrews, the reader begins to sense its value and responsibility in seeing the play come to its fitting conclusion, living in such a way as to honor the great cloud of witnesses whose story continues through the global church (Heb 11–12).

Historical Roots

Fourth, Hiebert cautions against any contextualization efforts that would divorce the receptor audience from the long history of the people of God throughout time. This issue is directly and consistently addressed throughout the TCC model. Furthermore, by using the book of Hebrews as the specific content, one capitalizes on its inclusion of the overarching biblical narrative in understanding and expressing its theology.

In reading Hebrews, the new culture is consistently directed back to the historical story in order to define the central terms of the gospel. In conceiving of the hermeneutical process as appropriate improvisation in Wright's five-act play, one also recognizes the inescapable narrative setting within which one does the work of theology. In so doing, the new culture is trained to retain the historical connection to the whole story so as to rightly understand atonement, the community of faith, their present role, and the theology that derives from the narrative. In sum, both in Wright's scheme and through the OBN presented in Hebrews, the narrative outline exerts its communicative power over individual words and concepts by way of relentless reminder of the lived history—past, present, and future—in which such words and concepts arise and make sense.

Unity of Cross Culture Churches

The fifth of Hiebert's concerns involves the recognition that, along with historical connectedness to the people of God, any contextualization effort should also produce a sense of global unity and participation. In other words, while one must embrace cultural appropriation of the Christian message, one should also reject contextualization that results in separatist or nationalistic expressions of faith that consciously maintain divisions between themselves and like-minded Christian communities throughout history and around the world. According to Hiebert, any element of one's contextualization that fosters such division should be discarded.

As noted above, both the content of Hebrews and the *telos* to which the five-act-play posture points include a picture of people of every tribe, tongue, and nation around the throne of God. The story ends with the expectation that there will be a multitude of cultures present in the new creation, and thus it points the act-5 community to embody and substantiate that reality in anticipation. It invites the new culture into a living global Christian history in the present.[36] It is likely that the missionary will be responsible for providing the data of church history, as the new culture may not have a means to access it. Furthermore, accounts of the church around the world may need to be provided by the outsider.

---

36. Hiebert, *Anthropological Reflections*, 90.

However, through the subsequent trialogue, lessons learned from historical councils, figures, and disagreements may be brought to bear on issues at hand while also considering contemporary issues facing the church around the world. Such attention to the global scope of the ongoing play fosters connection between the new culture to a second history in which it now participates.

Avoid Uncritical Acceptance of Culture

Hiebert's sixth concern is that the contextualizer will include too little critique of the host culture for fear of causing offense or out of a desire to retain as much of the culture as possible. The TCC model responds to this concern by maintaining an ongoing dialogue between the missionary and the new culture. This dialogue expects each culture to do the work of hermeneutics in order to produce theology, but it also requires an openness on the part of both the missionary and the new culture in order to challenge and refine "conclusions" and aspects of the other's theology.

Within Wright's scheme, all the members of the troupe must be subject to scrutiny and willing to scrutinize their fellow actors. As questionable theological decisions are made or suspicious applications are put forward, the trialogue creates a public space for critique. This model strives to be a conduit of "iron sharpening iron." For that to be the case, each theologian must be willing to receive and give correction. By utilizing the book of Hebrews as the content with which the contextualization process begins, the Western Christian sits under Scripture itself with the audience and is subject to critique of his or her own improper cultural accommodations. Therefore, through the TCC, the missionary demonstrates that neither the sending culture nor the receiving culture are beyond the scrutiny of Scripture.

Avoid Syncretism

Finally, in summation of all that has been said above, Hiebert warns against any forms of syncretism whereby non-Christian practices and beliefs are allowed to comingle with the testimony of Scripture. Addressing this concern, both the TCC and the book of Hebrews capitalize on the OBN that sets forth YHWH as a jealous and exclusive God who then claims Jesus the Messiah to be *the* Way, Truth and Life.³⁷ Hebrews itself warns the reader to leave the camp and the old ways of approaching God in order to draw near through Christ alone (Heb 13:13). Likewise, by attending to the Day of Atonement and the surrounding narrative in Leviticus involving Nadab and Abihu, the reader is exposed to the results of approaching God in a strange or unprescribed way.

Likewise, by inviting a new culture to find their place in Hebrews' presentation of the OBN, the text itself invites the audience to discover the God who tells the one story of the one world in which the one God is at work. Each culture—including the missionary's home culture—smuggles bits of syncretism into the new life of a Christian. The process of sanctification and trialogue, however, aims to biblically eradicate such issues by way of "the expulsive power of a new affection" in the gospel of the king and his kingdom.³⁸ The TCC is simply an invitation to the worldwide community of Christians to humbly read Scripture together, listen to its message, and apply it in such a way as to display the beauty of the story before the watching world. While the TCC responds to Hiebert's concerns, it also capitalizes on the strengths of the three alternative models for contextualization among Muslims that were highlighted in the introduction while avoiding the weaknesses.

Three Models and Their Concerns

As noted above, this endeavor began by assessing various models of ministry to Muslims that fit under the umbrella of a high view of Scripture. The three models were examined and each exhibited besetting weaknesses along with positive elements. It remains for this project to demonstrate, if only in brief, that the proposed TCC model along with Hebrews as its initial content can both mitigate some of the besetting weaknesses of the three models and retain the positive elements within its approach. Following, then, is a brief breakdown of how the proposed model stands up to the three categories on offer.

---

37. John 14:6.
38. Chalmers, *Expulsive Power*.

Combative Models

While the combative model is perhaps the least helpful of the three models considered in this book, it is not without positive aspects. In fact, while the posture of the combative models is often unhelpful, it is the approach that is most likely to highlight the fact that the Qur'an and the Bible are incompatible at some of the most central points. For one intent on communicating a biblical perspective on atonement in Christ to an audience influenced by the Qur'an, then, it is important to be able to recognize the junctures at which the teaching of the Qur'an and the teaching of the Bible part ways.

By using the book of Hebrews as the initial content employed by the TCC model proposed herein, one can yet highlight the points of divergence between the Bible and the Qur'an while avoiding the posture of debate that characterizes so much of the combative approach to ministry among Muslims. Because the text of Hebrews highlights the distinctive way that the vocabulary of *kaffara* functions, the purpose of sacrificial ritual, and the overarching metanarrative that the Christ event claims to continue, points of divergence will naturally arise. However, they will arise in the context of Hebrews' demonstration that the Christ event fits in the OBN.

Since Hebrews defines atonement through its presentation of the OBN, the alternative story conflicts with the Qur'an rather than conflicting as an isolated doctrinal proposition. In other words, the OBN presentation explains why Jesus died on the cross rather than getting caught in an irreconcilable argument about the issue with someone arguing from the Qur'an's denial of the crucifixion and resurrection.[39] The OBN, then, not only argues for Jesus's death, but explains how it fits with biblical atonement.

---

39. It should be noted that Reynolds's article, "Muslim Jesus," 237–58, argues that the Qur'an does not argue that Jesus did not die, but rather that it is concerned to demonstrate that the Jews were not responsible for killing Jesus. While this is a possible interpretation, it is more likely that one's dialogue partner will understand the Qur'an's message in the traditional sense to mean that Jesus was not crucified nor did he die. For the traditional account from the most widely respected biography of Muhammad, see Guillaume, *Life of Muhammad*, 276.

Conversational Models

The burden of the conversational models discussed within this project is to communicate contextually and to recognize that the context has influence over the communication process. However, as the introduction contended, one of the negative aspects that emerges from such models is that the discussion regarding contextualization practice almost exclusively begins at the point of expression and application rather than beginning with the selection of an appropriate portion of the Bible.

Again, by employing the book of Hebrews within the TCC model proposed in this chapter, one can accommodate cultural nuances by sitting under the text with another person or group of people from within whose culture the message will be contextualized. Such a process allows the receiver culture to participate in the work of appropriation and theologizing from within their own dialogue with both Scripture and the Sender. Therefore, the TCC encourages the receiver culture to engage in the work of hermeneutics and application from the earliest stages rather than viewing contextualization as a process that the foreigner does prior to engaging with the receiver.

Furthermore, and in response to the weakness of the conversational model, this book has argued that the gravity of the contextualization process begins with the selection of appropriate Scripture. By proposing that contextualization among Muslims begins by mutual examination of the book of Hebrews, the TCC model claims and demonstrates reliance on the Bible from the very beginning of the encounter.

OBN Models

Finally, while this project finds OBN models to be the most helpful of the three, the introduction noted that these models fall short of ideal in that they require the sender to select, compile, and arrange the stories to be considered within an OBN presentation. In so doing, the sender inadvertently exerts formative influence on the understanding of the OBN. Rather than allowing the text to drive its own storyline, such models require the missionary to pick and choose which stories to highlight and which to leave out.

The beauty of the OBN as it is presented in Hebrews, however, is that it flows out of a book within the canon of Scripture itself. The TCC model applied to Muslim ministry intends to include a missionary sitting with a Muslim or formerly Muslim audience, unpacking the logic and narrative of Hebrews, and walking with the audience through the references Hebrews makes to the various components of the Hebrew Bible. Thus, an advantage the TCC has over other OBN models is that, in a situation where the missionary is no longer able to continue meeting with the audience, Hebrews itself expresses the OBN. Therefore this model does not require anyone to compile stories.

Ideally, however, the sender will remain a part of the trialogue, helping the receiver to discover the HB referents to which Hebrews is pointing, and discussing appropriate contextual expression of the Bible's message. Furthermore, rather than relying on a series of stories that reinforce the missionary's theological conclusions, the structure of the letter allows the book's own logical sequence and inclusion of such stories to explain the purpose of creation, the effects of the fall, atonement and the Christ event, and the end to which all things are going. Thus, both audiences under Scripture encounter the challenge and authority of the Bible, working out improvisation together.

Conclusions and Further Research

The TCC model presented in this chapter intends to hold together the supreme authority of the Bible with the reality that expression of theology and meaning within a variety of cultures will result in a cultural mosaic of Christianity. Though the work of theology under the TCC model includes a dialogue between two cultures under Scripture, seeking ways of improvisation together, this does not require that both cultures subsequently exhibit the unchanging truths of Scripture in the same manner.

What it does allow for, however, is a broader understanding of how broadly and beautifully the global church can apply the gospel and its implications meaningfully. In a sense, a missionary and a host culture sitting under Scripture together, differently expressing the same truths, is an advance celebration of the scene around the throne in Revelation 7, wherein people from each of the world's cultures will bring praise in their language to the one God dwelling in the midst of his people.

Summary

As this project comes to a close, it will be helpful to review the findings offered herein before considering what additional research might be required. The project began with the intention to argue that Christ's fulfillment of the Day of Atonement, as presented in the book of Hebrews, exposes distinct worldview differences between the Qur'an and Bible, and can be used to challenge qur'anic claims to completing prior revelation. In order to do so, chapters 2–4 sought to understand the teaching of Leviticus, Hebrews, and the Qur'an as they each address the idea of atonement from each text's own perspective. In so doing, and following the anthropological insights of Ninian Smart and N. T. Wright, it became apparent that atonement as a doctrine intermingles with ritual, metanarrative, and worldview in each text. Thus, adjustment to one's doctrine affects one's practice and understanding of ritual. An alternative conception of ritual, then, also affects the metanarrative one tells and rehearses, which subsequently alters one's worldview.

Atonement: Leviticus, Hebrews, and the Qur'an

Beginning with the doctrine of atonement as it appears and is explained through the ritual of the Day of Atonement as prescribed in Leviticus 16–17, chapter 2 followed Jay Sklar by demonstrating that atonement in the priestly literature of the HB involves a concept cluster including sacrifice, forgiveness/ransom, purification, and blood. Blood serves as the linchpin for the concept, serving as a symbol of life presented before God on behalf of his people that exhibits the power to stand for the corporate life of Israel that is forfeited by her collective sins. Blood also provides a cleansing of the holy place, camp of Israel, and people of Israel themselves due to its power to counteract the defilement of sin that encroaches on the camp.

Chapter 3 showed that when Hebrews picks up the ritual of the Day of Atonement (Heb 9–10), the author intends not only to reveal the Christ event as the completion of the Yom Kippur ritual, but also as the extension of the story in which Yom Kippur is embedded. Therefore, atonement and the annual sacrificial ritual that effected it for Israel is continued and completed once for all for the author of Hebrews because Jesus is the *telos* to which it pointed. Again, Hebrews' presentation of atonement demonstrates continuity with ancient Israel's understanding of God's purposes in creation, the damage caused by the fall, and God's provision of a remedy for such damage so that he might dwell in the midst of his people. The Qur'an does not exhibit the same kind of continuity.

Continuity: Hebrews and the Qur'an

Having investigated the claim to continuity that both Hebrews and the Qur'an make regarding prior revelation, it became apparent that both texts mean something different when they claim continuity. For the book of Hebrews, the Christ event is the proper continuation and extension of the same story told and rehearsed in ancient Israel's practice of the Day of Atonement. By retelling this story in the light of the Christ event, the author of Hebrews bends the arc of ancient Israel's metanarrative to and through Jesus, maintaining and expanding the worldview of ancient Israel while claiming the eternal effects of her atonement rituals in Christ.

Such a presentation of continuity, based in the unchanging purposes of God to create a people and dwell in their midst, stands in stark contrast to what the Qur'an intends when it claims to continue and perfect the religion that precedes it. For the Qur'an, chapter 4 and 5 revealed that the component parts of biblical atonement—sacrifice, forgiveness/ransom, and purification—are disconnected due to a distinct teaching on the role of blood. By removing blood's substitutionary and cleansing role from its teaching on forgiveness and purification, the Qur'an exposes multiple levels of conflict between its teaching and the teaching that precedes it.

Hebrews: Communication and Challenge

Finally, chapter 5 addressed the fact that the book of Hebrews provides a means of both confronting the Qur'an with an alternative metanarrative that makes sense of the world and includes attention to the details of previous revelation in laying claim to rightly continue the history stretching back through ancient Israel and even back to creation itself. Such a challenge, however, capitalizes on an OBN structure by which it overcomes several of the communication barriers that emerge from the divergent worldviews produced by the Qur'an's metanarrative and the metanarrative of the book of Hebrews.

The OBN structure of Hebrews overcomes the lexical barriers surrounding the concept of atonement in Arabic (*kaffara*) by positioning reference to atonement within the larger narrative setting in which it occurs. Thus, rather than allowing a biblical instance of the word to be filled with prior and divergent qur'anic meaning, the function of Jesus's atonement for sins is explained as a dual process of providing purification for sins and cleansing through the presentation of his blood in the heavenly tabernacle.

Likewise, ritual barriers prove surmountable by using Hebrews. Its OBN connection between ancient Israel's perception of sacrifice and the Christ event as the final sacrifice allows the audience to see the different function that sacrifice plays in the Bible to what it does in the Qur'an. For the Qur'an, sacrifice exists as a heavenly indication that a new dispensation of revelation has descended. Thus sacrifice is an ebenezer of remembrance and reminder to observe the tenets of the faith to which such a sacrifice points. For Hebrews, as for Leviticus, however, sacrifice is intimately connected to the process of effecting what Jay Sklar referred to as a "ransom-purgation" for sin.

Finally, due to its narrative shape, the argument of Hebrews invites the reader into the metanarrative that it tells, and in so doing, provides context for its doctrinal claims that Christ's sacrifice and his session at the right hand of God provides an eternal atonement that is the perfected form of the Yom Kippur sacrifice which was always but a shadow. By rehearsing and retelling ancient Israel's story, using the creation, fall, redemption, restoration framework of the OBN, Hebrews' content also forms and produces a worldview in which the teaching of atonement fits. At each juncture within Hebrews' presentation of the OBN, then, it weaves the thread of the single purpose of God dwelling with his people and receiving their worship.

Areas for Further Research

One of the limiting factors of this project was the focus on the Christian doctrine of atonement. While Hebrews provides helpful material for explaining atonement in Christ to an audience unfamiliar with the OBN, it would benefit the missiological community for someone to investigate other core doctrines in order to select portions of Scripture that would be appropriate for conveying a biblical perspective on them.

Furthermore, this book remained self-consciously focused on the Qur'an and its teaching. As indicated in the introduction, this decision arose from a desire to reach a broader audience, not distinguishing between Sunni and Shia' Muslims, or Turkish and Indonesian expressions of Islam. However, since the secondary teachings of Islam through the *Sunnah*, various schools of Islamic jurisprudence (*fiqh*), and one's geographical and cultural context exert formative pressure on individual expressions of the faith, it would behoove the missiological community to apply and adjust the findings of this research to the various contexts and branches of Islam in which missiologists intend to work and communicate.

Finally, using Hebrews as the initial content employed by the TCC model allows for significant exposure to Old Testament themes and narrative that find their fulfillment in Christ. While the book is replete with warnings and general commands for living as the new-covenant people in Christ, there is not much attention given to the idea of the church and the development of disciples. This leaves room and even demand for other scholars to suggest what content might be best to use in the formation of churches and the continuous development of disciples.

Conclusion

Ultimately, then, through its teaching on atonement, the Qur'an takes a fundamentally divergent worldview trajectory by telling an alternative story in which sacrifice plays a different role and the word atonement means something other than what the Bible means. Therefore, when one conditioned by the Qur'an encounters the claims regarding atonement presented in Hebrews, both points of conflict and communication barriers arise. At the same time, such points of conflict reveal key differences that a Christian communicator must acknowledge between the two systems prior to ensuring that communication has occurred.

Embracing such points of conflict, the preceding chapters have demonstrated that the OBN presentation in Hebrews is able to define atonement in context, explain its understanding of sacrifice in terms of the atoning ritual of Yom Kippur, and invite the audience to encounter the story of the people of God as a metanarrative that produces the worldview in which Hebrews' understanding of atonement makes sense. Thus, despite the conflict that arises by using Hebrews, such conflict is overcome through the power of an alternative narrative. For all of the previous reasons, then, we can conclude that Christ's fulfillment of the

Day of Atonement, as presented in the book of Hebrews, does expose distinct worldviews between the Qur'an and Bible, and it can be used to challenge qur'anic claims to completing prior revelation.

Bibliography

Abdo, Geneive. *No God but God: Egypt and the Triumph of Islam.* Oxford: Oxford University Press, 2000.
Accad, Martin. "Muḥammad's Advent as the Final Criterion for the Authenticity of the Judeao-Christian Tradition: Ibn Qayyim Al-Jawziyya's 'Hidayat Al-Hayara Fi Ajwibat Al-Yahud Wa-'l-Nasara." In *Three Rings: Textual Studies in the Historical Trialogue of Judaism, Christianity, and Islām,* edited by Barbara Roggema et al., 217–36. Dudley, MA: Peeters, 2005.
Adang, Camilla. *Muslim Writers on Judaism and the Hebrew Bible: From Ibn Rabbani to Ibn Hazm.* New York: Brill, 1996.
Ahmad, Mirza Tahir. *Christianity: A Journey from Facts to Fiction.* Surry: Bath, 1994. https://www.alislam.org/library/books/Christianity-A-Journey.pdf.
Akin, Daniel L. *1, 2, 3, John.* New American Commentary 38. Nashville: B&H, 2001.
Al-Bukhari. *Sahih Bukhari.* http://www.sahih-bukhari.com/Pages/Bukhari_3_31.php.
———. *Summarized Sahih Al-Bukhari: Arabic-English.* Translated by Muḥammad Muhsin Khan. Riyadh, Saudi Arabia: Darussalam, 1996.
Al-Faruqi, Isma'il R. *Islam.* Niles, IL: Argus, 1979.
Al Jazeera Centre for Studies. "The Arab Spring: Results of The Arab Youth Opinion Poll." *Reports* (blog), *Aljazeera Centre for Studies,* July 30, 2013. http://studies.aljazeera.net/en/reports/2013/07/.
Al-Tabari. "Tafsīr As-Saffaat 107." In *Ayat Al-Qur'an Al-Karīm.* http://quran.ksu.edu.sa/tafseer/tabary/sura37-aya107.html.
Anderson, C. P. "Who Are the Heirs of the New Age in the Epistle to the Hebrews?" In *Apocalyptic and the New Testament,* edited by Joel Marcus and Marion L. Soards, 255–77. Sheffield: JSOT, 1989.
Anyabwile, Thabiti. *The Gospel for Muslims: An Encouragement to Share Christ with Confidence.* Chicago: Moody, 2010.
Armstrong, Karen. *Muḥammad: A Biography of the Prophet.* London: Phoenix, 1993.
Asad, Muhammad, trans. *The Message of the Qur'an.* London: The Book Foundation. http://al-quran.info/#33.
Ashford, Bruce, ed. *Theology and Practice of Mission.* Nashville: B&H, 2011.
Attridge, Harold. *Hebrews: A Commentary on the Epistle to the Hebrews.* Hermeneia: A Critical and Historical Commentary on the Bible. Minneapolis: Fortress, 1989.
Attridge, Harold, et al. "Loving God and Neighbor Together: A Christian Response to *A Common Word Between Us and You*: An Unprecedented Breakthrough?" *IJFM* 24 (Winter 2007) 215–17.

Aulen, Gustaf. *Christus Victor.* Translated by A. G. Hebert. Austin: Wise Path, 2016.
Aziz-us-Samad, Ulfat. *Islām and Christianity.* Cairo: Al Falah Foundation, 2003.
Backhaus, Knut. "How to Entertain Angels." In *Hebrews: Contemporary Methods—New Insights,* edited by Gabriella Gelardini, 148–75. Leiden: SBL, 2008.
Bailey, Kenneth E. *Jesus Through Middle Eastern Eyes: Cultural Studies in the Gospels.* Downers Grove, IL: IVP Academic, 2008.
Barr, James. *The Concept of Biblical Theology: An Old Testament Perspective.* Minneapolis: Fortress, 1999.
Bartholomew, Craig G., and Michael W. Goheen. *Christian Philosophy: A Systematic and Narrative Introduction.* Grand Rapids: Baker, 2013.
———. *The Drama of Scripture: Finding Our Place in the Biblical Story.* 2nd ed. Grand Rapids: Baker, 2014.
———. "Story and Biblical Theology." In *Out of Egypt: Biblical Theology and Biblical Interpretation,* edited by Craig Bartholomew et al., 144–71. Grand Rapids: Zondervan, 2004.
Bauckham, Richard. *Bible and Mission.* Grand Rapids: Baker Academic, 2003.
Bauckham, Richard, et al., eds. *The Epistle to the Hebrews and Christian Theology.* Grand Rapids: Eerdmans, 2009.
Bavinck, J. H. *The Church Between Temple and Mosque: A Study of the Relationship Between the Christian Faith and Other Religions.* Grand Rapids: Eerdmans, 1981.
Bebbington, David. *Evangelicalism in Modern Britain: A History from the 1730s to the 1980s.* Grand Rapids: Baker, 1989.
Beilby, James K., and Paul R. Eddy, eds. *Four Views of the Atonement.* Downers Grove, IL: InterVarsity, 2006.
Belakhdar, Naoual, et al., eds. *Arab Revolutions and Beyond: Change and Persistence.* Proceedings of the International Conference, Tunis, November 12–13, 2013.
Bernard, Jody. "Anti-Jewish Interpretations of Hebrews: Some Neglected Factors." *Meliliah* 11 (2014) 25–52.
Bevans, Stephan B. *Models of Contextual Theology.* Rev. and exp. ed. Maryknoll, NY: Orbis, 2002.
Bishop, Eric F. F. "The Epistle to the Hebrews and the Religion of Islam." *The Muslim World* 28 (October 1938) 345–60.
Bloch, Abraham P. *The Biblical and Historical Background of the Jewish Holy Days.* New York: Ktav, 1978.
Boda, Mark. *A Severe Mercy: Sin and Its Remedy in the Old Testament.* Winona Lake, IN: Eisenbrauns, 2009.
Bosch, David. *Transforming Mission.* 20th anniversary ed. Maryknoll, NY: Orbis, 2011.
Bridger, Scott. *Christian Exegesis of the Qur'ān: A Critical Analysis of the Apologetic Use of the Qur'ān in Select Medieval and Contemporary Arabic Texts.* Ann Arbor, MI: ProQuest, 2013.
Brinner, William. "An Islamic Decalogue." In *Studies in Islamic and Judaic Traditions 1,* edited by William M. Brinner and Stephen D Ricks, 67–84. Atlanta: Scholar's Press, 1989.
Brown, Jonathan A. C. *Hadith: Muhammad's Legacy in the Medieval and Modern World.* Oxford: Oneworld, 2009.
Brown, Rick. "Biblical Muslims: Insider Movements: The Conversation Continues." *IJFM* 24 (Summer 2007) 65–74.

———. "Selecting and Using Scripture Portions Effectively in Frontier Missions: The First Foot Forward in Scripture Selection?" *IJFM* 18 (Winter 2001) 10–25.

———. "The 'Son of God': Understanding the Messianic Titles of Jesus." *IJFM* 17 (Spring 2000) 41–52.

———. "Why Muslims Are Repelled by the Term 'Son of God.'" *EMQ* 43 (2007) n.p. https://www.emqonline.com/node/2083.

Bruce, F. F. *The Epistle to the Hebrews*. NICNT. Grand Rapids: Eerdmans, 1964.

Cate, Patrick O. "Gospel Communication from Within." In *Encountering the World of Islam*, edited by Keith Swartley, 67–84. Tyrone, GA: Authentic, 2005.

Chalmers, Thomas. *The Expulsive Power of a New Affection*. Edited by William Hanna. Edinburgh: Constable, 1855.

Chapman, Colin. *Cross and Crescent: Responding to the Challenge of Islam*. 2nd ed. Downers Grove, IL: InterVarsity, 2007.

———. "The God Who Reveals." In *Muslims and Christians on the Emmaus Road*, 127–47. Monrovia, CA: MARC, 1989.

———. "Rethinking the Gospel for Muslims." In *Muslims and Christians on the Emmaus Road*, 105–25. Monrovia, CA: MARC, 1989.

Chilton, Bruce D., and Jacob Neusner, eds. *Classical Christianity and Rabbinic Judaism*. Grand Rapids: Baker, 2004.

Clark, David K. *To Know and Love God: Method for Theology*. Wheaton, IL: Crossway, 2003.

Cockerill, Garreth. *The Melchizedek Christology in Hebrews 7:1–28*. Ann Arbor, MI: University Microfilms International, 1979.

———. "To the Hebrews, to the Muslims: Islamic Pilgrimage as a Key to Interpretation." *Missiology* 22 (July 1994) 347–59.

Cox, Wade. "Hebrew and Islamic Calendar Reconciled." http://www.ccg.org/weblibs/study-papers/p053.html.

Cragg, Kenneth. *The Call of the Minaret*. 3rd ed. Oxford: Oneworld, 2003.

Crawford T. J. *The Doctrine of Holy Scripture Respecting the Atonement*. Edinburgh: Blackwood, 1871.

Curry, Theodore. "Mission to Muslims." In *Theology and Practice of Mission*, edited by Bruce R. Ashford, 222–37. Nashville: B&H, 2011.

Cuypers, Michel. *The Banquet: A Reading of the Fifth Sura of the Qur'an*. Miami: Convivium, 2009.

Danby, Herbert. *The Mishna*. London: Oxford University Press, 1933.

Douglas, Robert. "Ongoing Strategy Debate in Muslim Missions." *IJFM* 11 (April 1994) 69–73.

Droge, A. J. *The Qur'an: A New Annotated Translation*. Reprint, Bristol, CT: Equinox, 2015.

Dunn, James D. G. *Unity and Diversity in the New Testament: An Inquiry into the Character of Earliest Christianity*. 3rd ed. London: SCM Press, 2006.

Eberhart, Christian. "Characteristics of Sacrificial Metaphors in Hebrews." In *Hebrews: Contemporary Methods—New Insights*, edited by Gabriella Gelardini, 37–64. Leiden: Brill, 2005.

Eisenbaum, Pamela M. "Locating Hebrews within the Literary Landscape of Christian Origins." In *Hebrews: Contemporary Methods—New Insights*, edited by Gabriella Gelardini, 213–37. Leiden: Brill, 2004.

Ellingworth, Paul. *The Epistle to the Hebrews: A Commentary on the Greek Text*. NIGTC. Grand Rapids: Eerdmans, 1993.
Firestone, Reuven. "The Qur'ān and the Bible: Some Modern Studies of Their Relationship." In *Bible and Qur'ān: Essays in Scriptural Intertextuality*, edited by John C. Reeves, 1–22. Atlanta: SBL, 2003.
Fowden, Garth. *Before and After Muhammad: The First Millennium Refocused*. Princeton: Princeton University Press, 2014.
Gabriel, Mark A. *Jesus and Muhammad: Profound Differences and Surprising Similarities*. LakeMary, FL: Charisma, 2004.
Gathercole, Simon. *Defending Substitution: An Essay on Atonement in Paul*. Grand Rapids: Baker Academic, 2015.
Geiger, Abraham. "What Did Muḥammad Borrow from Judaism?" In *The Origins of the Koran: Classic Essays on Islām's Holy Book*, edited by Ibn Warraq, 165–226. New York: Prometheus, 1998.
Geiger, Kaden. *A Monk's Topical Bible A–D*. Monastic Series 3. Revelation Insight, 2010.
Geisler, Norman. *Systematic Theology: In One Volume*. Bloomington, MN: Bethany House, 2011.
Geisler, Norman L., and Abdul Saleeb. *Answering Islam: The Crescent in Light of the Cross*. 2nd ed. Grand Rapids: Baker, 2002.
Gelardini, Gabriella. "Hebrews, an Ancient Synagogue Homily for Tisha Be-Av: Its Function, Its Basis, Its Theological Interpretation." In *Hebrews: Contemporary Methods—New Insights*, edited by Gabriella Gelardini, 107–27. Leiden: SBL, 2008.
———. "The Inauguration of Yom Kippur According to the LXX and Its Cessation or Perpetuation According to the Book of Hebrews." In *The Day of Atonement: Its Interpretations in Early Jewish and Christian Traditions*, edited by Thomas Hieke and Tobias Nicklas, 225–54. Boston: Brill, 2012.
Gelardini, Gabriella, ed. *Hebrews: Contemporary Methods—New Insights*. Leiden: SBL, 2008.
Georges, Jayson, and Mark D. Baker. *Ministering in Honor-Shame Cultures: Biblical Foundations and Practical Essentials*. Downers Grove, IL: IVP Academic, 2016.
Gesink, Indira Falk. *Islamic Reform and Conservativism: Al-Azhar and the Evolution of Modern Sunni Islam*. Rev. ed. New York: Tauris, 2014.
Gliders, William K. "The Day of Atonement in the Dead Sea Scrolls." In *The Day of Atonement: Its Interpretations in Early Jewish and Christian Traditions*, edited by Thomas Hieke and Tobias Nicklas, 63–73. Boston: Brill, 2012.
Goheen, Michael W. *A Light to the Nations: The Missional Church and the Biblical Story*. Grand Rapids: Baker, 2011.
Grabbe, Lester L. *An Introduction to Second Temple Judaism: History and Religion of the Jews in the Time of Nehemiah, the Maccabees, Hillel and Jesus*. New York: T. & T. Clark, 2010.
Green, Joel B. "The Kaleidoscopic View." In *The Nature of the Atonement: Four Views*, edited by James Beilby and Paul R. Eddy, 157–85. Downers Grove, IL: IVP Academic, 2006.
Griffith, Sidney H. "*Al-Naṣārā* in the Qur'ān: A Hermeneutical Reflection." In *New Perspectives on the Qur'ān: The Qur'ān in Its Historical Context 2*, edited by Gabriel Said Reynolds, 301–22. Routledge Studies in the Qur'ān. New York: Routledge, 2011.

———. *The Bible in Arabic: The Scriptures of the "People of the Book" in the Language of Islām*. Princeton: Princeton University Press, 2013.

———. *The Church in the Shadow of the Mosque: Christians and Muslims in the World of Islam*. Princeton: Princeton University Press, 2008.

Guillaume, A., trans. *The Life of Muḥammad: A Translation of Ibn Ishaq's Sirat Rasul Allah*. Oxford: Oxford University Press, 1982.

Gwynne, Rosalind Ward. *Logic, Rhetoric, and Legal Reasoning in the Qur'an: God's Arguments*. New York: RoutledgeCurzon, 2004.

Haddad, Yvonne Yazbeck. *Contemporary Islām and the Challenge of History*. Albany: State University of New York Press, 1982.

Hahn, Scott W. "Covenant, Cult, and the Curse-of-Death." In *Hebrews: Contemporary Methods—New Insights*, edited by Gabriella Gelardini, 65–88. Leiden: Brill, 2005.

Hanapi, Mohd Shukri. "The Conceptual Elements of the Development Worldview in the Qur'an: A Study of Thematic Exegesis." *American International Journal of Social Science* 2 (May 2013) 40–55.

Hausfeld, Mark. "The Necessity for Retaining Father and Son Terminology in Scripture Translations for Muslims." In *Controversies in Mission: Theology, People, and Practice of Mission in the 21st Century*, 210–29. EMS Series 24. Pasadena: Carey, 2016.

Hays, Richard B. *Echoes of Scripture in the Gospels*. Waco, TX: Baylor University Press, 2016.

———. "Here We Have No Lasting City: New Covenantalism in Hebrews." In *The Epistle to the Hebrews and Christian Theology*, edited by Richard Bauckham, et al., 151–73. Grand Rapids: Eerdmans, 2009.

———. *Reading Backwards*. Waco, TX: Baylor University Press, 2014.

Hesselgrave, David. *Communicating Christ Cross-Culturally*. Grand Rapids: Zondervan, 1991.

Hesselgrave, David, and Edward Rommen. *Contextualization: Meaning, Methods, and Models*. Leicester: Apollos, 1989.

Hiebert, Paul. *Anthropological Insights for Missionaries*. Grand Rapids: Baker Academic, 1985.

———. *Anthropological Reflections on Missiological Issues*. Grand Rapids: Baker, 1994.

———. *Missiological Implications of Epistemological Shifts: Affirming Truth in a Modern/Postmodern World*. Harrisburg, TN: Trinity, 1999.

———. *Transforming Worldviews: An Anthropological Understanding of How People Change*. Grand Rapids: Baker Academic, 2008.

Hieke, Thomas, and Tobias Nicklas, eds. *The Day of Atonement: Its Interpretations in Early Jewish and Christian Traditions*. Boston: Brill, 2012.

Hill, Charles, and Frank James, eds. *The Glory of the Atonement: Biblical, Theological, and Practical Perspectives*. Downers Grove, IL: IVP Academic, 2004.

Holmes, Stephen R. "Death in the Afternoon: Hebrews, Sacrifice, and Soteriology." In *The Epistle to the Hebrews and Christian Theology*, edited by Richard Bauckham, et al., 229–52. Grand Rapids: Eerdmans, 2009.

Hooker, Morna D. "Christ, the 'End' of the Cult." In *The Epistle to the Hebrews and Christian Theology*, edited by Richard Bauckham et al., 189–212. Grand Rapids: Eerdmans, 2009.

Houssney, Georges. *Engaging Islam*. Boulder: Treeline, 2010.

Ibn Kathīr. "Tafsīr As-Saffaat 107." In *Ayat Al-Qur'an Al-Karīm.* http://quran.ksu.edu.sa/tafseer/katheer/sura37-aya107.html#katheer.

Ibn Warraq, ed. *The Origins of the Koran: Classic Essays on Islām's Holy Book.* New York: Prometheus, 1998.

———. *What the Koran Really Says: Language, Text, and Commentary.* Amherst, NY: Prometheus, 2002.

Jabbour, Nabeel. *The Crescent through the Eyes of the Cross.* Carol Stream, IL: NavPress, 2008.

———. "Islamic Fundamentalism: Implications for Mission." *IJFM* 11 (April 1994) 81–86.

———. "Relational Evangelism Among Muslims: Is There a Better Way?" *IJFM* 25 (Fall 2008) 151–56.

Ja'far, Muḥammad Kamal Ibrahim. "Appendix E: *Islām* Looks at History." In *Contemporary Islām and the Challenge of History*, edited by Yvonne Yazbeck Haddad, 174–80. Albany: State University of New York Press, 1982.

Jeffery, Arthur. "Ghevond's Text of the Correspondence Between 'Umar II and Leo III.'" In *The Early Christian-Muslim Dialogue: A Collection of Documents from the First Three Islamic Centuries (632–900 A.D.): Translations with Commentary*, edited by N. A. Newman, 57–132. Hatfield, PA: Interdisciplinary Biblical Research Institute, 1993.

Jenkins, Philip. *The Lost History of Christianity: The Thousand-Year Golden Age of the Church in the Middle East, Africa, and Asia—and How It Died.* New York: HarperOne, 2008.

Kalimi, Isaac. "The Day of Atonement in the Late Second Temple Period." In *The Day of Atonement: Its Interpretations in Early Jewish and Christian Traditions*, edited by Thomas Hieke and Tobias Nicklas, 75–96. Boston: Brill, 2012.

Kapic, Kelly M. "Typology, the Messiah, and John Owen's Theological Reading of Hebrews." In *Christology, Hermeneutics and Hebrews: Profiles from the History of Interpretation*, edited by Jon C. Laansma and Daniel J. Treier, 135–54. London: T. & T. Clark, 2013.

Kaskas, Safi, and David Hungerford. *The Qur'an: With References to the Bible.* Fairfax, VA: Bridges of Reconciliation, 2016.

Kateregga, Badru D., and David Shenk W. *A Muslim and a Christian in Dialogue: Christians Meeting Muslims.* Harrisonburg, VA: Herald, 2011.

Katsh, Abraham. *Judaism in Islām: Biblical and Talmudic Backgrounds of the Koran and its Commentaries.* Philadelphia: Bloch, 1954.

Laansma, Jon C., and Daniel J. Treier, eds. *Christology, Hermeneutics, and Hebrews: Profiles from the History of Interpretation.* New York: T. & T. Clark, 2014.

Lane, William L. *Hebrews 1–8.* WBC 47a. Dallas: Word, 1991.

———. *Hebrews 9–13.* WBC 47b. Dallas: Word, 1991.

Lavine, Baruch. *In the Presence of the Lord: A Study of Cult and Some Cultic Terms in Ancient Israel.* Leiden: Brill, 1974.

Leithart, Peter. *Deep Exegesis: The Mystery of Reading Scripture.* Waco, TX: Baylor University Press, 2009.

———. *Delivered from the Elements of the World: Atonement, Justification, Mission.* Downers Grove, IL: IVP Academic, 2016.

Levenson, Jon. *Inheriting Abraham: The Legacy of the Patriarch in Judaism, Christianity, and Islām.* Princeton: Princeton University Press, 2012.

Lewis, Bernard. *The Arabs in History*. New York: Hutchinson's University, 1950.
———. *Faith and Power: Religion and Politics in the Middle East*. New York: Oxford University Press, 2010.
———. *Islām in History*. New York: Library Press, 1973.
Licona, Michael R. *Paul Meets Muhammad: A Christian-Muslim Debate on the Resurrection*. Grand Rapids: Baker, 2006.
Lindars, Barnabas. *The Theology of the Letter to the Hebrews*. Cambridge: Cambridge University Press, 1991.
Little, Don. *Effective Discipling in Muslim Communities: Scripture, History, and Seasoned Practice*. Downers Grove, IL: IVP Academic, 2015.
Lodahl, Michael. *Claiming Abraham: Reading the Bible and the Qur'ān Side by Side*. Grand Rapids: Brazos, 2010.
Macquarrie, John. *Jesus Christ in Modern Thought*. 2nd ed. London: SCM Press, 2003.
Madrigal, Carlos. *Explaining the Trinity to Muslims: A Personal Reflection on the Biblical Teaching in Light of the Theological Criteria of Islam*. Pasadena: Carey, 2011.
Marshall, I. Howard. "Soteriology in Hebrews." In *The Epistle to the Hebrews and Christian Theology*, edited by Richard Bauckham et al., 253–79. Grand Rapids: Eerdmans, 2009.
Masri, Fouad. *Adha in the Injeel*. Indianapolis: Crescent Project, 2004.
Massey, Joshua. "Misunderstanding C–5: His Ways Are Not Our Orthodoxy." EMQ 40 (July 2004) n.p. https://www.scribd.com/document/66491460/Misunderstanding-C5-Unabr.
Mathews, Kenneth. *Genesis 11:27–50:26*. New American Commentary. Nashville: B&H, 2005.
McConville, Gordon J. *Being Human in God's World: An Old Testament Theology of Humanity*. Grand Rapids: Baker Academic, 2016.
———. *God and Earthly Power: An Old Testament Political Theology*. Nashville: B&H, 2006.
McGrath, Alister. *The Genesis of Doctrine: A Study in the Foundation of Doctrinal Criticism*. Grand Rapids: Eerdmans, 1990.
McIllwain, Trevor. *Building on Firm Foundations*. Sanford, FL: New Tribes Mission, 2005.
McKnight, Scot. *The King Jesus Gospel: The Original Good News Revisited*. Grand Rapids: Zondervan, 2011.
Medearis, Carl. *Muslims, Christians, and Jesus: Gaining Understanding and Building Relationships*. Minneapolis: Bethany, 2008.
Milgrom, Jacob. *Leviticus 1–16: A New Translation with Introduction and Commentary*. ABC 3. New York: Doubleday, 1991.
———. *Leviticus 17–22*. ABC 3A. New York: Doubleday, 2000.
———. *Leviticus 23–27*. ABC 3B. New York: Doubleday, 2001.
———. *Leviticus: A Book of Ritual and Ethics*. Continental Commentary. Minneapolis: Fortress, 2004.
Miller, James C. "Paul and Hebrews: A Comparison of Narrative Worlds." In *Hebrews: Contemporary Methods-New Insights*, edited by Gabriella Gelardini, 245–64. Leiden: Brill, 2004.
Mingana, A. "Patriarch Timothy I and the Caliph Mahdi: Dialogue." In *The Early Christian Muslim Dialogue: A Collection of Documents from the First Three Islamic Centuries (632–900 A.D.): Translations with Commentary*, edited by N.

A. Newman, 169–264. Hatfield, PA: Interdisciplinary Biblical Research Institute, 1993.

Moffitt, David M. *Atonement and the Logic of Resurrection in the Epistle to the Hebrews.* Supplements to *Novum Testamentum* 141. Leiden: Brill, 2013.

Moreau, A. Scott. *Contextualization in World Missions: Mapping and Assessing Evangelical Models.* Grand Rapids: Kregel Publications, 2012.

Moritz, Thorsten. "Reflecting on N. T. Wright's 'Tools for the Task.'" In *Renewing Biblical Interpretation*, edited by Craig Bartholomew et al., 1:172–97. The Scripture and Hermeneutics Series. Grand Rapids: Zondervan, 2000.

Muir, William. *The Apology of Al-Kindy: Written at the Court of Al Mamun (A.H. 215; A.D. 830)—In Defence of Christianity Against Islam.* London: Smith, Elder & Co., 1882.

Muller, Roland. *Honor and Shame: Unlocking the Door.* Bloomington, IN: Xlibris, 2001.

Musk, Bill. *Touching the Soul of Islam.* Sussex: MARC, 1995.

Nadwi, Shaykh Abul Hasan Ali. "Fast of Ashura." http://www.albalagh.net/general/fast_ashura.shtml.

Nanos, Mark D. "New or Renewed Covenantalism? A Response to Richard Hays." In *The Epistle to the Hebrews and Christian Theology*, edited by Richard Bauckham et al., 183–88. Grand Rapids: Eerdmans, 2009.

Nasr, Seyyed Hossein. *The Heart of Islam: Enduring Values for Humanity.* New York: HarperOne, 2002.

———. *Ideals and Realities of Islam.* Rev. and upd. ed. San Francisco: Aquarian, 1994.

Naugle, David K. *Worldview: The History of a Concept.* Grand Rapids: Baker, 2002.

Nelson, Richard D. "'He Offered Himself' Sacrifice in Hebrews." *Interpretation* 57 (2003) 251–65.

Neusner, Jacob. *Performing Israel's Faith: Narrative and Law in Rabbinic Theology.* Waco, TX: Baylor University Press, 2005.

Newbigin, Lesslie. *The Gospel in a Pluralist Society.* Grand Rapids: Eerdmans, 1989.

———. *The Open Secret: An Introduction to the Theology of Mission.* Rev. ed. Grand Rapids: Eerdmans, 1995.

———. *Truth and Authority in Modernity.* Valley Forge: Trinity Press International, 1996.

Ohlig, Karl Heinz, ed. *Early Islām: A Critical Reconstruction Based on Contemporary Sources.* New York: Prometheus, 2013.

———. *The Hidden Origins of Islām: New Research into its Early History.* Amhert, NY: Prometheus, 2010.

Omar, 'Abdul Manan. *Dictionary of the Holy Qur'an.* 2nd ed. Reprint, Hockessin, DE: Noor Foundation, 2010.

Omar, Irfan A., ed. *A Muslim View of Christianity: Essays on Dialogue by Mahmoud Ayoub.* Maryknoll, NY: Orbis, 2007.

Osborne, Grant. *The Hermeneutical Spiral.* Downers Grove, IL: InterVarsity, 1991.

Osman, Ghada. *The Christians of the Late 6th and Early 6th Century Mecca and Medina: An Investigation into the Arabic Sources.* Cambridge: Harvard University Press, 2001.

Packer, J. I. "Infallible Scripture and the Role of Hermeneutics." In *Scripture and Truth*, edited by D. A. Carson and John D. Woodbridge, 325–58. Grand Rapids: Zondervan, 1983.

Parshall, Phil. *Muslim Evangelism: Contemporary Approaches to Contextualization.* Rev. ed. Colorado Springs: Biblica, 2003.

———. "Rethinking the Gospel for Muslims." In *Muslims and Christians on the Emmaus Road*, edited by J. Dudley Woodberry, 105–25. Monrovia, CA: MARC, 1989.

Penn, Michael Philip. *When Christians First Met Muslims: A Sourcebook of the Earliest Syriac Writings on Islam*. Oakland: University of California, 2015.

Peters, F. E. *Judaism, Christianity, and Islām*. 3 vols. Princeton: Princeton University Press, 1990.

———. *Muḥammad and the Origins of Islām*. Albany: State University of New York Press, 1994.

Philips, Abu Ameenah Bilal. *The Evolution of Fiqh: Islamic Law and the Madh-habs*. Riyadh: International Islamic Publishing House, 2005.

Polen, Nehemia. "Leviticus and Hebrews . . . and Leviticus." In *The Epistle to the Hebrews and Christian Theology*, edited by Richard Bauckham et al., 213–27. Grand Rapids: Eerdmans, 2009.

Qureshi, Nabeel. *No God but One: Allah or Jesus?* Grand Rapids: Zondervan, 2016.

———. *Seeking Allah, Finding Jesus: A Devout Muslim Encounters Christianity*. Grand Rapids: Zondervan, 2014.

Rahman, Fazlur. *Major Themes of the Qurʾān*. 2nd ed. Chicago: University of Chicago Press, 2009.

Redditt, Paul. "Leviticus." In *Theological Interpretation of the Old Testament: A Book-by-Book Survey*, edited by Kevin J. Vanhoozer, 52–58. Grand Rapids: Baker Academic, 2008.

Reed, Lyman. *Preparing Missionaries for Intercultural Communication: A Bicultural Approach*. Pasadena: Carey, 1985.

Reisacher, Evelyn A., ed. *Toward Respectful and Understanding Witness among Muslims: Essays in Honor of J. Dudley Woodberry*. Pasadena: Carey, 2012.

Reynolds, Gabriel Said. "The Muslim Jesus: Dead or Alive?" *Bulletin of School of Oriental and African Studies* 72 (2009) 237–58.

———. "On the Presentation of Christianity in the Qurʾan and the Many Aspects of Qurʾanic Rhetoric." *Al Bayan-Journal of Qurʾan and Hadith Studies* 12 (2014) 42–54.

———. "On the Qurʾanic Accusation of Scriptural Falsification (*taḥrīf*) and Christian Anti-Jewish Polemic." *Journal of the American Oriental Society* 130 (2010) 189–202.

Reynolds, Gabriel Said, ed. *The Emergence of Islām: Classical Tradition in Contemporary Perspective*. Minneapolis: Fortress, 2012.

———. *The Qurʾān and its Biblical Subtext*. New York: Routledge, 2010.

———. *New Perspectives on the Qurʾān: The Qurʾān in Its Historical Context*. Routledge Studies in the Qurʾān 2. New York: Routledge, 2011.

Robinson, George. "The Gospel and Evangelism." In *Theology and Practice of Mission: God, the Church, and the Nations*, edited by Bruce R. Ashford, 76–91. Nashville: B&H, 2011.

Robinson, Neal. *Christ in Islam and Christianity*. Albany: State University of New York Press, 1991.

Roggema, Barbara, et al., eds. *The Three Rings: Textual Studies in the Historical Trialogue of Judaism, Christianity and Islām*. Dudley, MA: Peeters, 2005.

Rooker, Mark F. *Leviticus*. NAC 3A. Nashville: B&H, 2000.

Rubin, Uri. "Islamic Retellings of Biblical History." In *Adaptations and Innovations: Studies on the Interaction between Jewish and Islamic Thought and Literature from the Early Middle Ages to the Late Twentieth Century*, edited by Y. Tzvi Langermann and Josef Stern, 299–313. Paris: Peeters, 2007.

Rutherford, Bruce K. *Egypt after Mubarak: Liberalism, Islam, and Democracy in the Arab World*. Princeton: Princeton University Press, 2008.

Saad Eddin Ibrahim. *Egypt, Islam, and Democracy: Critical Essays*. Cairo: American University in Cairo Press, 2004.

Sachedina, Abdulaziz. "End-of-Life: The Islamic View." *The Lancet* (August–September 2005) 774–79.

Sailhamer, John H. *Introduction to Old Testament Theology: A Canonical Approach*. Grand Rapids: Zondervan, 1999.

Samir, Samir Khalil. "The Earliest Arab Apology for Christianity." In *Christian Arabic Apologetics During the Abbasid Period: 750–1258*, edited by Samir Khalil Samir and Jørgen S. Nielsen, 57–114. New York: Brill, 1994.

Sarna, Nahum M. *Exodus*. JPSTC. Philadelphia: Jewish Publication Society, 1991

———. *Exploring Exodus*. New York: Schocken, 1986.

Saunders, J. J. *A History of Medieval Islām*. New York: Barnes and Noble Inc., 1965.

Schenck, Kenneth. *Understanding the Book of Hebrews: The Story Behind the Sermon*. Louisville: Westminster John Knox, 2003.

Schimmel, Annemarie. *Islam: An Introduction*. Albany, NY: State University of New York Press, 1992.

Schlorff, Sam. *Missiological Models for Ministry to Muslims*. Philadelphia: Middle East Resources, 2006.

Schofield, Rodney. *Emerging Scriptures: Torah, Gospel, and Qur'ān in Christian Perspective*. Luwinga: Mzuni, 2014.

Schreiner, Thomas. "Penal Substitution View." In *The Nature of the Atonement: Four Views*, edited by James Beilby and Paul Eddy, 67–98. Downers Grove, IL: IVP Academic, 2006.

Shamoun, Sam. "Where Is the Blood? An Examination of the Biblical and Islamic View of Blood Atonement." http://www.answering-islam.org/Shamoun/bloodatonement.htm.

Sharma, Arvind. *Religious Studies and Comparative Methodology: The Case for Reciprocal Illumination*. Albany: State University of New York Press, 2005.

Shipman, Mike. *Any Three: Anyone, Anywhere, Anytime*. Monument, CO: WIGTake, 2013.

Shoemaker, Stephen J. *The Death of a Prophet: The End of Muḥammad's Life and the Beginnings of Islām*. Philadelphia: University of Pennsylvania Press, 2012.

Sinclair, Daniel: *A Vision of the Possible: Pioneer Church Planting in Teams*. Colorado Springs: Biblica, 2006.

Sire, James. *Naming the Elephant: Worldview as a Concept*. Downers Grove, IL: InterVarsity, 2015.

Sklar, Jay. *Leviticus*. Tyndale Old Testament Commentaries 3. Downers Grove, IL: IVP Academic, 2014.

———. *Sin, Impurity, Sacrifice, Atonement: The Priestly Conceptions*. Sheffield: Sheffield Phoenix, 2015.

Small, Keith E. *Textual Criticism and Qur'ān Manuscripts*. New York: Lexington, 2011.

Smart, Ninian. *Dimensions of the Sacred: An Anatomy of the World's Beliefs*. Berkeley: University of California Press, 1996.

———. *Worldviews: Crosscultural Explorations of Human Beliefs.* 3rd ed. Upper Saddle River, NJ: Prentice Hall, 2000.
Smith, Jane Idleman, and Yvonne Yazbeck Haddad. *The Islamic Understanding of Death and Resurrection.* Albany: State University of New York Press, 1981.
Smith, Steve, and Ying Kai. *T4T: A Discipleship Re-Revolution.* Monument, CO: WIGTake, 2011.
Smith, Wilfred Cantwell. *On Understanding Islām: Selected Studies.* New York: Mouton, 1981.
Spencer, Robert. *Did Muḥammad Exist? An Inquiry into Islām's Obscure Origins.* Wilmington, DE: Intercollegiate Studies Institute, 2012.
Stott, John. *The Cross of Christ.* 20th anniv. ed. Downers Grove, IL: IVP Academic, 2006.
Stuart, Douglas K. *Exodus: An Exegetical and Theological Exposition of Holy Scripture*, vol. 2. NAC. Nashville: B&H, 2006.
Synge F. C. *Hebrews and the Scriptures.* London: SPCK, 1959.
Tennent, Timothy C. *Christianity at the Religious Roundtable: Evangelicalism in Conversation with Hinduism, Buddhism, and Islam.* Grand Rapids: Baker Academic, 2002.
———. "Followers of Jesus (Isa) in Islamic Mosques: A Closer Examination of C-5 'High Spectrum' Contextualization." *IJFM* 23 (Fall 2006) 101–15.
Terry, John Mark. "Approaches to the Evangelization of Muslims." In *Encountering the World of Islam*, edited by Keith E. Swartley, 314–19. Atlanta: Authentic, 2005.
Teule, Herman. "Paul of Antioch's Attitude Towards the Jews and the Muslims: His 'Letter to the Nations and the Jews.'" In *Three Rings: Textual Studies in the Historical Trialogue of Judaism, Christianity, and Islām*, edited by Barbara Roogema et al., 91–110. Dudley, MA: Peeters, 2005.
Theological Education Fund. *Ministry in Context: The Third Mandate Programme of the Theological Education Fund (1970–1977).* Bromley, England: Theological Education Fund, 1972.
Torrey, Charles Cutler. *The Jewish Foundation of Islām.* New York: Bloch, 1933.
Travis, John. "The C1 to C6 Spectrum: A Practical Tool for Defining Six Types of 'Christ-centered Communities' ('C') Found in the Muslim Context." *EMQ* 34 (October 1998) 407–8.
———. "Messianic Muslim Followers of *Isa*: A Closer Look at C5 Believers and Congregations." *IJFM* 17 (Spring 2000) 53–59.
———. "Must All Muslims Leave Islam to Follow Jesus?" *EMQ* 34 (1998) 411–15.
Van Dyke, Cornelius. *Al Kitab Al Muquddis.* Cairo: Egypt Bible Society, 1972.
van Huyssteen, Wentzel. "Narrative Theology: An Adequate Paradigm for Theological Reflection?" *HTS Teologiese Studies* 45 (1989) 767–77.
VanderWerff, Lyle. "Christian Witness to Our Muslim Friends." *International Journal of Frontier Missions* 13 (July–September 1996) 111–16.
Vanhoozer, Kevin J. "The Atonement in Postmodernity: Guilt, Goats, and Gifts." In *The Glory of the Atonement*, edited by Frank James and Charles Hill, 367–404. Downers Grove, IL: IVP Academic, 2004.
———. *The Drama of Doctrine: A Canonical Linguistic Approach to Christian Theology.* Louisville: Westminster John Knox, 2005.
Wansborough, John. *The Sectarian Milieu.* Oxford: Oxford University Press, 1978.
Wasserstrom, Steven M. *Between Muslim and Jew: The Problem of Symbiosis Under Early Islām.* Princeton: Princeton University Press, 1995.

Wedderburn, A. J. M. "Sawing Off the Branches: Theologizing Dangerously." *Journal of Theological Studies* 56 (2005) 393–414.
Wenham, Gordon. *The Book of Leviticus*. NICOT. Grand Rapids: Eerdmans, 1979.
———. *Story as Torah*. Grand Rapids: Baker Academic, 2000.
Wensinck, A. J., et al., eds. *First Encyclopaedia of Islām 1913–1938*. Reprint, Leiden: Brill, 1993.
Wilde, Clare Elena. *Approaches to the Qurʾān in Early Christian Arabic Texts: 750–1258 CE*. Palo Alto, CA: Academica Press, 2014.
Williams, Mark. "Revisiting the C1–C6 Spectrum in Muslim Contextualization." *MIR* 39 (July 2011) 335–51.
Williams, Michael. "Systematic Theology as a Biblical Discipline." In *All for Jesus: A Celebration of the 50th Anniversary of Covenant Theological Seminary*, edited by R. A. Patterson and S. M. Lucas, 167–96. Fearn: Christian Focus, 2005.
Willi-Plein, Ina. "Some Remarks on Hebrews from the Viewpoint of Old Testament Exegesis." In *Hebrews: Contemporary Methods—New Insights*, edited by Gabriella Gelardini, 25–35. Leiden: Brill, 2005.
Wilson, S. G. *Related Strangers: Jews and Christians, 70–170 C. E*. Minneapolis: Fortress, 1995.
Wolters, Al. "Hebrews and Biblical Theology." In *Out of Egypt: Biblical Theology and Biblical Interpretation*, edited by Craig Bartholomew et al., 313–38. Grand Rapids: Zondervan, 2004.
Woodberry, J. Dudley, ed. "Contextualization Among Muslims: Reusing Common Pillars." *IJFM* 13 (October–December 1996) 171–86.
———. *Muslims and Christians on the Emmaus Road*. Monrovia, CA: MARC, 1989.
Wright, Christopher. *The Mission of God: Unlocking the Bible's Grand Narrative*. Downers Grove, IL: IVP Academic, 2006.
Wright, N. T. *How God Became King: The Forgotten Story of the Gospels*. New York: HarperOne, 2012.
———. *Jesus and the Victory of God*. Minneapolis: Fortress, 1996.
———. *The New Testament and the People of God*. Minneapolis: Fortress, 1992.
———. *Paul and the Faithfulness of God*. 2 vols. Minneapolis: Fortress, 2013.
———. *The Resurrection of the Son of God*. Minneapolis: Fortress, 2003.
Wu, Jackson. *One Gospel for All Nations*. Pasadena: William Carey, 2015.
Young, Frances M. "Christological Ideas in the Greek Commentaries." In *Christology, Hermeneutics and Hebrews: Profiles from the History of Interpretation*, edited by Jon C. Laansma and Daniel J. Treier, 33–47. New York: T. & T. Clark, 2014.
Zeghal, Malika. "Religion and Politics in Egypt: The Ulema of Al-Azhar, Radical Islam, and the State (1952–1994)." *International Journal of Middle East Studies* 31 (August 1999) 371–99.
Zellatin, Holger Michael. *The Qurʾān's Legal Culture: The Didascalie Apostolorum as a Point of Departure*. Tübingen: Mohr Siebeck, 2013.
Zsengellér, József. "The Day of Atonement of the Samaritans." In *The Day of Atonement: Its Interpretations in Early Jewish and Christian Traditions*, edited by Thomas Hieke and Tobias Nicklas, 139–61. Boston: Brill, 2012.
Zwemer, Samuel. "Atonement by Blood Sacrifice in Islām." *The Moslem World* 36 (1946) 187–92.

APPENDIX A

Kaffāra (Noun – Atonement) in the Qur'an

Noun – [كَفَّارَة] kaffāra: atonement, expiation[1]			
Reference	Qur'an – Arabic[2]	Muhammad Asad	Author's Comment
Qur'an 5:45	وَكَتَبْنَا عَلَيْهِمْ فِيهَا أَنَّ النَّفْسَ بِالنَّفْسِ وَالْعَيْنَ بِالْعَيْنِ وَالْأَنْفَ بِالْأَنْفِ وَالْأُذُنَ بِالْأُذُنِ وَالسِّنَّ بِالسِّنِّ وَالْجُرُوحَ قِصَاصٌ ۚ فَمَن تَصَدَّقَ بِهِ فَهُوَ كَفَّارَةٌ لَّهُ ۚ وَمَن لَّمْ يَحْكُم بِمَا أَنزَلَ اللَّهُ فَأُولَٰئِكَ هُمُ الظَّالِمُونَ	And We ordained for them in that [Torah]: A life for a life, and an eye for an eye, and a nose for a nose, and an ear for an ear, and a tooth for a tooth, and a [similar] retribution for wounds; but he who shall forgo it out of charity will <u>atone</u> thereby for some of his past sins. And they who do not judge in accordance with what God has revealed—they, they are the evildoers!	The refusal to take vengeance serves as an atonement (though Asad translates the concept verbally, it is nominal in the Arabic) for the one refusing vengeance.
Qur'an 5:89 (x2)	لَا يُؤَاخِذُكُمُ اللَّهُ بِاللَّغْوِ فِي أَيْمَانِكُمْ وَلَٰكِن يُؤَاخِذُكُم بِمَا عَقَّدتُّمُ الْأَيْمَانَ ۖ فَكَفَّارَتُهُ إِطْعَامُ عَشَرَةِ مَسَاكِينَ مِنْ أَوْسَطِ مَا تُطْعِمُونَ أَهْلِيكُمْ أَوْ كِسْوَتُهُمْ أَوْ تَحْرِيرُ رَقَبَةٍ ۖ فَمَن لَّمْ يَجِدْ فَصِيَامُ ثَلَاثَةِ أَيَّامٍ ۚ ذَٰلِكَ كَفَّارَةُ أَيْمَانِكُمْ إِذَا حَلَفْتُمْ ۚ وَاحْفَظُوا أَيْمَانَكُمْ ۚ كَذَٰلِكَ يُبَيِّنُ اللَّهُ لَكُمْ آيَاتِهِ لَعَلَّكُمْ تَشْكُرُونَ	GOD will not take you to task for oaths which you may have uttered without thought, but He will take you to task for oaths which you have sworn in earnest. Thus, the breaking of an oath must be <u>atoned</u> for by feeding ten needy persons with more or less the same food as you are wont to give to your own families, or by clothing them, or by freeing a human being from bondage; and he who has not the wherewithal shall fast for three days [instead]. This shall be the <u>atonement</u> for your oaths whenever you have sworn [and broken them]. But be mindful of your oaths! Thus God makes clear unto you His messages, so that you might have cause to be grateful.	An act of charity or a fast of three days serves as an atonement for a broken oath that was sworn in earnest.

1 'Omar, *Dictionary*, 490.

2 All citations and translations are taken from Asad, *Message of Qur'an*.

Reference	Qur'an – Arabic[2]	Muhammad Asad	Author's Comment
Qur'an 5:95	يَا أَيُّهَا الَّذِينَ آمَنُوا لَا تَقْتُلُوا الصَّيْدَ وَأَنْتُمْ حُرُمٌ ۚ وَمَنْ قَتَلَهُ مِنْكُمْ مُتَعَمِّدًا فَجَزَاءٌ مِثْلُ مَا قَتَلَ مِنَ النَّعَمِ يَحْكُمُ بِهِ ذَوَا عَدْلٍ مِنْكُمْ هَدْيًا بَالِغَ الْكَعْبَةِ أَوْ كَفَّارَةٌ طَعَامُ مَسَاكِينَ أَوْ عَدْلُ ذَٰلِكَ صِيَامًا لِيَذُوقَ وَبَالَ أَمْرِهِ ۗ عَفَا اللَّهُ عَمَّا سَلَفَ ۚ وَمَنْ عَادَ فَيَنْتَقِمُ اللَّهُ مِنْهُ ۗ وَاللَّهُ عَزِيزٌ ذُو انْتِقَامٍ	O you who have attained to faith! Kill no game while you are in the state of pilgrimage. And whoever of you kills it intentionally, [shall make] amends in cattle equivalent to what he has killed—with two persons of probity giving their judgment thereon—to be brought as an offering to the Ka'bah; or else he may <u>atone</u> for his sin by feeding the needy, or by the equivalent thereof in fasting: [this,] in order that he taste the full gravity of his deed, [while] God shall have effaced the past. But whoever does it again, God will inflict His retribution on him: for God is almighty, an avenger of evil.	Hunting and killing an animal while on *hajj* requires an atonement. This atonement can be acquired through similar means as those required for broken oaths: feeding the needy or fasting.

APPENDIX B

Kaffara (Verb – To Atone) in the Qur'an

Verb – [كفّر] *kaffara*: to atone, to cover, to efface, to redeem in the Qur'an[3]

Reference	Arabic	Muhammad Asad	Comment
Qur'an 2:271	إِن تُبْدُوا الصَّدَقَاتِ فَنِعِمَّا هِيَ ۖ وَإِن تُخْفُوهَا وَتُؤْتُوهَا الْفُقَرَاءَ فَهُوَ خَيْرٌ لَّكُمْ ۚ وَيُكَفِّرُ عَنكُم مِّن سَيِّئَاتِكُمْ ۗ وَاللَّهُ بِمَا تَعْمَلُونَ خَبِيرٌ	If you do deeds of charity openly, it is well; but if you bestow it upon the needy in secret, it will be even better for you, and it will <u>atone</u> for some of your bad deeds. And God is aware of all that you do.	This is the only instance of *kaffara* that does not have God as the agent.
Qur'an 3:193	رَّبَّنَا إِنَّنَا سَمِعْنَا مُنَادِيًا يُنَادِي لِلْإِيمَانِ أَنْ آمِنُوا بِرَبِّكُمْ فَآمَنَّا ۚ رَبَّنَا فَاغْفِرْ لَنَا ذُنُوبَنَا وَكَفِّرْ عَنَّا سَيِّئَاتِنَا وَتَوَفَّنَا مَعَ الْأَبْرَارِ	"O our Sustainer! Behold, we heard a voice1 call [us] unto faith, 'Believe in your Sustainer!'—and so we came to believe. O our Sustainer! Forgive us, then, our sins, and <u>efface</u> our bad deeds; and let us die the death of the truly virtuous!"	God is the agent who will *kaffara* the bad deeds of believers.
Qur'an 3:195	فَاسْتَجَابَ لَهُمْ رَبُّهُمْ أَنِّي لَا أُضِيعُ عَمَلَ عَامِلٍ مِّنكُم مِّن ذَكَرٍ أَوْ أُنثَىٰ ۖ بَعْضُكُم مِّن بَعْضٍ ۖ فَالَّذِينَ هَاجَرُوا وَأُخْرِجُوا مِن دِيَارِهِمْ وَأُوذُوا فِي سَبِيلِي وَقَاتَلُوا وَقُتِلُوا لَأُكَفِّرَنَّ عَنْهُمْ سَيِّئَاتِهِمْ وَلَأُدْخِلَنَّهُمْ جَنَّاتٍ تَجْرِي مِن تَحْتِهَا الْأَنْهَارُ ثَوَابًا مِّنْ عِندِ اللَّهِ ۗ وَاللَّهُ عِندَهُ حُسْنُ الثَّوَابِ	And thus does their Sustainer answer their prayer: "I shall not lose sight of the labour of any of you who labours [in My way], be it man or woman: each of you is an issue of the other. Hence, as for those who forsake the domain of evil, and are driven from their homelands, and suffer hurt in My cause, and fight [for it], and are slain—I shall most certainly <u>efface</u> their bad deeds, and shall certainly bring them into gardens through which running waters flow, as a reward from God: for with God is the most beauteous of rewards."	God is the agent who will *kaffara* the bad deeds of those who suffer for him and who are martyrs in the cause of following God.
Qur'an 4:31	إِن تَجْتَنِبُوا كَبَائِرَ مَا تُنْهَوْنَ عَنْهُ نُكَفِّرْ عَنكُمْ سَيِّئَاتِكُمْ وَنُدْخِلْكُم مُّدْخَلًا كَرِيمًا	If you avoid the great sins, which you have been enjoined to shun, We shall <u>efface</u> your [minor] bad deeds, and shall cause you to enter an abode of glory.	God is the agent who will *kaffara* the minor bad deeds of those who avoid great sins.

3 'Omar, Dictionary, 489–91. "Efface" has been included as it features in Asad's translation.

KAFFARA (VERB – TO ATONE) IN THE QUR'AN

Verb – [كفّر] *kaffara*: to forgive, to cover, to efface, to redeem

Reference	Arabic	Muhammad Asad	Comment
Qur'an 5:12	وَلَقَدْ أَخَذَ اللَّهُ مِيثَاقَ بَنِي إِسْرَائِيلَ وَبَعَثْنَا مِنْهُمُ اثْنَيْ عَشَرَ نَقِيبًا ۖ وَقَالَ اللَّهُ إِنِّي مَعَكُمْ ۖ لَئِنْ أَقَمْتُمُ الصَّلَاةَ وَآتَيْتُمُ الزَّكَاةَ وَآمَنْتُمْ بِرُسُلِي وَعَزَّرْتُمُوهُمْ وَأَقْرَضْتُمُ اللَّهَ قَرْضًا حَسَنًا لَأُكَفِّرَنَّ عَنْكُمْ سَيِّئَاتِكُمْ وَلَأُدْخِلَنَّكُمْ جَنَّاتٍ تَجْرِي مِنْ تَحْتِهَا الْأَنْهَارُ ۚ فَمَنْ كَفَرَ بَعْدَ ذَٰلِكَ مِنْكُمْ فَقَدْ ضَلَّ سَوَاءَ السَّبِيلِ	AND, INDEED, God accepted a [similar] solemn pledge from the children of Israel when We caused twelve of their leaders to be sent [to Canaan as spies]. And God said: "Behold, I shall be with you! If you are constant in prayer, and spend in charity, and believe in My apostles and aid them, and offer up unto God a goodly loan, I will surely efface your bad deeds and bring you into gardens through which running waters flow. But he from among you who, after this, denies the truth, will indeed have strayed from the right path!"	God is the agent who will *kaffara* the bad deeds of the faithful, admitting them to paradise in the end.
Qur'an 5:65	وَلَوْ أَنَّ أَهْلَ الْكِتَابِ آمَنُوا وَاتَّقَوْا لَكَفَّرْنَا عَنْهُمْ سَيِّئَاتِهِمْ وَلَأَدْخَلْنَاهُمْ جَنَّاتِ النَّعِيمِ	If the followers of the Bible would but attain to [true] faith and God-consciousness, We should indeed efface their [previous] bad deeds, and indeed bring them into gardens of bliss;	God is the agent who will *kaffara* bad deeds and admit the faithful to paradise.
Qur'an 8:29	يَا أَيُّهَا الَّذِينَ آمَنُوا إِنْ تَتَّقُوا اللَّهَ يَجْعَلْ لَكُمْ فُرْقَانًا وَيُكَفِّرْ عَنْكُمْ سَيِّئَاتِكُمْ وَيَغْفِرْ لَكُمْ ۗ وَاللَّهُ ذُو الْفَضْلِ الْعَظِيمِ	O you who have attained to faith! If you remain conscious of God. He will endow you with a standard by which to discern the true from the false, and will efface your bad deeds, and will forgive you your sins: for God is limitless in His great bounty.	God is the agent who will *kaffara* the bad deeds of those who are God-conscious.
Qur'an 29:7	وَالَّذِينَ آمَنُوا وَعَمِلُوا الصَّالِحَاتِ لَنُكَفِّرَنَّ عَنْهُمْ سَيِّئَاتِهِمْ وَلَنَجْزِيَنَّهُمْ أَحْسَنَ الَّذِي كَانُوا يَعْمَلُونَ	And as for those who attain to faith and do righteous deeds, We shall most certainly efface their [previous] bad deeds, and shall most certainly reward them in accordance with the best that they ever did.	God is the agent who will *kaffara* the bad deeds of those who are faithful and do righteous deeds.
Qur'an 39:35	لِيُكَفِّرَ اللَّهُ عَنْهُمْ أَسْوَأَ الَّذِي عَمِلُوا وَيَجْزِيَهُمْ أَجْرَهُمْ بِأَحْسَنِ الَّذِي كَانُوا يَعْمَلُونَ	And to this end, God will efface from their record the worst that they ever did, and give them their reward in accordance with the best that they were doing [in life].	God is the agent who will *kaffara* the worst deeds of those who bring the truth (v. 33)

KAFFARA (VERB – TO ATONE) IN THE QUR'AN

Verb – [كَفَّرَ] *kaffara*: to forgive, to cover, to efface, to redeem

Reference	Arabic	Muhammad Asad	Comment
Qur'an 47:2	وَالَّذِينَ آمَنُوا وَعَمِلُوا الصَّالِحَاتِ وَآمَنُوا بِمَا نُزِّلَ عَلَىٰ مُحَمَّدٍ وَهُوَ الْحَقُّ مِن رَّبِّهِمْ ۙ كَفَّرَ عَنْهُمْ سَيِّئَاتِهِمْ وَأَصْلَحَ بَالَهُمْ	whereas those who have attained to faith and do righteous deeds, and have come to believe in what has been bestowed from on high on Muhammad—for it is the truth from their Sustainer—[shall attain to God's grace:] He will <u>efface</u> their [past] bad deeds, and will set their hearts at rest.	God is the agent who will *kaffara* the bad deeds of those who are faithful and do righteous deeds.
Qur'an 48:5	لِيُدْخِلَ الْمُؤْمِنِينَ وَالْمُؤْمِنَاتِ جَنَّاتٍ تَجْرِي مِن تَحْتِهَا الْأَنْهَارُ خَالِدِينَ فِيهَا وَيُكَفِّرَ عَنْهُمْ سَيِّئَاتِهِمْ ۚ وَكَانَ ذَٰلِكَ عِندَ اللَّهِ فَوْزًا عَظِيمًا	[and] that He might admit the believers, both men and women, into gardens through which running waters flow, therein to abide, and that He might <u>efface</u> their [past bad] deeds: and that is, in the sight of God, indeed a triumph supreme!	God is the agent who will *kaffara* the bad deeds of believers and admit them to paradise.
Qur'an 64:9	يَوْمَ يَجْمَعُكُمْ لِيَوْمِ الْجَمْعِ ۖ ذَٰلِكَ يَوْمُ التَّغَابُنِ ۗ وَمَن يُؤْمِن بِاللَّهِ وَيَعْمَلْ صَالِحًا يُكَفِّرْ عَنْهُ سَيِّئَاتِهِ وَيُدْخِلْهُ جَنَّاتٍ تَجْرِي مِن تَحْتِهَا الْأَنْهَارُ خَالِدِينَ فِيهَا أَبَدًا ۚ ذَٰلِكَ الْفَوْزُ الْعَظِيمُ	[Think of] the time when He shall gather you all together unto the Day of the [Last] Gathering—that Day of Loss and Gain! For, as for him who shall have believed in God and done what is just and right, He will [on that Day] <u>efface</u> his bad deeds, and will admit him into gardens through which running waters flow, therein to abide beyond the count of time: that will be a triumph supreme!	On the Day of Judgment God will be the agent who will *kaffara* the bad deeds of those who have believed in God and done what is just and right.
Qur'an 65:5	ذَٰلِكَ أَمْرُ اللَّهِ أَنزَلَهُ إِلَيْكُمْ ۚ وَمَن يَتَّقِ اللَّهَ يُكَفِّرْ عَنْهُ سَيِّئَاتِهِ وَيُعْظِمْ لَهُ أَجْرًا	[for] all this is God's commandment, which He has bestowed upon you from on high. And unto everyone who is conscious of God will He <u>pardon</u> [some of] his bad deeds, and will grant him a vast reward.	God is the agent who will *kaffara* the bad deeds of those who are God-conscious.
Qur'an 66:8	يَا أَيُّهَا الَّذِينَ آمَنُوا تُوبُوا إِلَى اللَّهِ تَوْبَةً نَّصُوحًا عَسَىٰ رَبُّكُمْ أَن يُكَفِّرَ عَنكُمْ سَيِّئَاتِكُمْ وَيُدْخِلَكُمْ جَنَّاتٍ تَجْرِي مِن تَحْتِهَا الْأَنْهَارُ يَوْمَ لَا يُخْزِي اللَّهُ النَّبِيَّ وَالَّذِينَ آمَنُوا مَعَهُ ۖ نُورُهُمْ يَسْعَىٰ بَيْنَ أَيْدِيهِمْ وَبِأَيْمَانِهِمْ يَقُولُونَ رَبَّنَا أَتْمِمْ لَنَا نُورَنَا وَاغْفِرْ لَنَا ۖ إِنَّكَ عَلَىٰ كُلِّ شَيْءٍ قَدِيرٌ	O you who have attained to faith! Turn unto God in sincere repentance: it may well be that your Sustainer will <u>efface</u> from you your bad deeds, and will admit you into gardens through which running waters flow, on a Day on which God will not shame the Prophet and those who share his faith: their light will spread rapidly before them, and on their right; [and] they will pray: "O our Sustainer! Cause this our light to shine for us forever, and forgive us our sins: for, verily, Thou hast the power to will anything!"	God is the agent who will *kaffara* the bad deeds of those who repent and turn to God, and God will admit them into paradise.

APPENDIX C

Sacrificial Vocabulary in the Qur'an

Verb – [انحَر] _inhar_: to sacrifice[4]

Reference	Qur'an – Arabic	Muhammad Asad	Author's Comment
Qur'an 108:2	فَصَلِّ لِرَبِّكَ وَانْحَرْ	hence, pray unto thy Sustainer [alone], and sacrifice [unto Him alone].	This is the only verb in the Qur'an commanding the believers to sacrifice.

Noun – [ذبِح] _dhibih_: a sacrifice[5]

Reference	Qur'an – Arabic	Muhammad Asad	Author's Comment
Qur'an 37:107	وَفَدَيْنَاهُ بِذِبْحٍ عَظِيمٍ	And We ransomed him with a tremendous sacrifice,	In the Islamic system, the idea of sacrifice as a substitution or ransom seems anomalous.

Verb – [ذَبَحَ] _dhabaha_: to sacrifice, to slaughter[6]

Reference	Qur'an – Arabic	Muhammad Asad	Author's Comment
Qur'an 2:49	وَإِذْ نَجَّيْنَاكُمْ مِنْ آلِ فِرْعَوْنَ يَسُومُونَكُمْ سُوءَ الْعَذَابِ يُذَبِّحُونَ أَبْنَاءَكُمْ وَيَسْتَحْيُونَ نِسَاءَكُمْ وَفِي ذَٰلِكُمْ بَلَاءٌ مِنْ رَبِّكُمْ عَظِيمٌ	And [remember the time] when We saved you from Pharaoh's people, who afflicted you with cruel suffering, slaughtering your sons and sparing [only] your women—which was an awesome trial from your Sustainer;	The idea of slaughter here is related to war, not a religious rite.
Qur'an 2:67	وَإِذْ قَالَ مُوسَىٰ لِقَوْمِهِ إِنَّ اللَّهَ يَأْمُرُكُمْ أَنْ تَذْبَحُوا بَقَرَةً ۖ قَالُوا أَتَتَّخِذُنَا هُزُوًا ۖ قَالَ أَعُوذُ بِاللَّهِ أَنْ أَكُونَ مِنَ الْجَاهِلِينَ	AND LO! Moses said unto his people: "Behold, God bids you to sacrifice a cow." They said: "Dost thou mock at us?" He answered: "I seek refuge with God against being so ignorant!"	Moses gives the Israelites a command to sacrifice a cow and they pose many questions about how to do so.

4 'Omar, _Dictionary_, 555.

5 'Omar, _Dictionary_, 187.

6 'Omar, _Dictionary_, 187.

APPENDIX C 231

Reference	Qur'an – Arabic	Muhammad Asad	Author's Comment
Qur'an 2:71	قَالَ إِنَّهُ يَقُولُ إِنَّهَا بَقَرَةٌ لَا ذَلُولٌ تُثِيرُ الْأَرْضَ وَلَا تَسْقِي الْحَرْثَ مُسَلَّمَةٌ لَا شِيَةَ فِيهَا ۚ قَالُوا الْآنَ جِئْتَ بِالْحَقِّ ۚ فَذَبَحُوهَا وَمَا كَادُوا يَفْعَلُونَ	[Moses] answered: "Behold, He says it is to be a cow not broken-in to plough the earth or to water the crops, free of fault, without markings of any other colour." Said they: "At last thou hast brought out the truth!"—and thereupon they sacrificed her, although they had almost left it undone.	Moses gives the Israelites a command to sacrifice a cow and they pose many questions about how to do so.
Qur'an 5:3	حُرِّمَت عَلَيْكُمُ الْمَيْتَةُ وَالدَّمُ وَلَحْمُ الْخِنْزِيرِ وَمَا أُهِلَّ لِغَيْرِ اللَّهِ بِهِ وَالْمُنْخَنِقَةُ وَالْمَوْقُوذَةُ وَالْمُتَرَدِّيَةُ وَالنَّطِيحَةُ وَمَا أَكَلَ السَّبُعُ إِلَّا مَا ذَكَّيْتُمْ وَمَا ذُبِحَ عَلَى النُّصُبِ وَأَن تَسْتَقْسِمُوا بِالْأَزْلَامِ ۚ ذَٰلِكُمْ فِسْقٌ ۗ الْيَوْمَ يَئِسَ الَّذِينَ كَفَرُوا مِن دِينِكُمْ فَلَا تَخْشَوْهُمْ وَاخْشَوْنِ ۚ الْيَوْمَ أَكْمَلْتُ لَكُمْ دِينَكُمْ وَأَتْمَمْتُ عَلَيْكُمْ نِعْمَتِي وَرَضِيتُ لَكُمُ الْإِسْلَامَ دِينًا ۚ فَمَنِ اضْطُرَّ فِي مَخْمَصَةٍ غَيْرَ مُتَجَانِفٍ لِإِثْمٍ ۙ فَإِنَّ اللَّهَ غَفُورٌ رَحِيمٌ	FORBIDDEN to you is carrion, and blood, and the flesh of swine, and that over which any name other than God's has been invoked, and the animal that has been strangled, or beaten to death, or killed by a fall, or gored to death, or savaged by a beast of prey, save that which you [yourselves] may have slaughtered while it was still alive; and [forbidden to you is] all that <u>has been slaughtered</u> on idolatrous altars. And [you are forbidden] to seek to learn through divination what the future may hold in store for you: this is sinful conduct. Today, those who are bent on denying the truth have lost all hope of [your ever forsaking] your religion: do not, then, hold them in awe, but stand in awe of Me! Today have I perfected your religious law for you, and have bestowed upon you the full measure of My blessings, and willed that self-surrender unto Me shall be your religion. As for him, however, who is driven [to what is forbidden] by dire necessity and not by an inclination to sinning—behold, God is much-forgiving, a dispenser of grace.	In this passage believers are prohibited from eating the meat of animals that have been sacrificed on pagan altars.

APPENDIX C

Reference	Qur'an – Arabic	Muhammad Asad	Author's Comment
Qur'an 14:6	وَإِذْ قَالَ مُوسَىٰ لِقَوْمِهِ اذْكُرُوا نِعْمَةَ اللَّهِ عَلَيْكُمْ إِذْ أَنْجَاكُمْ مِنْ آلِ فِرْعَوْنَ يَسُومُونَكُمْ سُوءَ الْعَذَابِ وَيُذَبِّحُونَ أَبْنَاءَكُمْ وَيَسْتَحْيُونَ نِسَاءَكُمْ ۚ وَفِي ذَٰلِكُمْ بَلَاءٌ مِنْ رَبِّكُمْ عَظِيمٌ	And, lo, Moses spoke [thus] unto his people: "Remember the blessings which God bestowed upon you when He saved you from Pharaoh's people who afflicted you with cruel suffering, and slaughtered your sons, and spared [only] your women—which was an awesome trial from your Sustainer."	The idea of slaughter here is related to war and persecution, not a religious rite.
Qur'an 27:21	لَأُعَذِّبَنَّهُ عَذَابًا شَدِيدًا أَوْ لَأَذْبَحَنَّهُ أَوْ لَيَأْتِيَنِّي بِسُلْطَانٍ مُبِينٍ	[If so,] I will punish him most severely or will kill him unless he bring me a convincing excuse!	This is a threat of punishment rather than a religious rite involving sacrifice.
Qur'an 28:4	إِنَّ فِرْعَوْنَ عَلَا فِي الْأَرْضِ وَجَعَلَ أَهْلَهَا شِيَعًا يَسْتَضْعِفُ طَائِفَةً مِنْهُمْ يُذَبِّحُ أَبْنَاءَهُمْ وَيَسْتَحْيِي نِسَاءَهُمْ ۚ إِنَّهُ كَانَ مِنَ الْمُفْسِدِينَ	Behold, Pharaoh exalted himself in the land and divided its people into castes. One group of them he deemed utterly low; he would slaughter their sons and spare [only] their women: for, behold, he was one of those who spread corruption [on earth].	The idea of slaughter here is related to war and persecution, not a religious rite.
Qur'an 37:102	فَلَمَّا بَلَغَ مَعَهُ السَّعْيَ قَالَ يَا بُنَيَّ إِنِّي أَرَىٰ فِي الْمَنَامِ أَنِّي أَذْبَحُكَ فَانْظُرْ مَاذَا تَرَىٰ ۚ قَالَ يَا أَبَتِ افْعَلْ مَا تُؤْمَرُ ۖ سَتَجِدُنِي إِنْ شَاءَ اللَّهُ مِنَ الصَّابِرِينَ	And [one day,] when [the child] had become old enough to share in his [father's] endeavours,1 the latter said: "O my dear son! I have seen in a dream that I should sacrifice thee: consider, then, what would be thy view!" [Ishmael] answered: "O my father! Do as thou art bidden: thou wilt find me, if God so wills, among those who are patient in adversity!"	When Abraham tells his son about his vision that he is to slaughter his son, they both submit to God's will as seen in the vision.

APPENDIX C

Noun – [قربان] *qorban*: offering, sacrifice[7]

Reference	Qur'an – Arabic	Muhammad Asad	Author's Comment
Qur'an 3:183	الَّذِينَ قَالُوا إِنَّ اللَّهَ عَهِدَ إِلَيْنَا أَلَّا نُؤْمِنَ لِرَسُولٍ حَتَّىٰ يَأْتِيَنَا بِقُرْبَانٍ تَأْكُلُهُ النَّارُ ۗ قُلْ قَدْ جَاءَكُمْ رُسُلٌ مِنْ قَبْلِي بِالْبَيِّنَاتِ وَبِالَّذِي قُلْتُمْ فَلِمَ قَتَلْتُمُوهُمْ إِنْ كُنْتُمْ صَادِقِينَ	As for those who maintain, "Behold, God has bidden us not to believe in any apostle unless he comes unto us with <u>burnt offerings</u>"—say [unto them, O Prophet]: "Even before me there came unto you apostles with all evidence of the truth, and with that whereof you speak: why, then, did you slay them, if what you say is true?"	Jews are seen here rejecting Islamic teaching because it does not have a burnt offering associated with it and that is a criterion for authenticity as an apostle.
Qur'an 5:27	وَاتْلُ عَلَيْهِمْ نَبَأَ ابْنَيْ آدَمَ بِالْحَقِّ إِذْ قَرَّبَا قُرْبَانًا فَتُقُبِّلَ مِنْ أَحَدِهِمَا وَلَمْ يُتَقَبَّلْ مِنَ الْآخَرِ قَالَ لَأَقْتُلَنَّكَ ۖ قَالَ إِنَّمَا يَتَقَبَّلُ اللَّهُ مِنَ الْمُتَّقِينَ	And convey unto them, setting forth the truth, the story of the two sons of Adam—how each offered a <u>sacrifice</u>, and it was accepted from one of them whereas it was not accepted from the other. [And Cain] said: "I will surely slay thee!" [Abel] replied: "Behold, God accepts only from those who are conscious of Him."	Adam's sons both brought sacrifices, one being accepted, the other rejected. The implication is that the rejected sacrifice was brought by one who was not God-conscious.
Qur'an 46:28	فَلَوْلَا نَصَرَهُمُ الَّذِينَ اتَّخَذُوا مِنْ دُونِ اللَّهِ قُرْبَانًا آلِهَةً ۖ بَلْ ضَلُّوا عَنْهُمْ ۚ وَذَٰلِكَ إِفْكُهُمْ وَمَا كَانُوا يَفْتَرُونَ	But, then, did those [beings] whom they had chosen to worship as deities beside God, hoping that <u>they would bring them nearer</u> [to Him], help them [in the end]? Nay, they forsook them: for that [alleged divinity] was but an outcome of their self-delusion and all their false imagery.	This is a contested passage that may not refer merely to sacrifice, but also to acts of piety that draw one nearer to God.

---

7. 'Omar, *Dictionary*, 449–50.

Noun – [نُسُك] *nusuk*: a sacrifice, a rite, an act of worship[8]

Reference	Qur'an – Arabic	Muhammad Asad	Author's Comment
Qur'an 2:128	رَبَّنَا وَاجْعَلْنَا مُسْلِمَيْنِ لَكَ وَمِن ذُرِّيَّتِنَا أُمَّةً مُّسْلِمَةً لَّكَ وَأَرِنَا مَنَاسِكَنَا وَتُبْ عَلَيْنَا ۖ إِنَّكَ أَنتَ التَّوَّابُ الرَّحِيمُ	"O our Sustainer! Make us surrender ourselves unto Thee, and make out of our offspring a community that shall surrender itself unto Thee, and show us our <u>ways of worship</u>, and accept our repentance: for, verily, Thou alone art the Acceptor of Repentance, the Dispenser of Grace!"	The idea of this word group includes sacrifices among the system of acceptable ways to worship God given to a people.
Qur'an 2:196	وَأَتِمُّوا الْحَجَّ وَالْعُمْرَةَ لِلَّهِ ۚ فَإِنْ أُحْصِرْتُمْ فَمَا اسْتَيْسَرَ مِنَ الْهَدْيِ ۖ وَلَا تَحْلِقُوا رُءُوسَكُمْ حَتَّىٰ يَبْلُغَ الْهَدْيُ مَحِلَّهُ ۚ فَمَن كَانَ مِنكُم مَّرِيضًا أَوْ بِهِ أَذًى مِّن رَّأْسِهِ فَفِدْيَةٌ مِّن صِيَامٍ أَوْ صَدَقَةٍ أَوْ نُسُكٍ ۚ فَإِذَا أَمِنتُمْ فَمَن تَمَتَّعَ بِالْعُمْرَةِ إِلَى الْحَجِّ فَمَا اسْتَيْسَرَ مِنَ الْهَدْيِ ۚ فَمَن لَّمْ يَجِدْ فَصِيَامُ ثَلَاثَةِ أَيَّامٍ فِي الْحَجِّ وَسَبْعَةٍ إِذَا رَجَعْتُمْ ۗ تِلْكَ عَشَرَةٌ كَامِلَةٌ ۗ ذَٰلِكَ لِمَن لَّمْ يَكُنْ أَهْلُهُ حَاضِرِي الْمَسْجِدِ الْحَرَامِ ۚ وَاتَّقُوا اللَّهَ وَاعْلَمُوا أَنَّ اللَّهَ شَدِيدُ الْعِقَابِ	AND PERFORM the pilgrimage and the pious visit [to Mecca] in honour of God; and if you are held back, give instead whatever offering you can easily afford. And do not shave your heads until the offering has been sacrificed; but he from among you who is ill or suffers from an ailment of the head shall redeem himself by fasting, or alms, or [any other] <u>act of worship</u>. And if you are hale and secure, then he who takes advantage of a pious visit before the [time of] pilgrimage shall give whatever offering he can easily afford; whereas he who cannot afford it shall fast for three days during the pilgrimage and for seven days after your return: that is, ten full [days]. All this relates to him who does not live near the Inviolable House of Worship. And remain conscious of God, and know that God is severe in retribution.	There is a connection here between the ransoming of oneself and the performance of acts of charity, piety, sacrifice, and fasting that are associated with the *hajj*.

---

8 'Omar, Dictionary, 562.

APPENDIX C   235

Reference	Qur'an – Arabic	Muhammad Asad	Author's Comment
Qur'an 2:200	فَإِذَا قَضَيْتُم مَّنَاسِكَكُمْ فَاذْكُرُوا اللَّهَ كَذِكْرِكُمْ آبَاءَكُمْ أَوْ أَشَدَّ ذِكْرًا ۗ فَمِنَ النَّاسِ مَن يَقُولُ رَبَّنَا آتِنَا فِي الدُّنْيَا وَمَا لَهُ فِي الْآخِرَةِ مِنْ خَلَاقٍ	And when you have performed your <u>acts of worship</u>, [continue to] bear God in mind as you would bear your own fathers in mind—nay, with a yet keener remembrance!1 For there are people who [merely] pray, "O our Sustainer! Give us in this world"—and such shall not partake in the blessings of the life to come.	Acts of worship have been given to the believers, including the *hajj* and its sacrifice (v. 196).
Qur'an 6:162	قُلْ إِنَّ صَلَاتِي وَنُسُكِي وَمَحْيَايَ وَمَمَاتِي لِلَّهِ رَبِّ الْعَالَمِينَ	Say: "Behold, my prayer, and [all] my acts of worship, and my living and my dying are for God [alone], the Sustainer of all the worlds,"	Acts of worship including sacrifice and prayer are done for God alone.
Qur'an 22:34	وَلِكُلِّ أُمَّةٍ جَعَلْنَا مَنسَكًا لِّيَذْكُرُوا اسْمَ اللَّهِ عَلَىٰ مَا رَزَقَهُم مِّن بَهِيمَةِ الْأَنْعَامِ ۗ فَإِلَٰهُكُمْ إِلَٰهٌ وَاحِدٌ فَلَهُ أَسْلِمُوا ۗ وَبَشِّرِ الْمُخْبِتِينَ	And [thus it is:] unto every community [that has ever believed in Us] have We appointed [<u>sacrifice as] an act of worship</u>, so that they might extol the name of God over whatever heads of cattle He may have provided for them [to this end]. And [always bear in mind:] your God is the One and Only God: hence, surrender yourselves unto Him. And give thou the glad tiding [of God's acceptance] unto all who are humble.	This verse most clearly reveals the Qur'an's teaching on the episodic nature of revelation and the role that sacrifice has in distinguishing one dispensation from the next. Every people receives a distinguishing sacrifice as a part of their worship.

Reference	Qur'an – Arabic	Muhammad Asad	Author's Comment
Qur'an 22:67	لِكُلِّ أُمَّةٍ جَعَلْنَا مَنسَكًا هُم نَاسِكُوهُ ۖ فَلَا يُنَازِعُنَّكَ فِي الْأَمْرِ ۚ وَادْعُ إِلَىٰ رَبِّكَ ۖ إِنَّكَ لَعَلَىٰ هُدًى مُّسْتَقِيمٍ	UNTO every community have We appointed [different] <u>ways of worship</u>, which they ought to observe. Hence, [O believer,] do not let those [who follow ways other than thine] draw thee into disputes on this score, but summon [them all] unto thy Sustainer: for, behold, thou art indeed on the right way.	Again, this verse refers back to the idea that God has given a sacrifice to each people in order to distinguish them.

APPENDIX D

Ransom Vocabulary in the Qur'an

Verb – [فدى] *fada*: to ransom, to offer ransom[9]

Reference	Qur'an – Arabic	Muhammad Asad	Author's Comment
Qur'an 2:85	ثُمَّ أَنتُمْ هَٰؤُلَاءِ تَقْتُلُونَ أَنفُسَكُمْ وَتُخْرِجُونَ فَرِيقًا مِّنكُم مِّن دِيَارِهِم تَظَاهَرُونَ عَلَيْهِم بِالْإِثْمِ وَالْعُدْوَانِ وَإِن يَأْتُوكُمْ أُسَارَىٰ تُفَادُوهُمْ وَهُوَ مُحَرَّمٌ عَلَيْكُمْ إِخْرَاجُهُمْ ۚ أَفَتُؤْمِنُونَ بِبَعْضِ الْكِتَابِ وَتَكْفُرُونَ بِبَعْضٍ ۚ فَمَا جَزَاءُ مَن يَفْعَلُ ذَٰلِكَ مِنكُمْ إِلَّا خِزْيٌ فِي الْحَيَاةِ الدُّنْيَا ۖ وَيَوْمَ الْقِيَامَةِ يُرَدُّونَ إِلَىٰ أَشَدِّ الْعَذَابِ ۗ وَمَا اللَّهُ بِغَافِلٍ عَمَّا تَعْمَلُونَ	And yet, it is you who slay one another and drive some of your own people from their homelands, aiding one another against them in sin and hatred; but if they come to you as captives, you ransom them—although the very [act of] driving them away has been made unlawful to you! Do you, then, believe in some parts of the divine writ and deny the truth of other parts? What, then, could be the reward of those among you who do such things but ignominy in the life of this world and, on the Day of Resurrection, commitment to most grievous suffering? For God is not unmindful of what you do.	Ransoming captives apparently refers to selling back prisoners of war to their people.

9 'Omar, *Dictionary*, 419.

Reference	Qur'an – Arabic	Muhammad Asad	Author's Comment
Qur'an 2:229	الطَّلَاقُ مَرَّتَانِ ۖ فَإِمْسَاكٌ بِمَعْرُوفٍ أَوْ تَسْرِيحٌ بِإِحْسَانٍ ۗ وَلَا يَحِلُّ لَكُمْ أَن تَأْخُذُوا مِمَّا آتَيْتُمُوهُنَّ شَيْئًا إِلَّا أَن يَخَافَا أَلَّا يُقِيمَا حُدُودَ اللَّهِ ۖ فَإِنْ خِفْتُمْ أَلَّا يُقِيمَا حُدُودَ اللَّهِ فَلَا جُنَاحَ عَلَيْهِمَا فِيمَا افْتَدَتْ بِهِ ۗ تِلْكَ حُدُودُ اللَّهِ فَلَا تَعْتَدُوهَا ۚ وَمَن يَتَعَدَّ حُدُودَ اللَّهِ فَأُولَٰئِكَ هُمُ الظَّالِمُونَ	A divorce may be [revoked] twice, whereupon the marriage must either be resumed in fairness or dissolved in a goodly manner. And it is not lawful for you to take back anything of what you have ever given to your wives unless both [partners] have cause to fear that they may not be able to keep within the bounds set by God: hence, if you have cause to fear that the two may not be able to keep within the bounds set by God, there shall be no sin upon either of them for what the wife may give up [to her husband] <u>in order to free herself</u>. These are the bounds set by God; do not, then, transgress them: for they who transgress the bounds set by God—it is they, they who are evildoers!	Ransom is used in this context for a woman who wants to buy her freedom from her husband by paying him a settlement to hasten the divorce.
Qur'an 3:91	إِنَّ الَّذِينَ كَفَرُوا وَمَاتُوا وَهُمْ كُفَّارٌ فَلَن يُقْبَلَ مِنْ أَحَدِهِم مِّلْءُ الْأَرْضِ ذَهَبًا وَلَوِ <u>افْتَدَىٰ</u> بِهِ ۗ أُولَٰئِكَ لَهُمْ عَذَابٌ أَلِيمٌ وَمَا لَهُم مِّن نَّاصِرِينَ	Verily, as for those who are bent on denying the truth and die as deniers of the truth—not all the gold on earth could ever be their ransom. It is they for whom grievous suffering is in store; and they shall have none to succour them.	God will not accept any payment, no matter how great, for the lives of those who deny the truth.
Qur'an 5:36	إِنَّ الَّذِينَ كَفَرُوا لَوْ أَنَّ لَهُم مَّا فِي الْأَرْضِ جَمِيعًا وَمِثْلَهُ مَعَهُ <u>لِيَفْتَدُوا</u> بِهِ مِنْ عَذَابِ يَوْمِ الْقِيَامَةِ مَا تُقُبِّلَ مِنْهُمْ ۖ وَلَهُمْ عَذَابٌ أَلِيمٌ	Verily, if those who are bent on denying the truth had all that is on earth, and twice as much, to offer as ransom from suffering on the Day of Resurrection, it would not be accepted from them: for grievous suffering awaits them.	God will not accept any payment, no matter how great, for the lives of those who deny the truth.
Qur'an 10:54	وَلَوْ أَنَّ لِكُلِّ نَفْسٍ ظَلَمَتْ مَا فِي الْأَرْضِ <u>لَافْتَدَتْ</u> بِهِ ۗ وَأَسَرُّوا النَّدَامَةَ لَمَّا رَأَوُا الْعَذَابَ ۖ وَقُضِيَ بَيْنَهُم بِالْقِسْطِ ۚ وَهُمْ لَا يُظْلَمُونَ	And all human beings that have been doing evil would surely, if they possessed all that is on earth, offer it as ransom [on Judgment Day]; and when they see the suffering [that awaits them], they will be unable to express their remorse. But judgment will be passed on them in all equity; and they will not be wronged.	God will not accept any payment, no matter how great, for the lives of those who deny the truth.

APPENDIX D 239

Reference	Qur'an – Arabic	Muhammad Asad	Author's Comment
Qur'an 13:18	لِلَّذِينَ اسْتَجَابُوا لِرَبِّهِمُ الْحُسْنَىٰ ۚ وَالَّذِينَ لَمْ يَسْتَجِيبُوا لَهُ لَوْ أَنَّ لَهُم مَّا فِي الْأَرْضِ جَمِيعًا وَمِثْلَهُ مَعَهُ لَافْتَدَوْا بِهِ ۚ أُولَٰئِكَ لَهُمْ سُوءُ الْحِسَابِ وَمَأْوَاهُمْ جَهَنَّمُ ۖ وَبِئْسَ الْمِهَادُ	of those who have responded to their Sustainer with a goodly response, and of those who did not respond to Him. [As for the latter,] if they possessed all that is on earth, and twice as much, they would surely offer it as ransom [on the Day of Judgment]: a most evil reckoning awaits them, and their goal is hell: and how evil a resting-place!	God will not accept any payment, no matter how great, for the lives of those who deny the truth.
Qur'an 37:107	وَفَدَيْنَاهُ بِذِبْحٍ عَظِيمٍ	And We ransomed him with a tremendous sacrifice,	The idea of ransom here does not seem congruent with Islamic theology as Abraham and his son both showed their faithfulness in submission, so there remains a question as to why a sacrifice was given in place of the son, and why it was referred to as a ransom.
Qur'an 39:47	وَلَوْ أَنَّ لِلَّذِينَ ظَلَمُوا مَا فِي الْأَرْضِ جَمِيعًا وَمِثْلَهُ مَعَهُ لَافْتَدَوْا بِهِ مِن سُوءِ الْعَذَابِ يَوْمَ الْقِيَامَةِ ۚ وَبَدَا لَهُم مِّنَ اللَّهِ مَا لَمْ يَكُونُوا يَحْتَسِبُونَ	But if those who are bent on evildoing possessed all that is on earth, and twice as much, they would surely offer it as ransom from the awful suffering [that will befall them] on the Day of Resurrection: for, something with which they had not reckoned before will [by then] have been made obvious to them by God.	God will not accept any payment, no matter how great, for the lives of those who deny the truth.
Qur'an 70:11	يُبَصَّرُونَهُمْ ۚ يَوَدُّ الْمُجْرِمُ لَوْ يَفْتَدِي مِنْ عَذَابِ يَوْمِئِذٍ بِبَنِيهِ	though they may be in one another's sight: [for,] everyone who was lost in sin will on that Day but desire to ransom himself from suffering at the price of his own children.	On Judgment Day, sinners will be so desperate to save themselves that they would offer their own children in ransom.

Noun – [فدية] *fidya*: a ransom[10]

Reference	Qur'an – Arabic	Muhammad Asad	Author's Comment
Qur'an 2:184	أَيَّامًا مَعْدُودَاتٍ ۚ فَمَن كَانَ مِنكُم مَّرِيضًا أَوْ عَلَىٰ سَفَرٍ فَعِدَّةٌ مِّنْ أَيَّامٍ أُخَرَ ۚ وَعَلَى الَّذِينَ يُطِيقُونَهُ فِدْيَةٌ طَعَامُ مِسْكِينٍ ۖ فَمَن تَطَوَّعَ خَيْرًا فَهُوَ خَيْرٌ لَّهُ ۚ وَأَن تَصُومُوا خَيْرٌ لَّكُمْ ۖ إِن كُنتُمْ تَعْلَمُونَ	[fasting] during a certain number of days. But whoever of you is ill, or on a journey, [shall fast instead for the same] number of other days; and [in such cases] it is incumbent upon those who can afford it to make <u>sacrifice</u> by feeding a needy person. And whoever does more good than he is bound to do does good unto himself thereby; for to fast is to do good unto yourselves—if you but knew it.	Here a ransom for missing obligatory days of fasting is paid by feeding a needy person.
Qur'an 2:196	وَأَتِمُّوا الْحَجَّ وَالْعُمْرَةَ لِلَّهِ ۚ فَإِنْ أُحْصِرْتُمْ فَمَا اسْتَيْسَرَ مِنَ الْهَدْيِ ۖ وَلَا تَحْلِقُوا رُءُوسَكُمْ حَتَّىٰ يَبْلُغَ الْهَدْيُ مَحِلَّهُ ۚ فَمَن كَانَ مِنكُم مَّرِيضًا أَوْ بِهِ أَذًى مِّن رَّأْسِهِ فَفِدْيَةٌ مِّن صِيَامٍ أَوْ صَدَقَةٍ أَوْ نُسُكٍ ۚ فَإِذَا أَمِنتُمْ فَمَن تَمَتَّعَ بِالْعُمْرَةِ إِلَى الْحَجِّ فَمَا اسْتَيْسَرَ مِنَ الْهَدْيِ ۚ فَمَن لَّمْ يَجِدْ فَصِيَامُ ثَلَاثَةِ أَيَّامٍ فِي الْحَجِّ وَسَبْعَةٍ إِذَا رَجَعْتُمْ ۗ تِلْكَ عَشَرَةٌ كَامِلَةٌ ۗ ذَٰلِكَ لِمَن لَّمْ يَكُنْ أَهْلُهُ حَاضِرِي الْمَسْجِدِ الْحَرَامِ ۚ وَاتَّقُوا اللَّهَ وَاعْلَمُوا أَنَّ اللَّهَ شَدِيدُ الْعِقَابِ	AND PERFORM the pilgrimage and the pious visit [to Mecca] in honour of God; and if you are held back, give instead whatever offering you can easily afford. And do not shave your heads until the offering has been sacrificed; but he from among you who is ill or suffers from an ailment of the head shall <u>redeem</u> himself by fasting, or alms, or [any other] act of worship. And if you are hale and secure, then he who takes advantage of a pious visit before the [time of] pilgrimage shall give whatever offering he can easily afford; whereas he who cannot afford it shall fast for three days during the pilgrimage and for seven days after your return: that is, ten full [days]. All this relates to him who does not live near the Inviolable House of Worship. And remain conscious of God, and know that God is severe in retribution.	Fasting, sacrificing, participation in worship and piety, and charity serve as a ransom by which one may redeem himself in the case of not being able to participate in the fasting or the pilgrimage.

---

10 'Omar, *Dictionary*, 419.

APPENDIX D   241

Reference	Qur'an – Arabic	Muhammad Asad	Author's Comment
Qur'an 47:4	فَإِذَا لَقِيتُمُ الَّذِينَ كَفَرُوا فَضَرْبَ الرِّقَابِ حَتَّىٰ إِذَا أَثْخَنتُمُوهُمْ فَشُدُّوا الْوَثَاقَ فَإِمَّا مَنًّا بَعْدُ وَإِمَّا فِدَاءً حَتَّىٰ تَضَعَ الْحَرْبُ أَوْزَارَهَا ۚ ذَٰلِكَ وَلَوْ يَشَاءُ اللَّهُ لَانتَصَرَ مِنْهُمْ وَلَٰكِن لِّيَبْلُوَ بَعْضَكُم بِبَعْضٍ ۗ وَالَّذِينَ قُتِلُوا فِي سَبِيلِ اللَّهِ فَلَن يُضِلَّ أَعْمَالَهُمْ	NOW WHEN you meet [in war] those who are bent on denying the truth, smite their necks until you overcome them fully, and then tighten their bonds; but thereafter [set them free,] either by an act of grace or against ransom, so that the burden of war may be lifted: thus [shall it be]. And [know that] had God so willed, He could indeed punish them [Himself]; but [He wills you to struggle] so as to test you [all] by means of one another. And as for those who are slain in God's cause, never will He let their deeds go to waste:	This use of ransom refers to selling back captives of war to their people so as to ease the burden of war.
Qur'an 57:15	فَالْيَوْمَ لَا يُؤْخَذُ مِنكُمْ فِدْيَةٌ وَلَا مِنَ الَّذِينَ كَفَرُوا ۚ مَأْوَاكُمُ النَّارُ ۖ هِيَ مَوْلَاكُمْ ۖ وَبِئْسَ الْمَصِيرُ	"And so, no ransom shall be accepted today from you, and neither from those who were [openly] bent on denying the truth. Your goal is the fire: it is your [only] refuge—and how evil a journey's end!"	There is no ransom that will be accepted for those who deny the truth.

Index

BIBLE

Old Testament

Genesis
12:1–3	97
17:7–8	74
22	119, 151
22:1–19	150
22:9	150

Exodus
6:6–7	74
12	53, 97
16	142
19:1–6	85
19:5	53
19:5–6	53
21:28–32	50
25:8	174
28:4	86
29:45–46	53, 55
29:46	75
32	54
32:30	54
33:14–17	54, 68, 174
33:16	71
34:29	56
34:32	56
40:34–38	56

Leviticus
4:15	72
4:31	122
5:17–19	72
8–10	86
9:8–24	70
10:1–2	53, 70
12:1–8	47, 52
16	6, 49, 58, 59, 60, 67, 82, 84, 107, 126
16:1	70
16:1–2	53, 58
16:2	70
16:3	65, 90
16:4	58, 65, 90
16:5	65, 90
16:6	64, 65, 90
16:7–10	65, 90
16:11	38, 52, 64
16:11–19	61
16:14–19	65, 90
16:15–22	65, 90
16:16	61, 122
16:20–22	60
16:21	72
16:22	72
16:24	64
16:24–25	65, 90
16:27	61, 91
16:30	71, 121
16:33	122
16–17	37, 56, 58, 65, 76, 95, 101, 106, 172, 176, 177, 181, 198, 207
17:10–16	139
17:11	51, 60, 62, 72
17:11–14	51, 65, 90
22:17–33	59

INDEX

Leviticus (*continued*)
22:20	59
22:31–33	68, 74
22:33	59
23:26–32	58
25:38	68
26:11–12	174
26:13	68
26:44–45	68

Numbers
3:5–13	86

Deuteronomy
4:9–14	158
4:20	141
4:38–39	141
6:6	141
6:12	158
6:24	141
7:7	108
7:11	141
7:18	158
8:1	141
8:2	158
9:1	141
9:26	108
11:12	141
13:15	108
15:15	108

Psalms
25	85
95:11	107
110:4	86

Jeremiah
31:31–34	88, 92, 103

New Testament

Matthew
28:18–20	185

John
6	142
17	142

Acts
1:8	185
15	25
15:19–21	140
15:28–29	140
15:29	139

1 Corinthians
8	25
13:12	195
15:14–19	20

Galatians
5:1–15	80

2 Timothy
3:16	195

2 Peter
1:21	195

Hebrews
1:1	97
1:1–2	44, 170, 181
1:1–4	99, 169
1:3	95, 160, 169, 170, 171, 176, 181
1:4	169
2:2	169, 175
2:3	174
2:4	99
2:10	97
2:14–15	83, 108, 109
2:14–18	170
2:17	95, 107, 160, 171, 176, 177, 181
2:18	7
3:7	174
3:7–15	85
3:7–18	181
3:11	107
3:15	174
3:17–18	108
4:3	107, 174
4:5	174
4:6–11	98

INDEX 245

4:7–9	85	9:22–28	101, 181
4:7–11	175	9:26	102
4:8–11	98	9:28	102
4:8–12	162	10:1	101
4:9–13	174	10:1–10	92
4:11	85	10:1–18	44
4:14–16	104, 181	10:3–4	87
4:15	95	10:5	100
5:9–10	159	10:5–10	88
6:4	99, 100, 106	10:9–10	91
6:19–20	87	10:9b	94
7–10	82, 171	10:10	83, 87, 88, 93, 103, 104
7:1–29	89		
7:5	85	10:11	100
7:11–14	88	10:11–12	89
7:12	88	10:11–14	159
7:13–17	86	10:12	87
7:14	86	10:12–14	95, 160, 177
7:15–28	86	10:12–18	92
7:16	86, 87, 108	10:14	91, 104, 178
7:17	86	10:15	99
7:18	79	10:15–22	103, 104
7:18–19	181	10:19–20	93
7:18–22	92	10:19–21	159
7:20–28	87	10:19–22	83, 99, 103, 104, 160, 177
7:23–24	88		
7:26–28	89, 90	10:19–25	181
7:27	89, 95, 160	10:20	99, 100, 105
8:1	83	10:22	104, 178, 181
8:1–2	177	10:22–23	178
8:2	84	10:25	102
8:5	84, 92, 93, 101	11	97, 150
8:8–12	88	11:13–16	155
8:13	98	11:16	102, 174
9:1–2	84	11:17–19	150, 155, 167
9:6–14	173	11:39–12:2	95
9:7	82	12:2	169
9:8	99, 105, 158	12:1–3	155
9:11–12	104	12:2	97, 150
9:11–14	83, 84, 105	12:18	103
9:11–22	92, 178	12:18–24	98, 174
9:12	82, 108	12:18–28	181
9:13	178	12:22	156
9:13–14	177	12:22–24	173
9:14	99	12:25–29	100
9:21	82	12:28	98, 174
9:22	82, 158, 176, 178	13:10–12	91
		13:12–13	105

INDEX

Hebrews (*continued*)
13:11	91
13:13	99, 100, 192, 203
13:13–14	181
13:14	85, 98, 102, 162, 174

Revelation
7:9–12	193

QUR'AN

Sura 2
2:30–39	155
2:30a	154
2:35–36	157
2:36	157
2:37	157
2:49	230
2:52	125
2:67	230
2:71	231
2:85	237
2:89	113
2:91	113
2:97	175
2:128	234
2:136	113
2:184	240
2:196	135, 160, 234, 243
2:200	235
2:214	163
2:229	238
2:230	154
2:271	6, 122, 227

Sura 3
3:91	238
3:183	233
3:193	121, 227
3:195	121, 227

Sura 4
4:31	227
4:163	115

Sura 5
5	140, 141, 160, 162
5:1–11	160
5:2	138
5:3	37, 114, 139, 141, 143,6 150, 154, 160, 162, 231
5:3a	139
5:3b	114
5:6	160
5:7–11	161
5:12	228
5:12–15	113
5:13–19	175
5:27	233
5:36	238
5:41	123
5:44–48	43
5:44–50	113
5:45	225
5:46–47	115
5:48	44
5:48b	163, 178
5:65	228
5:48b	163
5:89	225
5:95	226
5:114	141, 142, 143

Sura 6
6:162	235

Sura 7
7:158	128

Sura 8
8:29	228

Sura 10
10:54	238

Sura 13
13:18	239
13:39	130

Sura 14
14:6	137, 232

INDEX 247

Sura 22	
22	160, 161
22:23–24	161
22:32	138
22:34	137, 139, 235
22:34–38	161
22:34a	143
22:36–37	137, 159
22:37	132, 138, 140
22:37a	138
22:67	137, 236
22:67a	143
Sura 27	
27:21	232
Sura 28	
28:4	232
Sura 29	
29:7	228
Sura 37	
37	1758
37:85	154
37:94–96	154
37:99–113	150, 154
37:102	232
37:102–103	154
37:103–106	165
37:106	136
37:107	135, 230, 239

Sura 46	
46:9	130
46:28	233
Sura 47	
47:2	229
47:4	241
Sura 48	
48:5	229
Sura 51	
51:47–48	155
Sura 57	
57:15	241
Sura 64	
64:9	229
Sura 65	
65:5	229
Sura 68	
68:8	229
Sura 70	
70:11	239
Sura 108	
108:2	230

www.ingramcontent.com/pod-product-compliance
Lightning Source LLC
Chambersburg PA
CBHW050848230426
43667CB00012B/2203